SOCIAL THEORY FOR ALTERNATIVE SOCIETIES

Social Theory for Alternative Societies

Matt Dawson

First published 2016 by
PALGRAVE

Palgrave in the UK is an imprint of Macmillan Publishers Limited, registered in England, company number 785998, of 4 Crinan Street, London, N1 9XW.

Palgrave Macmillan in the US is a division of St Martin's Press LLC, 175 Fifth Avenue, New York, NY 10010.

Palgrave is a global imprint of the above companies and is represented throughout the world.

Palgrave® and Macmillan® are registered trademarks in the United States, the United Kingdom, Europe and other countries.

ISBN 978–1–137–33733–7 hardback
ISBN 978–1–137–33732–0 paperback

This book is printed on paper suitable for recycling and made from fully managed and sustained forest sources. Logging, pulping and manufacturing processes are expected to conform to the environmental regulations of the country of origin.

A catalogue record for this book is available from the British Library.

A catalog record for this book is available from the Library of Congress.

Printed and bound by CPI Group (UK) Ltd, Croydon, CR0 4YY

Contents

Acknowledgements

One argument made in this book is that social theorists develop ideas for alternative societies based upon the circumstances they find themselves in. The same is true of someone who decides to write a book like this; the decision to do so will inevitably be influenced by the circumstances in which I live and the people around me. Consequently, the acknowledgements page is an important part of such a book by recognising all the influences which allowed this book to be written.

The first, and biggest, thanks goes to the honours students who took my 'Sociological Alternatives: Ways to Change the World' course at the University of Glasgow in 2013 and 2015. The idea for this book actually began as the idea for that course. Inevitably, when developing such a course, there's a bit of fear that you're actually the only one who cares and that students will find all this material, which you care about so deeply, dull. Thankfully, both classes were exactly the opposite. In your enthusiasm for the topic, criticisms and compliments of the theorists we discussed and truly impressive essays you reassured me that actually I wasn't the only one who cared and that there was something to this sociological alternatives topic. I consider myself immensely lucky to have had such sharp students on the course to date and have no doubt those to come will be equally so. I hope anyone reading this book finds the topic as interesting as you all seemed to.

My next set of thanks goes to those who have read sections of this manuscript, provided comments and, perhaps more important, assured me that I was on the right track. Especial thanks here to Charlie Masquelier and Luke Martell who read all, or almost all, the manuscript and provided really valuable comments and further readings. Others who have been kind enough to cast their eye over material include Emma Jackson, Roona Simpson and Sarah Burton. I'm really grateful to all of you for that.

In many ways writing a book which traces a history of social theory is an arrogant act. After all, these theorists could, and do, have whole volumes devoted to their work. Therefore, a book like this requires lots of reading from the author and, in doing so, you can't help but recognise that you're fulfilling the old adage of standing on the shoulders of giants. As the author of this book I owe a great deal to the authors cited here who have devoted their time to discussion of these theorists, filling out the details of intellectual history we all so dearly rely on. This is academic labour which in times of 'impact' is increasingly hard to justify to the powers that be. We should continue to justify it since any discipline which loses such contributions is inevitably poorer.

Material from the G.D.H. Cole archives quoted in the introduction is reproduced with the kind permission of the Warden and Fellows of Nuffield College,

Oxford. My thanks to the staff at Nuffield College library for facilitating access to the archive.

I also owe thanks to those at Palgrave for their assistance in preparing this volume. Anna Reeve was important to this book being written as a result of her enthusiasm for the project and encouragement to submit the initial proposal, for which I am very grateful. Lloyd Langman and Nicola Cattini have then been an excellent source of support and encouragement during the production of the volume. This includes bearing with an event unknown to this point: an academic missing a deadline. My thanks also to Palgrave's reviewers who provided valuable comments which have improved this text.

Finally, huge, huge thanks to the friends and family who supported (or, at some points, simply put up with) me during writing this book. Some of them have already been mentioned but I would like to thank my parents for their continual support along with friends Lucy, Susie and Kirsteen. Thank you all so much.

Introduction

The year is 1950. G.D.H. Cole, at this point holder of one of the few jobs in the world dedicated to the research and teaching of social theory, the Chichele Professorship of Social and Political Theory, is welcoming students to Oxford and his course 'Prolegomena to Social and Political Theory'. After expressing his hopes that they find the course useful Cole begins to discuss the reasons why they might be there. He acknowledges some may be taking the course because they are required to for their degree, while others may simply be curious. Despite this, he detects another interest which has drawn students to his lectures on this cold January morning: the desire to change the world. He therefore decides to devote his first lecture to the theme of 'The Subject Matter of Social Theory' and argues that doing social theory inevitably leads to a desire for social change since 'no one who studies his [sic] own or a like society can possibly help carrying his judgements with him into his work ... This must be so, because he is a citizen as well as a scientist' (Cole 1950:9). Such problems are, for Cole, especially pressing for the students in the room who will become sociologists. It is perhaps easier to be objective as an outsider studying 'other' societies, but this is much more challenging for the sociologist studying their own society. They will inevitably have preferences about what should be done; after all, we cannot be entirely 'disinterested' when studying the things which impact our everyday lives (Cole 1950:10).

So, Cole asks, is social theory doomed to be simply the reflection of right and wrong, good and bad, held by an individual at a particular time? Cole strikes a tone of pessimism and optimism for his students. He suggests 'it is a vain hope that we shall be able to keep our personal predilections, ideals and dislikes out of our thinking' yet also argues that studying social theory gives us certain tools to think about good and bad. As he puts it:

> All we can hope or wish to do is to know, as nearly as possible, when we are trying to see things as they are and when we are appraising them as good or bad, either from the standpoint or our own wishes and values, or from any other. (Cole 1950:3)

It is in this spirit that Cole encourages his students not to ignore or expunge their own personal values from their thinking but rather to keep ideas of the 'good society' (a later topic on the course) in their mind. Then, they should use the tools of social theory to criticise these notions and assess whether their idea of 'good' would be the same for all.

This book is written in the spirit of what Cole told his students on that day in Oxford. In what follows I will present a history of social theory which focuses on how theorists have attempted to come up with ideas for this 'good', or alternative, society. This has become an increasingly forgotten history. When we think of social theory we often say that it is 'scientific ways of thinking about social life' (Harrington 2005:1) or a 'worked-up version of what we all know anyway, if often in semi-conscious ways' (Inglis and Thorpe 2012:4) concerning the 'articulation of the moves, problems and themes' emerging from the social world (Turner 2010:1) and therefore 'an attempt to bring order' to the research findings of social scientists (Calhoun et al. 2012:1). In short, social theory is abstract, conceptual and general claims made about the social world. Such definitions can be found in many books with theorists seen as focused on explanation and/or critique. It is common to trace a story of social theory coming to grips with 'modernity' (Mouzelis 2008), capitalism (Giddens 1971), communication (Habermas 1985, 1987) or interaction (Dennis et al. 2013); alternatively some present this as a story of critique (Calhoun 1995) or as one-sided, reflecting the worldview of men (Marshall and Witz 2004), mostly from Europe and the 'West' (Bhambra 2007). In most cases, social theory is a discussion of the social world as it is and has come to be, rather than what it could be. Missing here is the way in which social theory has discussed alternatives.

While some have discussed the approaches of particular schools of thought, such as feminism (Sargisson 1996) and postcolonialism (Venn 2006) to alternatives, there has been no attempt to date to discuss the ways in which social theorists as a whole have used their tools to say not only what was wrong or bad about society as currently constituted but how it could be improved. It is this story which this book traces. Social theory is not just concerned with the world as it is but, as we shall see, is often concerned with how the world could be. Like any story of social theory this is diverse, with many characters, ideas and paths followed or not followed. We will encounter social theorists who provided detailed blueprints of an alternative world to be implemented by the elites of which they are part, others who spent their time on the streets attempting to make a better world and those who thought that it was the responsibility of others to fully outline the alternative. All of these perspectives are an invitation to think of social theory as concerned in diverse ways with how the world could be.

As the contents page of this book indicates, this history takes in many of the 'giants' of social theory such as Marx, Durkheim, Du Bois and Giddens. This book also combines such figures with lesser known names, at least within contemporary social theory, such as Henri Lefebvre, Selma James and Ruth Levitas. While some of these writers would not identify themselves as 'sociologists' they all, as we shall see, make use of sociological insight when constructing their ideal society. Therefore, this book is not an attempt to cover the 'key' theorists in sociology (though some of these are covered) but rather to look at how this attempt to create a new society is shared by sociologists throughout the history of the discipline. This is not a 'sideline' activity engaged in by just a few figures but rather a central part of what makes sociology and social theory the discipline it is. I shall be calling this the search for 'sociological alternatives'.

Sociological alternatives

When sociologists construct a vision of the good society, or when they suggest changes to society as currently constituted, they are engaging in the construction of what I will term in this book 'sociological alternatives'. These sociological alternatives contain three parts:

1. The identification of a problem, or problems, with society as currently constituted: this is the 'critical' part of social theory. Here elements of society, or the whole of society, are condemned for the evils they produce. In what comes we will see such problems as including excessive economic inequality, alienation from what makes us human, individualism, male privilege and inadequate democracy, amongst others.
2. The suggestion of an alternative: here, in response to the problem(s) identified in the first stage, sociologists suggest some changes. As we shall see these can be large-scale changes requiring revolution and a fundamentally different structure (for example, the shift from capitalism to communism) or, they can be more small-scale measures of reform (such as changes to the education system). But even such small changes are said to have major implications more broadly.
3. A justification of how the alternative solves the problem(s): here the alternative offered is justified via its ability to solve the problem(s) identified in step 1. Importantly, at this point, it doesn't matter if the justification is unconvincing. A poorly justified sociological alternative is still a sociological alternative.

It is important for all three of these elements to be present. Doing step 1 without those that follow is to engage in 'critical sociology', condemning society without the idea of an alternative. Furthermore, offering an alternative without a critique is, as we shall see in Chapter 3, what Marx and Engels criticised 'utopian socialists' for: to assume you can start with a blank slate. Finally, if a justification is not offered it is hard to understand the reasons why the alternative is more attractive than what we have at the moment.

Let's take an example, in this case one from education. At this point we have ample evidence that a privileged class background gives some students an advantage through their holding of cultural capital (Bourdieu and Passeron 1977, Sullivan 2001). Therefore, my critique could be that this leaves those lacking such an advantage 'playing catch-up' to their more privileged peers upon entering school. This reproduces privileged and disadvantaged classes. I can then offer a variety of ideas for how to lessen such an advantage. For example, I could say children from less advantaged backgrounds should get extra tuition outside of school hours to assist their education. The justification for this may be that while it will not remove the inequalities present when students enter the education system it will help to eradicate some advantages gained due to background. This may have the added benefit of reducing disadvantage for

these children later in life by narrowing the gap in educational achievement due
to class background. Consequently, while this initially seems quite a small-scale
policy it actually has a wider social value; it ensures we move closer to a more
equal society. Therefore, extra tuition could be said to be a useful instrument of
social mobility and consequently a well-justified sociological alternative.

At this point the reader may wish to critique this alternative; it may be said
that inequalities of class are too extreme to be overcome solely by private tuition. Alternatively, it could be said that the issue with such a policy is that
tutors are likely to be from a privileged class themselves and therefore will
favour, and reproduce, those qualities in their students. Finally, we may question the practicalities of deciding who these 'disadvantaged' children deserving
of extra tuition are. Indeed, some of these issues are common to recent educational reforms which purport to overcome inequalities of class (Gillies 2005).

However, while we may not be convinced of the value of this alternative, it
does demonstrate how alternatives emerge from sociological insight. Imagine
we didn't know about the impacts of class inequalities on education. In this
case, my alternative would probably be different and I may argue that every
child should have extra tuition. After all, doesn't every child have the right to
equal opportunities to achieve as much as they can in education? We might call
such an approach, which relies upon a moral precept rather than sociological insight, a 'philosophical alternative' since it is based upon abstract moral
claims of what is right and wrong. It is only the sociological knowledge of
how inequalities are experienced and felt that allows this alternative to become
one about overcoming inequalities. Indeed, our philosophical alternative of
extra tuition for every child may make the problem worse by further entrench-
ing, and perhaps extending, the advantages of children from privileged backgrounds. Therefore, a 'sociological' alternative is defined by having all three
of the above elements. Some alternatives may start from small-scale instances
such as the above or from a broader claim (as in the advocacy of some form of
socialism); however, all are united in imagining a new, better society.

When discussing the sociological alternatives offered in this book I will follow this three-step process, first identifying the critique and then outlining the
alternative before finishing with the justification. As the book goes on we will
see that some sociologists offer a more extensive discussion of one or two of
these steps but not the others. For example, while Marx and Engels were quite
clear on steps 1 and 3, they were much more reticent on step 2. Alternatively,
while the feminist campaign to ban pornography was very strong on steps 1
and 2 it was less impressive on step 3. Moreover, we will see that the way sociologists offer alternatives differs greatly. Durkheim and Mannheim produced
books and articles which provided quite detailed blueprints about what should
happen. Others, such as Mead, instead devoted their time to trying to construct
alternatives in the here and now. As I will highlight throughout the book, and
return to in the 'Conclusion', such differences do not automatically make any
one sociological alternative better or worse than others, but rather reflect differing ideas in the discipline about how sociologists should offer alternatives
and what sociology is for.

Layout of the book

When Cole gave his students that advice about the purpose of social theory he was well aware that his view was not shared by all (Cole 1957). Indeed, when Cole constructed a sociological alternative in his conception of Guild Socialism (Cole 1920) his idea of sociology alienated him from many sociologists of his era (Dawson and Masquelier 2015). Chapter 1 will therefore begin with the question of whether sociologists should offer alternatives by tracing the debate on value-freedom from its initial propagation by Max Weber up to the current day. While this is hardly a settled debate, we will see that many have questioned Weber's key claims about the possibility (or desirability) of a value-free sociology. This is then reflected in Chapters 2–8 which are devoted to outlining the sociological alternatives offered by a variety of theorists. Chapters 2–4 are devoted to classical writers (Marx and Engels, Durkheim and Du Bois) while Chapters 5–8 are devoted to two or more thinkers who are linked by a common theme of their alternative (democracy, neo-Marxism, feminism and cosmopolitanism). Each of these chapters follows the threefold model of sociological alternatives outlined above. Chapters 9 and 10 are then focused on questions of how sociologists should go about offering alternatives through the two themes of utopianism and public sociology. Since these chapters aren't concerned with outlining alternatives but rather the means by which they can be offered, they will not follow the threefold model. The 'Conclusion' then summarises the debates outlined in the book and returns to the story of sociological alternatives.

Any book such as this which is devoted to the study of particular theorists or schools is inevitably limited in its scope and therefore must be selective in the writings it covers. Consequently, there are usually particular omissions or overemphasis in the positions and theorists represented. This is the case with this book. The theorists and schools discussed here have been chosen for particular reasons. I discuss such reasons in each chapter; however, they can be summarised here under four categories.

Firstly, in Chapters 2–4 I chose Marx and Engels, Durkheim and Du Bois since they are key classical writers. This indicates that some attempt to develop alternatives was a significant occupation during sociology's formative years. It was partly such tendencies which, as we shall see in Chapter 1, writers such as Weber contested in their hope to form sociology on a value-free basis and which led to a wider quest to separate out 'scientific sociology' from 'social reform' (Deegan 2006, Rocquin 2014).

Secondly, for Chapters 5–8, in order to indicate the various areas in which subsequent social theorists have been active I have taken a different approach. While, as mentioned above, there are some 'key' writers covered in these chapters I have attempted to choose cases which complement each other and provide different perspectives across the book. These differ not just on the form of alternatives but also on the role of intellectuals. For example, in Chapter 5 it would have been possible to draw upon writers other than Mead and Mannheim to discuss democracy. But these two cases serve as ideal types of the two extremes possible in the advocacy of democracy (either as a bottom-up or a top-down project). In doing so, as is explored in the conclusion to that chapter, it opens up a discussion on the role of sociologists as, to use Zygmunt Bauman's (1987) terms, 'legislators and interpreters'. Therefore, theorists in these chapters are partly chosen for illustrative reasons.

Thirdly, in choosing writers less frequently discussed in sociology today or remembered for different contributions – for example, when Lefebvre is discussed it tends to be for his work on the city, Mead for his idea on the social self and Mannheim is remembered primarily for his contribution to the sociology of knowledge – I am hoping to contribute to a wider project of moving away from what Law (2014:299) terms 'turn-taking' in social theory; a process in which previous theories are dismissed without further consideration as simply no longer of relevance. Instead, there is value in what Anderson et al. (1985:57–60) term a 'charitable reading', namely treating social theories as conceived by intelligent people hoping to respond to the circumstances they found which have distinct strengths and weaknesses. This is in opposition to what Law terms 'theory-baiting' (Law 2014:8–10) in order to define those who do not fit the current 'turn' as mistaken or deluded. This means that, as the reader will note, I do not engage in systematic critique of each theorist discussed here (though I do mention some criticisms made by others). This is an intentional strategy of letting the theorists stand on their own merits and, as discussed below, opening up further conversation on the role of social theory rather than, as is inevitably the case when discussing alternatives, providing criticisms shaped by what I imagine to be the ideal society (which I have outlined elsewhere, Dawson 2013).

Finally, the above means that these writers have not primarily been chosen due to the relevance for what they advocate to the society we confront today. The reason for this is that, as highlighted above, part of my goal here is to provide a history of sociological alternatives which also offers us ideas about the role of sociologists in social change. Therefore, while I believe all the theorists discussed here have something valuable to tell us, and I highlight forms of contemporary relevance throughout, their primary contribution today may be for this latter point. This is not to say that the alternatives offered here can be classed into 'out of date' or 'still relevant' – if we adopt the charitable reading it maybe that they all have valuable contributions to make to the type of society we may, or may not, want to live in – rather that this was not the primary consideration when the choices, and omissions, were made.

My hope is that the theories covered here will allow us to think of social theory as orientated towards questions of what should be as well as what is. Such a perspective can then encourage discovering and developing the ideas for alternatives found across the various perspectives of social theory. To quote Bauman (2008:236) I hope this story of social theory is 'a response and a new opening' in a conversation of what sociology is 'for', to which we will return in the 'Conclusion'.

Should Sociologists Offer Alternatives? Value-Free and Critical Sociologies

This book concerns ideas for alternatives offered by social theory – as I have termed them, sociological alternatives. Such a topic leads to an obvious initial question: should sociologists even offer alternatives? This will be discussed in this opening chapter.

Of course, the very fact that this book continues beyond this chapter suggests that sociologists have offered alternatives. However, as we shall see, while doing so some have been restrained by the possibilities they felt were available to intellectuals (as for Marx and the Marxists who followed) whereas others have fully embraced the supposed potential for sociology to provide clear guidelines for an alternative society (for example, Durkheim and Mannheim). Therefore, this question will remain with us throughout the text.

Before that, this chapter traces a history of some of the key debates concerning 'value-free' and 'critical' sociology; these hold differing views on the role of sociologists in offering alternatives. This will begin with the writings of Max Weber, which advocated a divide between empirically testable 'facts' and individually decided 'values'. Then, we will turn to the 'Becker/Gouldner debate'. Both writers diverged from Weber's distinction but had a disagreement on whether sociologists should be on the side of the underdog or of values. Then, we will discuss the position of Dorothy Smith, which critiques the truth claims of mainstream sociology. Finally, this chapter will discuss what it means to do 'critical' sociology, most notably, Bauman's advocacy for sociology as a 'science of freedom'. First, we need to consider what it means to be 'normative'.

Normativity and sociology

To ask if sociology should offer alternatives is to ask if it should be normative. This is a term used very broadly in the literature. It can alternatively mean having a particular position and viewpoint (for example, being a socialist), making claims as to what is 'good' and 'bad', having certain goals to achieve or defining the socially sanctioned 'norm' (heterosexuality is a normative sexuality, asexuality is a 'non-normative' sexuality). However, if we consult a dictionary of sociology we find 'normative theory' defined as 'hypotheses or other statements about what is right or wrong, desirable or undesirable, just or unjust in society' (Scott and Marshall 2005:453), a definition which will be used here. Therefore, to be normative is to make statements about what 'should' or 'ought' to happen.

We are all normative beings. We continually make statements about what we, others or indeed society as a whole 'should' do. In doing so we may draw upon moral guidelines (as in the claim 'this isn't fair') or social rules themselves (if someone sends you a gift you should send them a thank you note). Sociologists are of course interested in these normativities. They seek to understand how we come to develop our beliefs and 'why things matter to people' (Sayer 2011).

But is it correct for sociology itself to make such normative statements? Sociology, as a field of knowledge and programme of research, could be seen as defined more by statements about what 'is' or 'has been' rather than what 'should be'. Indeed, if we return to our dictionary of sociology we find that the entry for normative theory continues to say:

> The majority of sociologists consider it illegitimate to move from expla-
> nation to evaluation. In their view sociology should strive to be value-free,
> objective, or at least to avoid making explicit value judgements ... The
> majority of sociological enquiries are therefore analytical and explana-
> tory. They do not pose normative questions such as 'Which values ought
> to provide for social order?' and 'How ought society to organise itself?'
> (Scott and Marshall 2005:453)

As we shall see, many social theorists have in fact rejected such a position. Nevertheless, the claim of our sociology dictionary does emerge from a key writer in the discipline: Max Weber (1864–1920).

Max Weber: the value dispute

Weber once remarked that 'endless misunderstandings and a great deal of terminological – and hence sterile – conflict have taken place about the term "value-judgement"' (Weber 1949a:10) and, in many ways, this is as true of the years following Weber's writings as it was then. In the repetition of Weber's claims on value-freedom a somewhat simplified version of his argument has been produced which I will refer to as the 'standard' version. This standard version is, as we shall see, fundamentally opposed to any form of normative theory. However, if we return to Weber's writings and their context, we will see a much more complex argument which, while still opposed to such activity in our role as sociologists, contains an awareness of the difficulties of obtaining value-freedom and recognises how we can offer alternatives outside the role of sociologist.

We begin with the standard version which, while simplified, does draw upon some of the key assertions found in Weber's writings. Here we have the claim that Weber draws a distinction concerning the role of our values in the stages of the research process. Initially it is true that the topics we choose to research will be influenced by values. These can be either our own personal values (as in the things we find interesting/have experience of) or 'cultural values' which society as a whole is interested in (Weber 1949b:56, 61). For example, sociologists may research inequality because they personally consider it important – perhaps due to a political belief in its unjust nature – or since as a society we are interested in knowing, and tackling, forms of inequality.

However, once we actually begin research, we should be 'value-free' and not let our personal values and beliefs enter into the research process. The justification for this position rests upon a split between facts and value-judgements. Facts rely upon 'our capacity and need for *analytically ordering* empirical reality in a manner which lays claim to *validity* as empirical truth' (Weber 1949b:58) in that their being proven 'wrong' or 'right' relies upon empirical evidence. The claim that 'water boils at 100 degrees Celsius' is a fact since it can be empirically demonstrated by, in normal conditions at ground level, water continually boiling at 100 degrees. If water were to suddenly boil at a different temperature we would be forced to reject the claim. Value-judgements on the other hand are 'practical evaluations of the unsatisfactory or satisfactory character of phenomena subject to our influence' (Weber 1949a:1) and therefore involve normative claims about what is good or bad. Unlike facts, 'to *judge* the *validity* of such values is a matter of *faith*' (Weber 1949b:55). We believe certain things to be good due to faith in a religious sense or according to a certain set of moral precepts. Neither of these, for Weber, are empirically testable but rather, as beliefs, are beyond the claims of an empirical science.

How does this split work in practice? Let us continue with the example of inequality. As we have seen, values may lead us to research this issue but once we begin our research we need to avoid such value-judgements. This means that we could highlight the nature of inequality in our society, what the top and bottom 10 per cent earn, how this has changed over time, the groups most likely to be found at the top and bottom of the scale and so on. All of these claims are empirical facts, which can be tested by analysing data. But we cannot from this analysis say 'such undesirable inequalities show the unjustness of the capitalist system' since this would be a value-judgement. The opposite claim that 'such desirable inequalities show the benefits of capitalism as an economic system which rewards hard work and talent' is equally based on faith. Neither statement can be fully proven or disproven but rather both are based upon beliefs of what makes a good society (Weber 1949b:66). Indeed, some have accused sociologists of automatically, based upon their own left-of-centre political position, seeing inequality as 'bad' (Saunders 1995), reflecting a wider 'resentment' towards capitalism among sociologists (Cushman 2012). Of course, such writers are replacing one value-judgement with another where such inequalities are positive or inevitable elements of the good capitalist society (Black 2014:775).

What does this mean for sociological alternatives? Sociologists can, for Weber, discuss alternatives offered by others – ideas for lessening inequality, such as socialism, can be analysed according to their social origin and underpinning assumptions (Weber 1949b:67–9) – but since ultimately ideas about what we should do are ones of personal value 'it can never be the task of an empirical science to provide binding norms and ideals from which directives for immediate practical activity can be derived' (Weber 1949b:52). Or, as Weber put it in the introduction to *The Protestant Ethic and the Spirit of Capitalism*:

> He who yearns for seeing should go to the cinema ... Nothing is farther from the intent of these thoroughly serious studies than such an attitude. And, I might add, whoever wants a sermon should go to a conventicle ... It is true that the path of human destiny cannot but appall him who surveys a section of it. But he will do well to keep his small personal commentarie [sic] to himself, as one does at the sight of the sea or of majestic mountains, unless he knows himself to be called and gifted to give them expression in artistic or prophetic form. In most other cases the voluminous talk about intuition does nothing but conceal a lack of perspective toward the object, which merits the same judgment as a similar lack of perspective toward men. (Weber 1930:xli)

Consequently, the 'standard' reading of Weber seems to resolutely close down the possibility of sociological alternatives. It is here that a further reading of Weber's views, and the context in which they were offered, yields a more sophisticated discussion concerning the role of sociologists. This reading, while still opposed to sociological alternatives, highlights the potential difficulties of obtaining value-freedom.

Weber's work on value-freedom occurred as part of what became known as the *werturteilsstreit* or 'value dispute' in German sociology during the years preceding World War I. Weber and his colleagues, considered at the time a radical left wing of sociology, aligned themselves and their idea of value-freedom against a group of scholars who advocated normative social analysis largely in order to aid the German government. At the time, it was a conflict Weber and his colleagues lost, with the 1914 meeting of the Association for Social Policy being so hostile to value-freedom that, sensing his defeat, Weber simply got up and left (Dahrendorf 1968:1–4). As this indicates, the German context in which these ideas were offered was a politically charged atmosphere and many of the protagonists, including Weber, were heavily involved in politics (Mommsen 1974). Therefore, those holding to the doctrine of value-freedom were hardly impartial when it came to normative questions and shared Weber's view that 'an *attitude of moral indifference* has no connection with *scientific* "objectivity"' (Weber 1949b:60) and his suggestion that 'nor need I discuss further whether the distinction between empirical statements of fact and value-judgments is "difficult" to make. It is' (Weber 1949a:9). Part of the purpose of the debate was to allow both activities, that of science and politics, to exist alongside each other (Dahrendorf 1968). Scholars could hold on to their strongly held political beliefs yet still work with those who, equally strongly, held the opposite view. To do this, Weber created a separation between the roles of 'citizen' and 'sociologist' in two areas: research and teaching.

As we saw, Weber argued values can influence the choice of research topic. He also suggested values can influence the choice of how that research is conducted, specifically the measures we choose as relevant for the task. A good example of this for Weber is economic research, much of which takes economic growth as its focus (Weber 1949b:85). This position was largely unchallenged for much of the history of economics but is, for Weber, a fundamentally capitalist conception of what defines a 'strong' economy. The emergence of socialist economics, emerging from a different conception, questions this and highlights the value-claims in capitalist research (Weber 1949b:86). This makes the dividing lines between values and facts much less clear since, as Weber put it:

> In the *method* of investigation, the guiding 'point of view' [values] is of great importance for the *construction* of the conceptual scheme which will be used in the investigation. In the mode of their *use*, however, the investigator is obviously bound by the norms of our thought just as much here as elsewhere. For scientific truth is precisely what is *valid* for all who *seek* the truth. (Weber 1949b:84)

Therefore, sticking with our example, once we decide economic growth is our measure then the socialist and capitalist researcher should come to the same conclusion. But it is likely given their contrasting values that our researchers may have chosen different methods for investigation.

Consequently, when values influence not just our topic but how we research this it puts an additional demand on the researcher to be aware of their impact; to use contemporary parlance, we must be reflexive. Weber suggests that at the bare minimum, if researchers do offer value-judgements they must make very clear that they are value-judgements, beyond the reach of empirical claims (Weber 1949b:110). Furthermore, when doing so, we should realise that for most the value-judgement they reach is shaped 'to a quite significant degree by the degree of affinity between it and his class interests' (Weber 1949b:56). This was something Weber made clear in his own normative claims concerning economic policy where he argued 'I am a member of the bourgeois classes. I feel myself to be a bourgeois, and I have been brought up to share their views and ideals' (Weber 1895:23).

Therefore, Weber does highlight the difficulties of obtaining value-freedom and the role of values in the research process. What space does this leave for sociologists to outline possible alternatives? Weber's example here takes the form of a thought exercise: imagine someone approached you as a sociologist and asked 'should I be a syndicalist?'. Syndicalism is a form of anarchist theory which we could replace with 'environmentalist', 'socialist', 'libertarian', 'feminist' and so on. In such a case Weber (1949a:18) argues you can respond with three points:

1. The unavoidable means of creating a syndicalist society
2. The unavoidable side effects which would happen as a result
3. The conflicting value-judgements which would emerge along the way

In doing so, you may show that being a syndicalist is 'useless'. The means of creating such a society may be unavailable. Or it would be possible to create such a society but the side effects of it (for example, loss of individual freedom) would be worse than the problems now. Or the conflicting value-judgements may be unanswerable (would they be willing to jail, or even kill, those who disagree with their ideal society?). Nevertheless, while:

> You may demonstrate to a convinced syndicalist ... that his action will result in increasing the opportunities of reaction, in increasing the oppression of his class, and obstructing its ascent – and you will not make the slightest impression upon him. If an action of good intent leads to bad results, then, in the actor's eyes, not he but the world, or the stupidity of other men, or God's will who made them thus, is responsible for evil. (Weber 1921:120–1)

In short, the question of whether to advocate syndicalism, or any of the alternatives offered in this book, is a value-judgement. While sociologists can advise as to the practicalities of such ideas, they cannot advise on their ultimate value. This highlights a key element of Weber's writings. We will all, sociologists and non-sociologists, have values we hold and are, at the minimum, 'occasional' politicians by voting, expressing political opinions or taking part in political action (Weber 1921:83). For Weber, this is not only inevitable but to be encouraged. However, in our professional work as a 'sociologist' we need to leave such values behind and be value-free. This reinforces a divide between the citizen and the sociologist who operate in different spaces:

> To take a practical political stand is one thing, and to analyse political structures and party positions is another. When speaking in a political meeting about democracy, one does not hide one's personal standpoint; indeed, to come out clearly and take a stand is one's damned duty. The words one uses in such a meeting are not means of scientific analysis but means of canvassing votes and winning over others. They are not ploughshares to loosen the soil of contemplative thought; they are swords against the enemies: such words are weapons. It would be an outrage, however, to use words in this fashion in a lecture or in the lecture-room. (Weber 1922:145)

This leads us onto the second element of Weber's discussion of value-freedom: teaching.

A striking element of Weber's writings on value-freedom is how much space is given over to teaching. In some of these, including the famous 'Science as a Vocation' lecture (Weber 1922), teaching is more prominent than research. Here, as in research, Weber sees values as not appropriate. This is due to the role of teachers, which is to impart facts and methodology (Weber 1949a:1–10). Much like in the *werturteilsstreit* Weber found himself in the opposite corner to a general acceptance of value-judgements as part of a lecturer's role. The reason for this was the 'competition for students' whereby lecturers develop a 'cult of personality' in order to attract students to their class (Weber 1949a:6, 9). The easiest way to do this was to adopt the role of the preacher or 'prophet'. Lecturers who discuss their beliefs and urge their students onto action are, inevitably for Weber, much more interesting to listen to, since they will speak with passion (Weber 1949a:2). Other, non-prophet-like, lecturers tend to be defined by 'calm rigour, matter-of-factness and sobriety'; in short, they're boring (Weber 1949a:4).

The problem with the role of the prophet is that whereas there are professional credentials which demonstrate one's competence to teach freely (such as degrees in the subject) there is 'no specialised qualification for personal prophecy, and for this reason it is not entitled to that privilege of freedom' (Weber 1949a:4). It is especially problematic when such prophecy is done in a lecture hall since here it gains a cloak of 'science' and is given more credit than simply the personal prophecy of the individual speaking. As we saw above, Weber thought the appropriate place for such prophecy was the church.

However, as in his views on research, Weber acknowledges the complexity of his position. The question of the role of values in teaching is in fact an 'unresolvable question – unresolvable because it is ultimately a question of evaluation' (Weber 1949a:8). Saying what lecturers should do is ultimately based upon a value-judgement of what you think universities are for. For Weber, universities are for the training of scholars and the further enriching of the national culture (Weber 1895). Therefore, this requires value-freedom. A different conception, say of universities as the breeding ground for a ruling class intelligentsia as advocated by Mannheim in Chapter 5, would lead to a different conclusion. Consequently, Weber acknowledges that others may not agree with him and instead may believe that value-claims can enter into lectures. In that case Weber suggests two qualifications. Firstly, as in research, when value-claims are made by lecturers they must be clearly identified as such. Secondly, if value-claims are allowed then 'all party-preferences' should be 'granted the opportunity of demonstrating their validity on the academic platform' (Weber 1949a:6–7). For Weber, the latter condition was not recognised at the time due to the reluctance to allow Marxists and anarchists to lecture. We may now question whether we would allow neo-Nazis to lecture and, if not, we may not satisfy Weber's conditions.

Even if these conditions are met, Weber still advises against value-claims in teaching. He argues that teaching should be concerned with providing 'inconvenient facts' by challenging the views of the students (Weber 1922:147). Doing so will, for Weber, increase the respect accorded to the lecturer when they leave the classroom and express their values. Here we return to the split of our roles as citizens and sociologists, leading Weber to say:

> In the press, in congresses and associations, in essays – in short, in any form which is available equally to every other citizen – [the lecturer] may (and ought to) do whatever his God or his demon calls him to do.

> But what the present-day student should learn from his teachers above all, at least in the lecture hall, is, first, to fulfil a given task in a workman-like manner; secondly, definitely to recognise facts, even those may be personally uncomfortable, and to distinguish them from his own evaluations; and thirdly, to subordinate himself to the task and to repress the impulse to exhibit his personal tastes or other sentiments unnecessarily. (Weber 1949a:5)

Therefore, lecturers can speak their values in any forum available to all citizens, but should not do so in their role as lecturers (Weber 1949a:5). Therefore, alternatives are not the responsibility of sociologists as researchers or teachers, though they will hold normative beliefs as citizens. This split in the ascribed roles of sociologist and citizen is central to the Becker/Gouldner debate.

The Becker/Gouldner debate

Despite Weber's defeat in the *werturteilsstreit*, the idea of value-freedom quickly became dominant in the years preceding, and following, World War II. There are reasons for this, some of which we will explore below, but the key one was sociology's search for scientific respectability. Claiming to be value-free aligned sociology with 'expert' and scientific knowledge and allowed sociologists to claim they did not threaten any social formation with political views (Seubert 1991). It also ensured sociologists who were also involved in schemes for reform, such as Robert Park, could define such work as separate to their 'scientific' work as sociologists and, therefore, not worthy of academic comment (Deegan 2006). This was especially prominent in American sociology which searched for this scientific recognition in order to lose its previous association with community activism suggested in the work of, among others, Park's wife Clara Cahill Park and Jane Addams who collaborated with Mead and other female sociologists in her efforts for social reform (Deegan 1988, Turner 2014).

Into this context stepped Alvin Gouldner and his 1962 article 'Anti-Minotaur: The Myth of a Value-Free Sociology', which began with the following:

> This is an account of a myth created by and about a magnificent mino-taur named Max – Max Weber, to be exact; his myth was that social science should and could be value-free. The lair of this minotaur, although reached only by a labrynthian logic and visited only by a few who never return, is still regarded by many sociologists as a holy place. In particular, as sociologists grow older they seem impelled to make a pilgrimage to it and to pay their respects to the problem of the relations between values and social science … Today, all the powers of sociology … have entered into a tacit alliance to bind us to the dogma that 'Thou shalt not commit a value judgment' especially as sociologists. Where is the introductory textbook, where the lecture course on principles, that does not affirm or imply this rule? (Gouldner 1962:199)

As this quote indicates, for Gouldner value-freedom was a 'myth' in both sense of the term. It was a myth since it wasn't possible beyond a very small selection of possible cases (if at all) but it was also mythical given that, despite this, sociologists continued to believe in it. Indeed, a belief in value-freedom was one of the things that made one a sociologist. Problematically, for Gouldner, those who worshipped at the altar had not read the gospel; few had actually read Weber's work and in particular the careful and complicated lines which, as we saw above, Weber drew between a value-laden citizen and a value-free sociologist. When we recognise those complex lines there are three criticisms we can make of this myth for Gouldner.

Firstly, it is of its time and place. The Germany of the first decade of the twentieth century was, as we saw, a highly politically charged and confrontational arena. In any one academic meeting it may be possible to find anarchists, Marxists, liberals, conservatives and nationalists. In that context any political debate was largely impossible and Weber's claim for value-freedom 'was a proposal for an academic truce. It said, in effect, if we all keep quiet about our political views then we may all be able to get on with our work' (Gouldner 1962:202). This was especially notable in Weber's views on teaching, where an attempt to keep politics out of the classroom was encouraged by the fact that a lecturer's income, and potential for promotion, was linked directly to student numbers in their lectures (Gouldner 1962:201). None of these conditions still hold for Gouldner; not only are lecturers now promoted primarily on the basis of their research but the universities of the early 1960s America, along with wider society, were marked by their unpolitical nature. Therefore, instead of discouraging political debate it may be better to encourage it and therefore extend the political engagement and pluralism of society more broadly (Gouldner 1962:202).

Secondly, the distinction Weber makes between a value-heavy citizen and a value-free sociologist is untenable. In making this distinction Weber is separating the two traditions of reason and faith. For Gouldner, this allows Weber to have his cake and eat it too since it means the reasonable, rational sociologist could, in Weber's case, praise the rationalisation of society while the romantic citizen with faith could also condemn the disenchantment it created (Gouldner 1962:210). Weber 'wanted the play to be written by a classicist and to be acted by romanticists' (Gouldner 1962:211). Such a split is impossible for Gouldner since it demands cutting our personality in two. It is also unstable since it robs knowledge of its moral components and 'leaves feeling smugly sure only of itself and bereft of a sense of common humanity' (Gouldner 1962:212). Amoral knowledge does not relate to the types of lives we live; instead knowledge is always changed with moral ideas. For example, our idea of what 'poverty' is will always be shaped by moral ideas of the good life and, most likely, the (im)moral causes of such poverty.

Finally, the myth of value-freedom has been damaging for sociology. By arguing sociology is purely a profession with no commitment to values it means sociologists can sell their skills to the highest bidder. An example of this is 'doing market research designed to sell more cigarettes, although well aware of the implications of recent cancer research' (Gouldner 1962:204). This was not an unusual activity for sociologists (see Berger 2011:169–75).

Therefore, as a result of this, Gouldner encourages us to slay the minotaur and its doctrine of value-freedom, allowing space for normative claims. A similar message would, initially, appear to be contained in Howard Becker's classic article 'Whose Side Are We On?' (1967). Whereas Gouldner's argument was largely theoretical, Becker's referred to the process of research and the frequent accusations against sociologists of 'bias'. This, for Becker, reflects the nature of sociological research which is inevitably one-sided: we always look at the social world through the eyes of our participants. What is significant here is that, given the broadly left-leaning political position of sociologists, 'we usually take the side of the underdog' (Becker 1967:244). This is not a problem to be solved, rather, as we shall see, it is an inevitability to be acknowledged (Becker 1967:245).

The accusation of bias engendered by such research can be understood with reference to what Becker terms the 'hierarchy of credibility'. Defined as 'any system of ranked groups' (Becker 1967:241) this involves a situation where one group has power over a group below it and therefore is able to direct their daily activities and define their position. Given their politics sociologists tend to take the group at the bottom of the hierarchy; sociologists tend to research the working class and not the bourgeoisie, prisoners rather than guards and protesters rather than politicians. This can then lead to claims of bias in two ways. In an 'apolitical' situation no one has questioned the hierarchy of credibility and therefore sociological research is seen as misleading by taking the underdog's position. After all, 'everyone knows' that teachers do what is best for students, so why ask the children themselves? Everyone knows that prisoners have, by definition, wronged against society and are there to be punished, so why ask what they think the value of prison is? Consequently, since 'no one proposes that addicts should make and enforce laws for policemen, that patients should prescribe for doctors, or that adolescents should give orders to adult' (Becker 1967:241), sociological research is biased in seeking their views.

The second situation is a political situation. Here the hierarchy of credibility has been called into question; the subordinate group has questioned the superordinate and their right to rule. The best example of this is a riot or large-scale protest. In such a situation, both sides have their spokespeople and arguments they wish to make. Such spokespeople will view sociological arguments not through their validity but rather through how they help their cause. Those findings which don't help will inevitably be termed 'biased'. In this case spokespeople 'base the accusation not on failures of technique or method, but on conceptual defects' and 'accuse the sociologist not of getting false data but of not getting all the data relevant to the problem' (Becker 1967:245). In such a political situation it is therefore inevitable that we end up on one side or the other: we are on the side of the rioters or the police.

The immediate response to such an argument is that sociologists should endeavour not to cover one but all sides. This, for Becker, is impossible:

> By pursuing this seemingly simple solution, we arrive at a problem of infinite regress. For everyone has someone standing above him who prevents

him from doing things just as he likes. If we question the superiors of the prison administrator, a state department of corrections or prisons, they will complain of the governor and the legislature. And if we go to the governor and the legislature, they will complain of lobbyists, party machines, the public and the newspapers. There is no end to it and we can never have a 'balanced picture' until we have studied all of society simultaneously. I do not propose to hold my breath until that happy day. (Becker 1967:247)

Instead 'the question is not whether we should take sides, since we inevitably will, but rather whose side we are on' (Becker 1967:239) which, for Becker, should be the side of the underdog. While such one-sidedness is an inevitability we should seek to 'use our theoretical and technical resources to avoid the distortions that might introduce into our work ... and field as best we can the accusations and doubts that will surely be our fate' (Becker 1967:247). A good example of such an approach can be found in Lumsden's (2012) work on 'boy racers' in Scotland. Lumsden found that through her work with this group – who were largely condemned by others and dictated to by the police trying to limit their driving – she increasingly sought to 'take their side' and put their case forward in the public sphere (for example, via media appearances to advocate their position). Therefore, being on the side of the underdog leads sociologists to consider, and advocate, solutions for improving their situation.

In many ways, Becker's position chimes with Gouldner's; both, for slightly different reasons, argue that value-freedom is an impossible position. However, there is a key difference, picked up on by Gouldner (1968) in a response to Becker. Whereas Gouldner argued sociologists should take the side of certain values, Becker thought they should take the side of groups creating, as Gouldner puts it, a 'sentiment-free social scientist' (Gouldner 1968:105). The reason for this takes us to Becker's research which was part of 'a school of thought that finds itself at home in the world of hip, drug addicts, jazz musicians, cab drivers, prostitutes, night people, drifters, grifters and skidders: the "cool world"' (Gouldner 1968:104). This desire to be with the cool world meant that Becker sided with *certain* underdogs against *certain* authority figures: the underdogs were the drug takers, the authority figures were the 'squares'. To be exact, the squares were the police who take the cool people's drugs or the managers who fired them. Often, the squares in such scenarios are not those with true power but rather middle managers and administrators – not as much 'top dogs' as 'middle dogs'. This meant that:

The new underdog sociology propounded by Becker is, then, a standpoint that possesses a remarkably convenient combination of properties: it enables the sociologist to befriend the very small underdogs in local settings, to reject the standpoint of the 'middle dog' respectables and notables who manage local caretaking establishments, while, at the same time, to make and remain friends with the really top dogs in Washington agencies or New York foundations. (Gouldner 1968:110)

Therefore, while Becker's approach may solve the problems of the split between the sociologist and citizen it does not solve the problem of turning sociology into a profession and putting its services up for sale. The emergence of the welfare state and the identification of sociologists with the left-of-centre parties which advocated this – the Democrats in the US, the Labour Party in the UK and so on – meant that Becker's focus on the under/middle dog dynamic allowed him to not take sides in the larger issues – the conflict between government and people, or capital and worker – which Gouldner saw as truly important. Instead, Becker's position allows sociologists to go to the true top dog, welfare state governments, and ask for funding to research the relation of under and middle dogs. Consequently it 'is the sociology of young men with friends in Washington' (Gouldner 1968:110). In opposition to Becker, Gouldner argues that 'it is to values, not factions, that sociologists must give their most basic commitment'; these values should be the recognition and intolerance of suffering (Gouldner 1968:116).

Therefore, the Becker/Gouldner debate has highlighted that if we do not accept the position of Weber on value-freedom, this is only the beginning of a wider conversation. This concerns not just the position of values in sociology but also the position of sociology in relation to other groups, such as underdogs and governments. Their debate opens up a key divide in what alternatives are for. From Becker's position we could say alternatives are for groups to lessen the problems confronted by the underdogs. For Gouldner, alternatives are focused on furthering certain values, such as lessening suffering. Similar debates continued in later years.

Further writings on value-freedom

Following the Becker/Gouldner debate there have been some interventions in favour of reasserting the idea of value-freedom. For Hammersley (1999) Gouldner engages in 'moral gerrymandering' by proclaiming a set of values as 'sociology's values'. Like Weber's claim for there being no qualifications in prophecy, Hammersley argues that there is nothing within sociology which suggests some values are 'better' than others. Instead 'sociology alone cannot tell us what it is itself *for*, in the sense of what it should stand for or aim at' (Hammersley 1999:4.1). Therefore, we should not seek to have sociology do something for which it isn't fit. Instead, we should return to the split between the sociologist and citizen. Also, for Black (2014), the dismissal of value-freedom by Becker and others has meant that 'much of what they call sociology is little more than the promotion of liberal or otherwise left-wing ideology' (Black 2014:764). Rather than proclaiming value-freedom as impossible we should recognise that value-freedom means simply not letting our values enter into matters of fact and stick to that creed.

For writers such as Hammersley and Black, attempts to jettison value-freedom discredit the truth claims of sociology and, ultimately, its attempt to be identified as a science. Science is based on universalism of knowledge (Merton 1973:267–78) and, as we have seen, values aren't universal. However, other writers have taken a different perspective on the importance of such universal knowledge, an example of which can be found in the work of Dorothy Smith.

For Smith, the claims of value-freedom and objectivity in social science have only been achieved by taking one position, the position of dominant men, and presuming this to be universal. This creates a particular approach to doing sociology:

> A sociology is a systematically developed consciousness of society and social relations. The 'established' sociology ... gives us a consciousness that looks at society, social relations and people's lives as if we could stand outside them, ignoring the particular local places in the everyday in which we live our lives. It claims objectivity not on the basis of its capacity to speak truthfully, but in terms of its specific capacity to exclude the presence and experience of particular subjectivities. Nonetheless, of course, they are there and must be. (Smith 1987:2)

Therefore, sociology has established itself as a truth-teller which stands outside, and above, people's experiences (Smith 1987:1–10). The value-freedom and objectivity this is seen to give are based upon the universality of its statements; they are the facts, not the values, which Weber prized so much. However, this rests upon two problems. Firstly, it is based upon removing particular voices and subjectivities. In this case, for Smith, the everyday experiences of women, their routinised activities of domestic work, childcare and relationships, are largely removed in favour of the macro-level discussion of topics such as industrial work, politics and public activity. Women exist 'outside the frame' (Smith 1987:61–9) and the knowledge presented is that of the male world, with its values converted into 'facts'. This is what Donna Haraway (2004:87) terms a 'god-trick' of claiming one can present a universal and objective picture of the world. Secondly, in doing so, sociology tends to present, and validate, the 'relations of ruling' in society. These rely upon a 'continual transformation of the local and particular actualities of our lives into abstracted and generalised forms' (Smith 1987:3). In order to control us governments, the law, business and educational institutions need to group us into abstract categories (such as the 'working class', 'students', 'offenders' and so on). Sociologists, by researching and helping give names to these groups, have helped establish the relations of ruling (Smith 1987:105–11) which, for Smith, reflects the fact that much sociology comes 'from the standpoint of men who do that ruling' (Smith 1987:2). Here, Smith shares Gouldner's fear about Becker's potential link to the top dog, and ruling relations, of the welfare state. But she adds an important gendered component.

Therefore, for Smith, claims for value-freedom have existed only through ignoring certain experiences and by validating the relations of ruling. The values of such, predominantly male, sociologists are presented as facts. Instead she advocates a 'sociology for women' – or, as she later put it, a 'sociology for people' (Smith 2005) – which starts from those particular experiences and everyday encounters which shape our knowledge and activity in the world (Smith 1987). This is a 'standpoint' theory in the sense that it seeks to see the world from a particular position (that of everyday women) and uses it to allow the 'absent experience ... to be filled with the presence and spoken experience of actual women' (Smith 1987:107).

Standpoint theories opened up a cleavage within feminism to the extent that they could be said to operate as 'successor sciences' (Stanley and Wise 1990). Some, such as Sandra Harding, have argued that standpoint theory produces truer scientific knowledge since the oppressed see both their own experience and that of the dominant, whereas the dominant only know their own experience. Therefore, it is truly universal (Harding 1987). However, as Stanley and Wise (1990:29–36) note, this relies upon a universal 'female' standpoint which isn't true given the various inequalities between women, a position Smith (1987:106–7) also holds. Therefore, Smith's version of standpoint theory does not imagine a privileged position for universal female experience and is less likely to claim successor science status. A similar claim is found in Haraway's (2004:87) suggestion that 'feminist objectivity' is defined by the 'limited location and situated knowledge' of intellectual claims, rather than the 'god-trick' of false universalism. This position advocates the extension of everyday forms of knowledge with an 'intersectional' awareness of how people may occupy many different social positions. This has been advocated most notably by black feminists who highlight that some feminist standpoints are actually those of white women (Crenshaw 1991, Collins 2000).

What do such discussions mean for value-freedom and sociological alternatives? They make three claims. Firstly, as we have seen, pre-existing definitions of value-freedom can only claim such status by marginalising particular experiences and claiming one view of the world as a universal fact. In this case, the values of the male world are presented as such facts. Secondly, in doing so such a sociology can be complicit in maintaining, and even extending, ruling institutions (similar to Gouldner's claim). And finally, we should be careful about claiming any kind of universal experience of a social world which is highly unequal and differentiated. Consequently, alternatives should be aware of these diverse subjectivities and not seek to universalise the experience of one group. Therefore, not only were the writings of Smith and others critical of claims for value-freedom, they also indicate a shift towards the idea of 'critical sociology'.

Critical sociology

The idea of sociology being 'critical' has now become ubiquitous; indeed, whereas Gouldner claimed a belief in value-freedom made you a sociologist, it could now be said a belief in being critical makes you a sociologist. To speak of a sociologist's work as 'uncritical' is 'a criticism verging on the insulting'

(Levitas 2013:99). Nevertheless, this is a relatively recent occurrence, from roughly the 1970s onwards, and has seen some criticisms, with Hammersley (2005) again arguing against and in favour of the split of sociologist and citizen. A 'critical' sociology is one which seeks not just to explain the social world but rather to see what is hidden and, in particular, to highlight the forms of power and inequality which exist. As a result, it will often take the position of the powerless against the powerful. In this sense, it follows on from Becker's idea of the sociology of the underdog but with a wider normative goal. Critical sociology, or, as it is also called, 'liberation sociology' (Feagin et al. 2015), aims not just to understand the underdog but to 'emancipate' them (Boltanski 2011); the goal is not to recount the inequities of society but to change them. In doing so, non-critical forms of sociology are condemned as something which 'helps as much as a painstaking description of the technology of making nooses helps the convict overcome his fear of the gallows' (Bauman 1978:193).

There are different ways in which critical sociology is advocated (see Sayer 2009) but one of the most comprehensive ones comes from Bauman (1976a). For him, sociology has two key elements. Firstly, it is concerned with the limits provided by 'second nature'. Whereas there are 'natural' limits to our behaviour (for example, we cannot fly) the social limits are second nature which restrict our behaviour, including the norms, values and inequalities found in the social world. Part of the sociological mission is to understand how second nature works and its role in shaping our action (Bauman 1976a:1–14). The second element is common sense; sociology 'is a sophisticated elaboration upon crude commonsense' (Bauman 1976a:28) and seeks to understand, and see what is underneath, commonsense claims about the world. As Bauman puts it, this involves '*defamiliarizing the familiar* and *familiarizing* (taming, domesticating) *the unfamiliar*' (Bauman 2011:171).

Such a conception of sociology is not wholly unique (see Berger 1963), and similar claims are often the basis for the innately critical nature of sociology (Back 2007). What is unique in Bauman's conception is his claim that such attributes are not necessarily transgressive. An awareness of what leads people to act in certain ways and how norms and values shape our perception of the world can be used in order to control those people. For example, workplaces can be shaped to engender certain forms of action (Bauman 1976a:35–9) and sociological knowledge can be used by totalitarian regimes (Bauman 1976b). This could also be done in a paternalistic way by shaping institutions to 'encourage' people to adopt healthy lifestyles akin to 'nudge theory' (White 2013). In doing so sociology:

> Saves the individual from the torments of indecision and the responsibility he is too weak to bear, by sharply cutting down the range of acceptable options to the size of his 'real' potential. The price it pays, however, for playing such a benign and charitable role is its essentially conservative impact upon the society it helps people to explain and understand. (Bauman 1976a:35)

Such an approach Bauman terms 'the science of unfreedom'. Here the goal is to lessen the scope of human freedom, for either paternalistic or authoritarian ends (Bauman 1976a:27–42). This highlights 'the intrinsically conservative role of sociology' found within its potential as the science of unfreedom (Bauman 1976a:36).

In opposition to such an approach Bauman advocates a 'science of freedom'. This seeks not only to highlight the limits to freedom but to transcend them, meaning that 'its struggle is not with commonsense, but with the practice, called social reality, which underlies it' (Bauman 1976a:75). Consequently:

> By doing its job – re-presenting human condition as the product of human action – sociology was and is to me a critique of extant social reality. Sociology is meant to expose the relativity of what is, to open the possibility for alternative social arrangements and ways of life, to militate against the TINA ('There Is No Alternative') ideologies and life philosophies. As an interpretation of human experience laying bare its invisible, hidden or covered-up links, the mission of sociology, as I understood it all along, was to keep other options alive. (Bauman 2008:238)

Therefore, a science of freedom aimed at emancipation is fundamentally concerned with expanding the potential for human freedom. In doing so, for Bauman, it raises the possibility of alternatives. While this is not a universal claim – critical theorists such as Adorno rejected the prospect of being 'terrorised into action' by engaging in utopian speculation (Adorno 1991:202) – it could be said that if we critique and say that something is negative or bad then we imply some idea of a 'good' society in which such negatives are removed. Such a perspective of sociology as the science of freedom is implicit in many of the sociological alternatives offered throughout this book.

We can take the key point from Bauman that sociology faces a choice between the science of freedom and of unfreedom. If it chooses the latter, as it seems writers like Becker, Gouldner and Smith advocate, then the question of alternatives is inevitable. A critical approach implies sociological alternatives. Indeed, as we shall see in Chapter 9, for Levitas, this is a utopian perspective.

Conclusion

In this chapter I have traced a brief history of debates on value-freedom and critical sociology. As we have seen, the initial push for value-freedom in sociology from Weber came in a particular context of a politically charged Germany and rested on a split between the sociologist and the citizen. The former was not able to offer value-judgements, but the latter was. This distinction was a key part of the critique offered by both Becker and Gouldner. However, this debate threw up a further question: might the advocacy of values just create a partisan sociologist who sides with the newly emergent welfare state? Such concerns were expanded upon by Smith, who highlighted not only the link between sociology and the relations of ruling but how these relied upon the universalisation of a male viewpoint at the expense of female subjectivities. In comparison to such a perspective, the idea of sociology as 'critical' has emerged in recent decades. But, as Bauman noted, this is not an intrinsic good; instead we have a choice between the science of freedom or unfreedom.

So, to return to the question which began this chapter: should sociologists offer alternatives? The answer, from the debates we have discussed in this chapter, ultimately relies upon a value-judgement: what is it that we wish sociology to be? If the goal is to imagine a science based upon the values of universalism (Merton 1973) then alternatives, as value-judgements, should be avoided or, at the very least, kept to a minimum and clearly highlighted as value-judgements. This does not mean we as individuals will not have values rather that these are kept out of our professional sociological work. If we reject the possibility of such a divide or, following Bauman, argue the question of a science of freedom or unfreedom is inevitable, then alternatives become part of the sociological project. As we shall see, for a variety of reasons, the social theorists covered in this book have shared this point of view and, in different ways, have argued that sociologists should offer alternatives.

Karl Marx and Friedrich Engels: 'Recipes for the Cook-Shops of the Future'

2

Given the topic of this book it would seem Karl Marx (1818–83) and Friedrich Engels (1820–95) were obvious inclusions; after all, it is difficult to think of any theorists more readily associated with an alternative than Marx and Engels are with communism. This is also significant given the large number of communist states which, proclaiming themselves as 'Marxist', emerged in the twentieth century. Therefore, there is particular value in discussing Marx and Engels as an example of a 'successful' sociological alternative, if we define success as influence in creative alternative societies. However, here we face a contradiction since although Marx and Engels are associated with communism they actually wrote very little about it. The title of this chapter comes from a claim of Marx, offered in the afterword to the second German edition of *Das Kapital*, that he would limit himself 'to the mere critical analysis of actual facts, instead of writing recipes for the cook-shops of the future' (Marx 1996a:17, Wyatt 2006). As we shall see, Marx and Engels offered multiple justifications for this reticence, the main one being that the construction of communism was the job of the revolutionary working class, not intellectuals. As Marx put it, the working class:

> have no ideas to realise, but to set free the elements of the new society with which old collapsing bourgeois society itself is pregnant. In the full consciousness of their historic mission, and with the heroic resolve to act upon it, the working class can afford to smile at the coarse invective of the gentlemen's gentlemen with the pen and inkhorn, and at the didactic patronage of well-wishing bourgeois-doctrinaires, pouring forth their ignorant platitudes and sectarian crotchets in the oracular tone of scientific infallibility. (Marx 1996b:188)

Yet it is worthwhile revisiting Marx and Engels' writings since, as the above quote demonstrates, they argued the new society would be an attempt to set free the emancipatory potential within capitalist society. Indeed, it was the fact that trends in capitalism pointed towards communism, as well as the need for immediate political strategy, which meant Marx and Engels were more forthcoming about communism than the above comments suggest. For some writers, these ideas indicate the differences between communism as imagined by Marx and Engels and the communist states which formed in the twentieth century (Bauman 1976b:101).

Following the definition of a sociological alternative developed in the 'Introduction' I will begin by outlining the critique Marx and Engels offered of capitalist society. I will then discuss the reasons for their reluctance to detail an alternative before turning to the fragmentary suggestions they did offer. Here I will reference the Paris Commune of 1871 which, while for Engels and later Lenin was an example of working-class power, for Marx it showed the challenges of achieving communism.

Marx and Engels' critique

Given the fame of Marx as a theorist of class the initial temptation may be to assume his and Engels' critique is one focused on inequality; this is not the case. While class is central to the critique of capitalism the inequality it produces was not its main fault. Marx was appalled by the poverty he saw as a young man in Germany and later in London (Lubasz 1976) and Engels produced a masterpiece of social history with his survey of 1840s Manchester in *The Condition of the Working Class in England* (Engels 1958). Nevertheless, we will find a stronger condemnation of inequality when we turn to the work of Durkheim in the next chapter.

Instead, it is useful to think of Marx and Engels' critique of capitalism as having three key components: alienation, exploitation and wastefulness. While the first two are broadly critiques of the lived experience of capitalism the final one is more of a structural critique. The three combined suggest the inevitable failure of capitalism, forming 'the long-term non-sustainability of capitalism thesis' (Wright 2010:90) where capitalism's internal laws mean it produces the conditions for its revolutionary overthrow. This then opens the way for the transformation of society to Marx and Engels' alternative: communism. As *The Communist Manifesto* puts it, 'the theory of the Communists may be summed up in the single sentence: Abolition of private property' (Marx and Engels 1992:18). We should understand private property here as the ownership by an individual, or groups of individuals, of what Marx terms the 'means of production' or 'material productive forces of society' (Marx 1992c:425), that is, the things used to produce the goods we consume. This would include factories and machinery up to office buildings, computers and raw materials. Capitalism as an economic system relies upon these being privately owned. Since, for Marx, 'changes in the economic foundation lead sooner or later to the transformation of the whole immense superstructure' (Marx 1992c:426) changing the way in which the means of production are used away from a capitalist system will change the rest of society. It is this which makes Marx a 'materialist' since he believes that the shape of society is not primarily determined by laws, politics or ideas but rather originates from the material conditions (Marx 1992c:425). A capitalist system, based upon private property, will produce a capitalist society. Consequently removing private property, and thereby replacing capitalism with communism, will make a communist society.

Alienation

To understand the importance of alienation for Marx it is first essential to understand what he thought made us human. For Marx, humans are defined by their ability to be creative and, in relation with nature, produce things to make our lives liveable and enjoyable, whether this be the homes in which we live, the products we use or the meals we eat; as he put it 'productive life is species-life' (Marx 1992a:328). Unlike animals, who produce only for immediate ends, humans are able to contemplate, design and produce for long-term needs. Capitalism destroys this and in doing so alienates, or 'estranges', us from what makes us human. In *The Economic and Philosophical Manuscripts of 1844* Marx outlines four types of alienation: from the product of our labour, from the labour process, from our 'species-being' and from other people (Marx 1992a:322–34). I will now discuss these one by one (see Ollman 1976 for a more detailed discussion of alienation).

Alienation from the product of our labour concerns the things we produce. When we go to work we produce something which does not, nor will in the future, belong to us. This is true whether we build cars, design computers or sell insurance, in no instance is there a fruit of our labour which we can point to as 'ours'. Therefore, for Marx, the product on which we work appears 'alien' to us (Marx 1992a:326) and rather than gaining a sense of value from it – the satisfaction of producing something yourself – all the value goes into the product which is then sold to someone else. To exacerbate matters when the product is sold the value of it is not returned to us but is appropriated by the capitalist in the form of profit.

This then leads onto the second form of alienation: from the work process. Under capitalism work is something we are compelled to do to survive; therefore, work becomes a means towards an end. As a result we are not productive because we want to but because we have to; as Marx puts it, 'labour is *external* to the worker … [who] feels miserable and not happy, does not develop free mental and physical energy, but mortifies his flesh and ruins his mind' (Marx 1992a:326). Therefore, rather than finding enjoyment in the distinctively human activity of productive labour we turn elsewhere:

> The result is that man (the worker) feels that he is acting freely only in his animal functions – eating, drinking and procreating, or at most in his dwelling and adornment – while in his human functions he is nothing more than an animal. (Marx 1992a:327)

We ignore our uniquely human activities of creativity and labour in favour of things which are purely animal. This form of alienation is made worse by the division of labour. Our work likely involves doing a small task repeatedly. For example, no one 'builds' a car; they may just apply the paint, attach the tyres or do the initial design. In addition we are likely only to have one occupation, meaning our ability to be creative in multiple fields is removed.

This is where we confront alienation from what Marx calls 'species-being': alienation from labour and the labour process are denying what makes us truly human. This also means we are alienated from other people. Our relationships with others become defined by capitalist relations, such as competition for jobs or promotion, the services we pay for or our formal relations with work colleagues. The result is that other individuals are treated merely as commodities and sources for our satisfaction, rather than truly well-rounded, or as Marx prefers, *universal* (Marx 1992a:327), people. Capitalism leaves 'no other nexus between man and man than naked self-interest, than callous "cash payment"' (Marx and Engels 1992:5).

Thus far I have spoken about how alienation affects workers but Marx argues it affects all classes, including the bourgeoisie (Marx 1992a:333–4). This group, being those who control the means of production, inevitably have relationships determined primarily by economic considerations. This is true of the workers they pay and monitor, as well as their competitors who they hope to outperform. In addition to this, rather than capital giving us the possibility of being creative, it often means the opposite. If I own a factory I cannot produce whatever I want but rather what will sell or what I have been contracted to produce. Therefore, the comfortable position of the bourgeoisie is no shelter from the deformities of alienation.

The result of this is that, for Marx, higher wages would be 'nothing more than better *pay for slaves* and would not mean an increase in human significance or dignity' (Marx 1992a:332). Capitalism, a system where work is a compulsion done for others in order to produce something which is not ours, inevitably creates alienation.

Exploitation

For Marx, capitalism is a system based upon a contradiction: producing goods, and therefore producing value, is a collective affair. People come together to make and sell a product; however, the money made from that product is appropriated by the capitalist. Thus wealth is produced socially but privately appropriated. This law of capitalism is the first step in understanding how it is a system based upon the exploitation of workers.

When one lives in a capitalist system there are two possible paths to earn a living. Either, one has capital in which case they can invest in the means of production and employ people to work for them. Or, one does not have capital in which case the only way to make a living is to sell your labour for a wage. The former is the position of the bourgeoisie, and the latter that of the proletariat (Marx 1976:899). The worker is dependent upon a capitalist for a wage and therefore 'the capitalist reproduces the worker as a *wage-labourer*' (Marx 1976:1063).

These wages are paid in return for working a certain number of hours. If I am paid £50 for a day's work it stands to reason that during that day I should produce £50 worth of value. However, this is not the basis of capitalism since

I must also produce profit for the capitalist employing me. Marx (1976:340) outlines the working day as such:

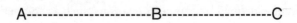

The point between A and B is the time in which I produce my £50 worth of value, and the point from B to C is when I am producing more value than my wage. I am, in effect, working for free in order to produce profit and wealth for a capitalist; it is 'unpaid labour' (Marx 1976:713). This unpaid labour, the point between B and C, is what Marx calls 'surplus value' which is the 'increment or excess' beyond which the capitalist has invested, in this case, by paying wages (Marx 1976:215).

Capitalism is a system based upon extracting as much surplus value, and thereby as much profit, as possible. This is done by pushing down wages to the lowest possible level and finding ways, either through pressure upon workers or greater use of machines, to increase the space between B and C representing surplus value; in contemporary parlance, there is pressure on the workers 'to do more for less'. The result is that capitalism is a:

> means of domination and exploitation of the producers; they distort the worker into a fragment of a man, they degrade him to the level of an appendage of a machine, they destroy the actual content of his labour by turning it into a torment ... they deform the conditions under which he works, subject him during the labour process to a despotism the more hateful for its meanness; they transform his life-time into working-time. (Marx 1976:799)

Therefore, for Marx, capitalism inevitably includes exploitation; the division of the population into workers and non-workers facilitates this. Nevertheless, as we shall see below, this process also contains the seeds of capitalism's destruction.

The wastefulness of capitalism

Another way for capital to increase the amount of surplus value is to expand globally. Globalization was an inevitable result of capitalism since 'the need of a constantly expanding market for its products chases the bourgeoisie over the entire surface of the globe. It must nestle everywhere, settle everywhere, establish connections everywhere' (Marx and Engels 1992:6). Globalization increases the number of workers producing surplus value and buyers of the products they produce. It also has the added advantage of pushing down wages in rich countries to compete with lower paid workers abroad (Marx 1976:749).

But here we encounter a problem: production in capitalism is done without reference to immediate need and, since it is in the *individual* interest of each capitalist to expand and produce as much as possible, *every* capitalist will produce as much as possible; we get what Marx terms 'production for production's sake' (Marx 1976:1037). Left unchecked this inevitably creates a crisis since goods are produced without any immediate buyer, meaning:

> No one knows how much of his particular article is coming on the market, nor how much of it will be wanted. No one knows whether his individual product will meet an actual demand, whether he will be able to make good his costs of production or even to sell his commodity at all. Anarchy reigns in socialized production. (Engels 1984:136)

Therefore, capitalism can be seen as wasteful in its production methods, with goods produced which later cannot be sold. Recent writers have also argued that Marx was making an ecological point here: capital will use up natural resources without any concern for the long-term health of the planet which is beyond their concern with immediate surplus value (Foster 2000). For example, some have argued Marx's theory includes some conception, albeit underdeveloped, of 'natural limits' to capitalist production which remain unrecognised in the push for capital accumulation and the resulting overproduction (Benton 1996:177). This overproduction means capitalism is prone to crisis as goods remain unsold. Such crises, by further pushing down wages and allowing large companies protected by their capital to buy up smaller competitors, tend towards the creation of a global market dominated by fewer and fewer monopolistic powers confronting an enlarged proletariat class (Marx 1976:1062).

As we have seen Marx and Engels criticise capitalism for the alienation it engenders in both the workers and the owners, the way it exploits the workers and its inherent wastefulness and tendency towards crisis. However, they also argue there is a long-term trend for the capitalist class to shrink to its most affluent members and for the ranks of the proletariat to expand. It is this process which gives them their belief in the inevitability of revolution.

The revolution

As we have seen, capitalism needs workers, indeed Marx argues that capitalism 'creates' workers by making individuals dependent on waged labour. But in creating this group it produces the contradiction between social production and private appropriation; this has 'manifested itself as the antagonism of proletariat and bourgeoisie' (Engels 1984:136). As we have seen, these groups have opposed interests under capitalism, occasionally conflicts break out and:

> the workers begin to form combinations against the bourgeois; they club together in order to keep up the rate of wages; they found permanent associations in order to make provision beforehand for those occasional revolts. Here and there the contest breaks out into riots. Now and then the workers are victorious, but only for a time. The real fruit of their battles lies, not in the immediate result, but in the ever-expanding union of the workers. (Marx and Engels 1992:12)

For Marx and Engels, real change in alienation and exploitation is impossible under capitalism; the system relies upon both as integral parts of its make-up. Therefore, the only way to remove these symptoms of capitalism is to attack the cause and overthrow it. Here the proletariat assume the role of what Marx terms a 'universal class' – so called since 'in their emancipation is contained universal human emancipation' (1992a:333). Capitalism 'creates its own grave-diggers' (Marx and Engels 1992:16). It creates a group of workers who share exploitation and alienation, expands their number, places them in close living quarters in cities and workplaces and gives them some education. In doing so capitalism generates the intellectual, environmental and political conditions for its eventual overthrow since ultimately the proletariat will realise their shared fate as the universal class.

This of course leaves the question of when and how this revolution will occur. The question of 'when' will be discussed in the next section. *How* this revolution will occur is, however, relatively clear in their work. The eventual revolution of the proletariat is one of *praxis*, a revolution in the way people conceive of their actions. In the case of the proletariat this requires a shift in class formation from, to use the Marxist terms, a class 'in itself' (a class of people which objectively exists) to a class 'for itself' (a class which not only objectively exists but is made up of individuals who act in the shared subjective interests of their class). While this is likely to occur as a result of increased knowledge amongst the working class – and the pressures of the increased deprivation of capitalism – communist parties, such as those Marx and Engels were involved in, have a part to play since they:

> are on the one hand, practically, the most resolute section of the working-class parties of every country, that section which pushes forward all others; on the other hand, theoretically, they have over the great mass of the proletariat the advantage of clearly understanding the line of march, the conditions, and the ultimate general results of the proletarian movement. (Marx and Engels 1992:17)

Therefore, Marx and Engels tie their critique of capitalism to a suggestion of how these problems will be overcome. It is the revolutionary proletariat who will strike the final blow against capitalism, ushering in communism. As this quote also suggests, Marx and Engels see this as a result of the historical trends of capitalist development.

Marx and Engels' alternative: communism

We have seen that Marx and Engels' critique of capitalism leads to the suggestion of its eventual revolutionary overthrow. However, at this point we return to the start of the chapter, namely that Marx and Engels were not willing to provide a detailed guideline as to when this would happen, or what communism would eventually look like. In short, they offer no 'blueprint' of a communist society. As was also highlighted at the start of the chapter Marx made a virtue out of this, claiming that it was the revolutionary proletariat who make communism, not the 'gentlemen's gentlemen with the pen and inkhorn' (Marx 1996b:188). There were other explanations for such reticence.

The question of 'when' the revolution will happen is absent from Marx and Engels' work. It is practically impossible to know when the revolution will come; to pretend that one knew, or to suggest a date in which it should happen, would mean 'that man can will the future' (Avineri 1968:217) and remove all power from the proletariat as the group who actually *make* revolution. Since Marx placed so much emphasis in the proletariat making revolution through *praxis*, this was inconceivable. Therefore, if one doesn't know when the revolution will happen, it is very difficult to know the conditions under which communism will be built. This is especially important for Marx since he suggests that revolution could happen in contrasting ways in different places. Speaking in 1871 he draws a distinction between two prospects:

> In England, for instance, the way to show political power lies open to the working class. Insurrection would be madness where peaceful agitation would more swiftly and surely do the work. In France a hundred laws of repression and a mortal antagonism between classes seem to necessitate the violent solution of social war. (Marx and Landor 1962:130)

Therefore, in a country like England communism may be achievable via the ballot box. As the working class gain the vote a peaceful election of communism is conceivable, whereas in France, as the Paris Commune (see below) showed, violence will probably be necessary. Given these varying trajectories any blueprint would seem useless, the birth and development of communism in the UK and France would be so divergent and the relations of those living under it so different that to provide a universal blueprint would be folly.

Consequently, Marx and Engels suggest that 'communism is for us not a *state of affairs* which is to be established ... We call communism the *real* movement which abolishes the present state of things' (Marx and Engels 1998:57). Since communism is a movement – as it was later called 'the theory of the *process* of liberation' (Screpanti 2007:140, my emphasis) – it can in the short term support a variety of other movements which 'bring to the front, as the leading question in each, the property question' (Marx and Engels 1992:39) without being dictated to by what a final blueprint suggests must be achieved.

Furthermore, Marx and Engels present their form of communism as 'scientific' since their conclusions, based upon the observable conditions and contradictions of capitalism, are:

> in no way based on ideas or principles that have been invented, or discovered, by this or that would-be universal reformer. They merely express, in

general terms, actual relations springing from an existing class struggle, from a historical movement going on under our very eyes. (Marx and Engels 1992:18)

In short, Marx and Engels' form of communism was based upon historical developments which showed possibilities for transformation beyond capitalism. We have seen this in the critique of capitalism and its links to the eventual revolution. This then forms the basis of another reason for rejecting the construction of a communist blueprint, found in Engels' comparison of their 'scientific' with others, 'utopian' socialism (Engels 1984).

Marx and Engels were far from the first to conceive of, and advocate, socialism. Many writers in the late eighteenth and nineteenth century had already done so, most notably the French philosophers Henri de Saint Simon (1760–1825) and Charles Fourier (1772–1837) as well as the Welsh businessman-turned-social reformer Robert Owen (1771–1858). Owen in particular had achieved a certain level of fame not only for his writings (it was rumoured even Napoleon, in exile on Elba, had managed to read, and comment upon, his *A New View of Society*) but as a man of action. Owen developed his New Lanark cotton mill in Scotland along humanitarian lines; formed new, but ultimately doomed, cooperative settlements such as New Harmony in Indiana, USA, and had a role in the London-based Trades Union. This final body in 1832 began the National Equitable Labour Exchange where workers could receive a voucher for their labour to be exchanged in stores – similar to an idea of Marx to be discussed below (for more details on Owen's socialism, see Cole 1930).

Despite a grudging respect for such figures, especially Owen who he saw as the father of social movements in the UK (Engels 1984:121), Engels was dismissive of their view of socialism for being 'utopian'. To be exact, each started not with the conditions of the society they confront but rather began by constructing the 'ideal' society, the blueprint of socialism. Once this 'new and more perfect system of social order' was constructed by the utopian all that was needed was to 'impose this upon society ... by propaganda and, whenever it was possible, by the example of model experiments' (Engels 1984:114). This relies upon what Engels termed 'the individual man of genius', that is, a brilliant man, such as Owen, thinking up the idea of socialism (Engels 1984:112). The individual man of genius comes to this realisation because of his brilliance and imagination, 'independent of time, space and of the historical development of man' (Engels 1984:122) not because of any study of the conditions of society and its long-term trends. To use the language of this book, Engels is arguing the socialisms of Owen et al. are not *sociological* but rather *philosophical* alternatives. They do not have a sociological understanding nor a critique of capitalist society such as that of Marx and Engels and, because of that, remain 'pure fantasies' (Engels 1984:114).

This is not only an intellectual problem for Engels but one of the construction of socialism. Reliance on an individual man of genius inevitably means placing a large amount of faith and power in that individual. Since St. Simon,

Fournier and Owen all disagreed on the nature of socialism, and since their visions were based on imagination rather than science, their followers could only trust their visionary and deride the vision of others. Marx had a similar view in his critique of anarchist thinkers who relied on blueprints (Avineri 1968:238–9).

So, as we have seen, Marx and Engels have clear justifications for their reluctance to provide a clearly elaborated alternative. Yet it would be untrue to say there was *no* suggestion of what communism would look like in their writings. Indeed, as Ollman (1977) has argued, even if the details of communism are sparse in Marx's work the *idea* of it is omnipresent. In order to criticise private property as alienating and exploitative one must be able to conceive of a society without private property: a communist society. Therefore, although the suggestions are sparse and perhaps less detailed than other theorists we will encounter in this book there is enough for us to perceive a general idea of what the communist alternative could look like, if not construct a blueprint. These suggestions come in three forms in the writings of Marx and Engels: communist strategy, the pre-existing conditions for communism and reflections on the Paris Commune.

Communist strategy

As we have seen Marx and Engels saw communism as a movement. While this movement may not know its final destination, like any political group, it needs some form of strategy for what it should be trying to achieve in the short term. *The Communist Manifesto*, a book written not only to let others know what communists stood for but also to let *communists* know, was the inevitable place for this (Hobsbawm 1998). The strategy suggested here is 'to raise the proletariat to the position of the ruling class, to win the battle for democracy' (Marx and Engels 1992:25); elsewhere a similar thought is expressed as the need to establish a 'dictatorship of the proletariat' (Marx 1978:127, 1996c:222). It has often been commented that these phrases are somewhat vague. However, as we have seen, Marx focused on the different ways of achieving proletariat power in different situations, so in countries like the UK 'winning the battle for democracy' could conceivably mean having members of the proletariat win the popular vote. Elsewhere it may mean large-scale agitation, violent or not, for an extension of the franchise or a new regime in which working-class power is more readily achievable. The *dictatorship* of the proletariat which would then be established may sound authoritarian to modern ears but the word 'dictatorship' did not have the same connotation in the time of Marx and Engels but rather meant a short-lived government granted exceptional powers by collective decision (Draper 1961:93). Therefore, communist strategy should be to obtain power for the proletariat; this group, as the revolutionary class, can then use this power to follow through on its historical mission (Marx and Engels 1992:25).

The *Manifesto* then provides the following list of demands (Marx and Engels 1992:25–6):

1. Abolition of property in land and application of all rents of land to public purposes.
2. A heavy progressive tax.
3. Abolition of all rights of inheritance.
4. Confiscation of the property of all emigrants and rebels.
5. Centralisation of credit in the hands of the State, by means of a national bank with State capital and an exclusive monopoly.
6. Centralisation of transport in the hands of the State.
7. Extension of factories and instruments of production owned by the State; the bringing into cultivation of wastelands, and the improvement of the soil generally in accordance with a common plan.
8. Equal liability of all to labour. Establishment of industrial armies, especially for agriculture.
9. Combination of agriculture with industry, promotion of the gradual elimination of the contradictions between town and countryside.
10. Free education for all children in public schools. Abolition of children's factory labour in its present form. Combination of education with industrial production.

This list has generated debate, focused upon whether or not it is communism. Some, such as Ollman (1977:10), argue these demands constitute the 'first stage' of communism and are to be put in place once the proletariat has defeated the bourgeoisie. Others, including Avineri (1968:204–8), argue that instead they are the things the state does *before* communism and which provide the basis for the 'universal suffrage' which Marx advocated. Universal suffrage here was more sophisticated than its usual meaning of everyone having the vote and rather meant abolishing 'the distinction between state and civil society' (Avineri 1968:204), by extending political power, held by the proletariat, into more and more areas.

Given Marx and Engels' lack of clarity about the list it is hard to know whether Avineri or Ollman was 'right'. However, Avineri seems to have the stronger case. As he points out, a key demand, in fact *the* communist demand, abolition of private property and the socialisation of the means of production, is not listed here. There is the removal of property of land but not the things used to produce (such as factories, machinery and so on). Indeed, the progressive taxation provision seems to imply the continuation of a bourgeoisie class who will be taxed. This can be explained by the fact it is the job of the revolutionary proletariat, not Marx and Engels as intellectuals, to determine how and when to appropriate the means of production once they have achieved political power. Avineri also highlights that in many ways this list is un-radical, reflecting changes which were occurring at the time (national banks and centralisation of transport) and indeed many have been realised in capitalist societies (free education and progressive taxation).

Therefore, returning to our earlier point, it is perhaps best to think of these ten demands not as a 'blueprint' for communism but rather immediate goals for the communist movement. Therefore, we must continue to look further in Marx and Engels' work for suggestions of the communist alternative.

The pre-existing conditions for communism

In an earlier quote we saw Marx argue that the proletariat hope 'to set free the elements of the new society with which old collapsing bourgeois society itself is pregnant'. We have also seen that this idea of communism emerging from capitalism was a key justification for Engels' defence of Marxism as 'scientific' rather than 'utopian' socialism.

Consequently, it would seem possible to highlight what these pre-existing conditions for communism are. This is exactly what Marx did in two pieces: the already mentioned *Economic and Philosophical Manuscripts* and *The Critique of the Gotha Programme*. The latter text was especially important; written as a detailed criticism of a draft plan of action for the German Social Democratic Workers Party it is forceful in its view that:

> Here we are dealing with a communist society, not as it *has developed* from first principles, but on the contrary, just as it *emerges* from capitalist society, hence in every respect – economically, morally, intellectually – as it comes forth from the womb, it is stamped with the birthmarks of the old society. (Marx 1996c:213)

Due to its parentage in capitalism Marx claims that communism would likely have two phases. These have since become known as the difference between socialism (first phase) and communism (second phase) although Marx never uses these terms, referring to 'crude communism' and 'communism' in the *Manuscripts* and the 'first' and 'higher' phase in the *Critique*. For ease I will use the second set of terms. These come close to a 'blueprint' of communism and thus it could be claimed Marx is contradicting himself. However, this can be defended as what Marx claims is likely to happen if the revolution occurred in the near future. Since we don't know when it will happen we can't guarantee this, but it may be useful as a guide.

The first phase of communism occurs once the proletariat have seized power, established their dictatorship and taken control of the means of production. Importantly, this doesn't mean property is abolished; property remains but is owned by the state. Rather than working for a capitalist, everyone works for the state, as Marx puts it 'the *community* as universal capitalist' (Marx 1992a:347). Therefore working conditions change little, but the way in which one is paid and goods distributed changes notably. Rather than being paid in a wage one gets a 'receipt of labour' which details how long one has worked. This receipt can then be used to 'withdraw from society's stores of the means of consumption an equal amount costed in labour terms' (Marx 1996c:213). So goods would be given a value not in terms of money but rather in terms of labour time; working more would mean being able to purchase more goods, the benefit here being that if one is given a receipt for all the labour they do there is no possibility of surplus labour and, as Marx puts it, 'the rights of producers is *proportional* to the labour they contribute' (Marx 1996c:214). Those who contribute more get more.

The upshot of this is that the first phase of communism is not an equal society – far from it in fact. Marx talks of the receipt system as containing a '*right to inequality*' (Marx 1996c:214) since, he suggests, some are 'physically or mentally superior' to others, meaning they can do more in less time and/or work longer. Also, Marx points out that some are married (note the gendered assumption here – married women clearly do not work) or have children, meaning they need more than others. The result of all this for Marx is that while the receipt system 'acknowledges no distinction of class' it does 'tacitly recognise unequal individual talent and hence productivity in labour as natural privileges' (Marx 1996c:214). Marx presents this inequality as an inevitable result of communism coming from capitalism; to go from a system of extreme inequality like capitalism to a system of equality overnight would not only be difficult practically but could be unjust morally. As Marx puts it, 'rights can never be higher than the economic form' and 'cultural development' of society (Marx 1996c:214). To introduce a right to equality without first having this economic and cultural development is impossible.

The first phase of communism then attempts not only to remove the exploitation of capitalism but also to engender this economic and cultural development. Marx suggests that given the strength of alienation under capitalism and the competition and distrust it creates between individuals a key aim of the first phase of communism is to create the 'cooperative' relationships between people as free producers rather than individuals divided by opposed class interests. This will inevitably take time but once it happens we have one of the key conditions for the higher phase of communism. With the development of cooperative relationships and a lack of class antagonism and conflict there is no more need for the 'socially repressive force' of the state (Engels 1984:147) and therefore this is removed or, as the later Leninist reading has it, 'withers away' (Lenin 1932). Since the state owned property in the first stage this also means that private property is finally removed; the higher phase of communism is 'the *positive* suppression of *private property*' (Marx 1992a:348). As a result no one 'owns' property but rather it becomes a common resource for all to use as they see fit.

The result of this is that we have no formal 'jobs' with no employer setting times for our shifts or other conditions. So it may be asked, would people continue to work? The answer to this for Marx is unequivocally yes. It is the alienation present within capitalism which has led us to think of productive activity as 'work', something we are forced to do in order to pay the bills. Remove that alienation, accomplished during the first stage of communism, and we will see labour as something we value and want to do; as Marx puts it, labour will become 'not merely a means to live but the foremost need in life' (Marx 1996c:214). By emphasising the centrality of labour and by providing the means of production to all communism is 'the complete restoration of man to himself as a *social*, that is human, being' (Marx 1992a:348); we can now cooperate in a friendly way to fulfil our fundamental human need to labour and be creative. What we produce is then distributed according to need and communism embodies the creed 'from each according to his ability, to each according to his needs' (Marx 1996c:215). We all contribute what our abilities allow us to do and the fruits of our labours are then distributed according to need. Such a system is impossible under the first phase of communism where alienated relationships remain; it is possible in the higher phase.

This vision of communism is also given a particular twist by Marx concerning the division of labour. As we saw earlier Marx saw this as one of the key elements of alienation; we were forced to do one job and, in particular, there was a strict divide between mental and physical labour. One was either a scientist or a plumber, being both was impossible. With the emergence of the higher phase of communism this is no longer the case; instead we do multiple jobs at a daily level. As Marx and Engels put it in a quote from *The German Ideology* which, despite its brevity, is perhaps the most detailed description of everyday life under communism they offered:

> as soon as the division of labour comes into being, each man has a particular, exclusive sphere of activity, which is forced upon him and from which he cannot escape. He is a hunter, a fisherman, a shepherd, or a critical critic, and must remain so if he does not want to lose his means of livelihood; whereas in communist society, where nobody has one exclusive sphere of activity but each can become accomplished in any branch he wishes, society regulates the general production and this makes it possible for me to do one thing today and another tomorrow, to hunt in the morning, fish in the afternoon, rear cattle in the evening, criticise after dinner, just as I have a mind, without ever becoming hunter, fisherman, shepherd or critic. (Marx and Engels 1998:53)

Since society provides people with the things they need to survive it is then possible to experiment in many different fields. Importantly, as the quote suggests, this removes the distinction between physical and mental labour; each is as productive as the other. Indeed:

> The exclusive concentration of artistic talent in particular individuals, and its suppression in the broad mass which is bound up with this, is a consequence of the division of labour ... In communist society there are no painters but only people who engage in painting among other activities. (Marx and Engels 1998:417–18)

The initial response upon hearing such a claim may be to doubt its plausibility; can people really excel in many fields? To explain how this would happen, it is worthwhile turning to education.

The final of the ten demands in *The Communist Manifesto* called for the abolition of child labour 'in its present form'. This qualification is central since, as much as it may surprise the modern reader, Marx was in favour of child labour, indeed he argues that 'a *general prohibition* of child labour is incompatible with the existence of large-scale industry and hence an empty, pious wish' (Marx 1996c:225). The reason for this concerned early-years education. Currently, the education system creates a strict division between academic and physical work. To be at school is to do academic work. In this system, for Marx, it is likely the children of the bourgeoisie succeed while proletarian children 'fail'. The result being that physical labour becomes that which children who have 'failed' at school do, while mental labour is for those that 'succeed'. This reproduces the false dichotomy between the two when both are as creative and fulfilling as each other (Marx 1976:618–19). Therefore, any communist system should provide an education which is 'both theoretical and practical' (Marx 1976:619) including child labour. This would ensure that from an early age children are not divided into one form of labour but rather develop the skills for both. From this point on it would seem a system of lifelong learning would allow us to experiment in different forms of creative physical and mental labour.

We have seen that Marx has suggestions for what communism could look like given the conditions at the time he wrote. I have noted at points how these changes could be seen to overcome the problems of capitalism. I will expand on this in the conclusion; before then there is one final factor to consider, an historical event which some have suggested was Marx's vision of communism come to life.

The Paris Commune

During the Franco-Prussian war of 1870–71 the city of Paris was under siege for just under four months. This was a period made famous by the citizens of the city turning to eating rats (although rat, due to the cost of making it edible, was a meal for the rich and most were left eating dog, bird, mice and cat) and using hot-air balloons to send messages to the outside world. After the French surrender and lifting of the siege the government remained in exile at Versailles and the people of Paris were left to rebuild the city. Throughout this period the animosity of the proletariat towards the government had been building. It was believed the latter had left the working class of Paris to the siege and, with the war over, were following Prussian requests to subdue their demands. These pressures were only increased by a variety of factors, including the order that the working-class districts of the city, armed during the siege as part of the National Guard, be disarmed; evacuation of Paris by much of its previous governing class and the government's claiming of overdue rents and bills which threaten to bankrupt many. All of these factors led to a revolt and capture of the city by the Paris Commune, a municipal government partly made up from, and mainly supported by, the working-class areas of the city. This was a short-run body, lasting from 18 March to 28 May 1871 before being brutally slaughtered in a government offensive later named 'bloody week' in which government troops were 'sheer savages, athirst for blood' (Cole 1954:161). During this week, roughly 25,000 people, the large majority being supporters of the Commune, were killed (see Cole 1954:134–73; Horne 2007:247–433).

During the Commune, and following it with the publication of *The Civil War in France*, Marx became somewhat of a media figure. Seen as the 'Red Terrorist Doctor' it was claimed he, being head of the First International (a collection of global socialist parties), was the man truly 'pulling the strings' of the Commune from his base in London (Horne 2007:430). The reality is that although there were members of the International in Paris in 1871, including some active in the Commune, Marx's influence was minimal and the lead was taken by followers of Auguste Blanqui. Marx, in a feeling he held for many fellow socialists of his time, had little respect for the Blanquists and was 'temperamentally out of sympathy with every one of the French groups' when the Commune began (Cole 1954:141). However, Marx's pamphlet on the Commune was to have an enormous impact upon Marxist communism from that point on.

What was important about the Commune for Marx was that it was a 'working-class government' (Marx 1996b:187). It included members of the working class and acted in their interests. Marx highlights four further elements of the Commune which gave it this character:

1. Universal suffrage and recall – not only was every resident of Paris given the vote, but elections became a system to 'serve the people' rather than to 'misrepresent the people' (Marx 1996b:185). This was achieved by frequent elections and a strict system of recall whereby 'Communards' (members of the Commune government) showing themselves to be incompetent or not following the will of the people could be swiftly removed.
2. A working wage – the Communards were paid the same wage as the workers they served in the government. Such wages, Marx notes sarcastically, were elsewhere considered one fifth of 'the minimum required for a secretary of a certain metropolitan school board' (Marx 1996b:188–9).
3. The election of the bureaucracy – any position of power – judges, police, functionaries and so on – was subject to election and recall and all were paid the working wage. The Commune almost immediately disbanded the regular police force and standing army to be replaced with elections in the former case and the National Guard in the latter. As Marx ironically points out this meant that 'the Commune made that catchword of bourgeois revolutions, cheap government, a reality' (Marx 1996b:187).
4. Its existence as a government of the universal class – the most important thing about the Commune for Marx was the very fact it existed, as he puts

it 'the great social measure of the Commune was its own working existence' (Marx 1996b:192). Some of the policies it enacted, such as an end to
night-time baking and limits on the ability of employers to punish workers,
although worthwhile in and of themselves, were more important as symbols
of proletariat power. Paris ruled by the Commune became 'radiant in the
enthusiasm of its historical initiative' (Marx 1996b:194).

So, given these conditions, and Marx's celebration of the Commune as a
working-class government, was it communism in action or even the dictatorship of the proletariat? This is important not only because it may give us some
detail of what communism would be but also because it could then act as guidance for the communist movements which followed.

Here we find a split between Marx on one side and Engels on the other.
Avineri (1968:239–49) highlights that *The Civil War in France* went through
multiple drafts. The earlier versions, written before bloody week and the later
canonisation of the Commune as proletarian government, are much more
focused on the Commune as a middle-class body. In doing so Marx focused
particularly on the origin of many of the leading Communards, arguing they
were of petty-bourgeois origin. This fracture and internal class contradictions
meant the Commune was doomed to fail. Even in the final, published, version
this view is still present. Here the Commune is referred to as the 'harbinger
of a new society' (Marx 1996b:209) not, importantly, an example of the new
society itself. In this version Marx also suggests the Commune was only able
to achieve power by winning the support of the 'great bulk of the Paris middle class – shopkeepers, tradesmen, merchants' (Marx 1996b:189). Thus the
Commune gained power partly because at that specific moment it was the only
group in Paris able to protect the interests of the middle classes. Not only did
this limit the immediate actions of the Commune, it would have greatly limited
any future actions; as Marx notes, the allegiance of the middle class was in
no way guaranteed (Marx 1996c:189). Indeed there is only one reference to
communism in the whole of *The Civil War in France,* when Marx makes an
adjacent point concerning how cooperative labour would inevitably require
communism; perhaps tellingly, the next paragraph begins 'the working class did
not expect miracles from the Commune' (Marx 1996c:188).

Therefore, the Commune was largely doomed to fail in Marx's eyes due to
its cross-class character and the fact that Communard Paris was only an island
in a sea of capitalism. While Marx highlights tactical errors which could have
extended the life of the Commune, such as their unwillingness to march on
Versailles, there is little suggestion extending its life would have created the
conditions for communism.

Twenty years after the fall of the Commune, and with Marx dead, Engels
wrote a new introduction to *The Civil War in France*. Here all doubt is removed
and Engels claims the Commune 'must necessarily have led in the end to communism' (Engels 1990:188). The failure of this to happen had nothing to do

with internal class conflict but was, for Engels, entirely tactical. Not only was the failure to expand an issue but even more important for Engels was the Communards' 'holy awe with which they remained standing respectfully outside the gates of the Bank of France … The bank in the hands of the Commune – this could have been worth more than ten thousand hostages' (Engels 1990:187). Had the Commune been more forceful its communist credentials would have shone through. Engels finishes the document with the following:

> Of late, the German philistine has once more been filled with wholesome terror at the words: Dictatorship of the Proletariat. Well and good, gentlemen, do you want to know what this dictatorship looks like? Look at the Paris Commune. That was the dictatorship of the Proletariat. (Engels 1990:191)

It is hard to think of a stronger statement of the distinctively *communist* nature of the Commune than something such as that from the co-author of *The Communist Manifesto*. Therefore, and perhaps unsurprisingly, the Commune became a model to future Marxists. Lenin cited it in the propaganda and party debates of the Bolsheviks in the revolutionary year of 1917 (Nimtz 2014:113–35). Indeed, it is rumoured that each day the USSR outlived the Commune he muttered 'Commune plus one' (Horne 2007:432). Unsurprisingly, he gave credence to Engels' reading, calling his 'Introduction' 'the last word' of Marxism on the topic (Lenin 1932:62). As a result, the lessons he took from the Commune were largely tactical. Like Engels he castigated its failure to take control of the bank and argued the Communards showed 'excessive magnanimity on the part of the proletariat: instead of destroying its enemies it sought to exert moral influence on them; it underestimated the significance of direct military operations in civil war' (Lenin 1962:477). Consequently, for Lenin the key lesson of the Commune was the need for the proletariat to 'break up' or 'shatter' the existing state apparatus and to 'start immediately the construction of a new one' (Lenin 1932:33, 42) as well as the importance of civil war to revolution (Lenin 1962). It could be argued these lessons – the need for radical state reconstruction, for the proletariat not to show magnanimity to its enemies and to immediately expand and take control of territory in a civil war – were the ones Lenin and some other Bolsheviks applied following the October Revolution, for better or worse.

Therefore, Marx and Engels' writings on the Commune as an alternative had a direct impact on the form which the sociological alternative of Marxist communism took upon its formation in the USSR. While it may be fair to claim Engels was the bigger influence on the question of the Paris Commune, and that even many Marxists disagree with the way in which the alternative was implemented, this does not change the fact that we have already seen in our first discussion the power of sociological alternatives to describe and create a new world.

Conclusion: would Marxist communism solve the problems of capitalism?

Marx and Engels conceived of capitalism as an inherently globalizing, yet crisis-ridden, system in which new international collaborations of the bourgeoisie continue to appropriate surplus value and dictate the conditions of alienated labour. As we have seen, despite their claim that they would not compose recipes for the cook-shops of the future the three factors of communist strategy, the pre-existing conditions for communism and the Paris Commune led them to provide a partial recipe. Having outlined this above, we can see that communism, at least in its higher phase, is a system whereby the means of production are communally available for all to use, where cooperative relationships exist between individuals, where the division of labour is no longer present and where the need to labour and being creative becomes the key thing driving individuals. Therefore, with this (admittedly partial) picture, we can turn to the third element of a sociological alternative outlined in the 'Introduction': would this system of communism solve the problems of capitalism? As we saw, Marx and Engels outlined three critiques of capitalism and therefore I shall go through these one by one.

Firstly, alienation. There are two ways in which communism could be said to remove alienation. The first of these is that, by removing the compulsion to labour as a means to an end, communism allows for individuals to engage in labour without compulsion. It is inevitable humans will labour for Marx, what communism allows is for this to be truly creative and free. Also, since we are no longer tied to a specific job we can perform many different tasks on a daily basis. Since the education system will privilege both mental and manual work, there is no longer a divide between the two, nor between artistic and non-artistic work; we can do both. Therefore, communism removes the alienation from species-being since we now become well-rounded, 'universal' individuals engaged with our creative abilities. The second surmounting of alienation concerns alienation from others. Since communism removes the division between bourgeoisie and proletariat as well as the competition between individuals, we now encounter others in cooperative relationships and as potential collaborators.

Secondly, exploitation. The key point here is the aforementioned removal of classes; without a bourgeoisie class there is no one to extract the surplus value of the worker's labour. In communism labour is done for its own enjoyment with the fruits of that labour then allocated on the basis of need by the community. Marx and Engels refer to this as embodying the principle of 'free development of each is the condition for the free development of all' (Marx and Engels 1992:26); by allowing all to labour and be creative the wider community is better off and all are able to explore their creativity. Without the class antagonism and reselling of goods for profit, this can finally occur without exploitation.

Finally, the wastefulness of capitalism. As we saw, the key point here was that capitalism is a system of 'production for production's sake'. Under communism this is removed, consequently labour and production are performed with reference to need. Our needs are fulfilled by the wider community. It must be acknowledged that Marx is sketchy on how exactly such a distribution would occur, especially given the passing of the state in the higher phase of communism. Nevertheless, it seems the development of cooperative relationships is a key element here; people would, in effect, look out for one another.

There are, of course, criticisms which could be raised against this system of communism which may, as in the above point, come back to the idea of it being unclear or poorly developed in Marx and Engels' writings. However, this criticism makes a negative out of a truly unique perspective claimed by Marx and Engels. Throughout this book we will be seeing how critique has led to suggestions of an alternative. Marx and Engels' contribution is to argue that, unlike the position of Weber, while the alternative emerges from scientifically discovered laws critique must be normative (for example, the idea humans should labour freely) and social theory should be very clear whose side it is on. Yet since social theorists will not be the ones creating the change it is not their responsibility to detail it. To do so is to pretend that sociologists somehow magically have the power to see into the future and know the conditions under which this alternative will be created. Therefore, for Marx and Engels, sociological alternatives are attempts to locate the conditions for change within the current system, not to create that alternative from thin air. As we move through the book we will see sociologists who both agree and disagree with this statement.

If you visit Marx's grave in Highgate Cemetery, London, you'll find the following, the famed thesis 11 on Feuerbach (Marx 1992b:423), inscribed:

The philosophers have only *interpreted* the world in various ways; the point is to change it.

As a statement in favour of sociological alternatives, this is iconic; what makes it Marxist is that the philosophers (or, in this case, sociologists) will not detail the change.

Émile Durkheim: Curing the Malaise

3

Whereas Marx may have appeared an obvious inclusion in this book, Émile Durkheim (1858–1917) may, initially, seem a less evident choice. Indeed, it was common for twentieth-century sociologists to present Durkheim as a conservative concerned with maintaining the status quo (Coser 1960), cast as the naïve 'anti-hero' to the radical Marx (Davies 1994). This reflects Durkheim's role in inspiring the conservative tradition within functionalism (Strasser 1976). Increasingly it has been acknowledged that Durkheim was actually a radical critic of the inequalities and immorality of capitalism (Sirianni 1984, Stedman Jones 2001, Dawson 2013). He did not limit himself to critique but, much more than Marx, was willing to provide a blueprint of an alternative which attempted to create greater equality and provide a just moral system. This is a pressing task for Durkheim since contemporary societies may 'be said to be a mission of justice' (Durkheim 1984:321) in which sociologists must:

> make use of our liberties to seek out what we must do and to do it, to smooth the functioning of the social machine, still so harsh on individuals, to place within their reach all possible means of developing their abilities without hindrance, to work finally to make a reality of the famous precept: to each according to his labour. (Durkheim 1973:55–6)

This chapter will show how Durkheim outlined a society which, with democratic 'corporations', moral education and the banning of inheritance, allows individuals to live a full and just life. These corporations, in the form of cooperatives, will also be part of our discussion in the next chapter on Du Bois. I will begin by outlining how Durkheim thought we should criticise society before turning to the specific critique he offered. This concerned what he saw as the malaise of contemporary society which I will suggest had three components: moral, economic and political. From here we will see how Durkheim's alternative hoped to lessen, and ultimately remove, this malaise.

In recent years there has been a shift towards a 'new cultural Durkheim' where, rather than emphasising concepts such as the division of labour, anomie and socialism – seen as ideas from Durkheim's 'first century' – ideas such as ritual, the sacred and collective representations are now central (Smith and Alexander 2005:31). This is part of the 'turn-taking' discussed in the 'Introduction' where particular visions of theorists become dominant and others are rejected. However, this chapter is very much focused on these so-called 'first-century' concepts since it is these, not the cultural concepts, that are central to Durkheim's alternative. In doing so, I hope to demonstrate the value of these concepts for Durkheim's sociological vision. Therefore Durkheim is particularly relevant for this book since the very basis of his sociological method, with its distinction of normal and pathological social facts, creates a 'constant preoccupation' with 'practical questions' (Durkheim 1982:160) concerning how society can, and should, be ordered. This is manifested in factors such as the division of labour and anomie. This opens up a different space for sociological alternatives to that found in the work of Marx and Engels and, as we shall see, Durkheim uses this to conceive of a radical alternative to the society he confronted.

Durkheim's *Rules of Sociological Method* and critique

The first step in constructing a sociological alternative is critique and, in the case of Durkheim, the way in which he outlines the role of critique is important. Here we turn to Durkheim's *Rules of Sociological Method* and one of his most well-known concepts: 'social facts'.

Social facts are, for Durkheim, 'the beliefs, tendencies and practices of the group taken collectively' (Durkheim 1982:54) which provide a:

> way of acting, whether fixed or not, capable of exerting over the individual an external constraint; or: which is general over the whole of a given society whilst having an existence of its own, independent of individual manifestations. (Durkheim 1982:59)

So, as an example Durkheim often used, morality is a social fact since it provides a set of prohibitions which limit the behaviours considered (in)appropriate in different situations (Durkheim 1961:42). Since these rules are developed by society, rather than individuals, they exert influence upon us and limit the activities we should or should not do. This means social facts are independent of individuals: the morality of our society exists before we enter into it and will remain there after we die. This does not mean moral rules remain unchanged. But there will always be a social morality external to the individual in which some precepts remain stable over time (Durkheim 1953:61). This is why, in Durkheim's famous claim, social facts must be treated as 'things', which we are able to study in the same way as observable phenomena (Durkheim 1982:60).

How do we study social facts? Here Durkheim is clear that 'the function of a social fact must always be sought in the relationship that it bears to some social end' (Durkheim 1982:134). To stick with our example, to understand why certain moral rules are developed and followed, we need to understand how they relate to certain essential functions and precepts of society. For example, moral prohibitions on killing or harming others clearly have important social functions; we need to be able to live without fear for society to reproduce itself. While this rule may be universal others will be time-specific; the social fact must apply to the society in which we live. As Durkheim argues, it must fit the 'complexity' (mono vs multi-cultural), 'evolution' (time) and 'species' (nationality) of our society. It is in the distinction between normal and pathological social facts that we find the basis of critique for Durkheim.

Put simply, 'normal' social facts are those which are appropriate for a given society, and 'pathological' ones are those which are not. A pathological social fact may be one which was appropriate to an earlier time or to a less 'complex' society but is no longer appropriate. For example, Durkheim defends the secular education developed in France in the early twentieth century as appropriate to a multi-religious society such as France at that point of time; therefore, it is normal. Two hundred years previous to this a wholly Catholic education would have been normal and a secular education pathological (Durkheim 1961). This separation of normal and pathological social facts forms the basis of sociological critique; anything which is pathological is open to critique. As an example, and prefiguring what we will discuss later in the chapter, Durkheim argues:

> to know whether the present economic state ... with the lack of organisation that characterises it, is normal or not, we must investigate what in the past gave rise to it. If the conditions are still those appertaining to our societies, it is because the situation is normal, despite the protest that it stirs up. If, on the other hand, it is linked to that old social structure which ... is now increasingly dying out, we shall be forced to conclude that this now constitutes a morbid state, however universal it may be. (Durkheim 1982:95)

Does the 'disorganised' (free market, unregulated) economy of Durkheim's and our own time fit the conditions of contemporary society, including its key ends and the things it values? If so, it is normal and should be accepted even if we personally dislike it. If not, it is open to critique even if we personally value it. This is why, for Durkheim, sociology is not only critical but is also a discipline concerned with the aforementioned 'practical questions'. As we shall see, Durkheim's sociology asks questions such as: how should we run the workplace? How should we educate our children? How should we elect our leaders? What should we do with the wealth of the dead? Such practical concerns are the inevitable outcome of Durkheim's concern with social facts and mean that while his sociology aims to 'liberate us from all [political] parties' (Durkheim 1982:161) it is fundamentally concerned with locating 'evil' and encouraging us to 'set resolutely to work' removing that evil (Durkheim 1952:359). Consequently, in order to discover which contemporary social facts are normal and pathological we must first locate the key value of our current society.

Durkheim's critique: the 'malaise'

Durkheim lived through a period that later came to be known as the *Fin de Siècle* (literally, end of an era) which was known for the 'pessimism, cynicism and ennui' felt by many intellectuals during 1880–1910 (Meštrović 1991:2). In particular, there was a fear that the advances of industrial capitalism and technology had a destructive impact on society. While we must be careful not to exaggerate the connection, Durkheim was certainly part of this mood; his writings make frequent reference to what he termed 'our collective malaise' (Durkheim 1959:7). It was this malaise, the pathological social facts and the feeling that something had gone wrong which Durkheim critiqued and hoped to change with his sociological alternative. Importantly, as the below indicates, although Durkheim was very aware of inequality, he did not see this malaise as solely affecting the working class, arguing instead that it was 'general over the whole of society' (Durkheim 1899:143).

Before turning to this we must, following Durkheim's methodology, establish the key principles of society; what is it that allowed society to function and therefore could be seen as its central values? Here Durkheim was clear in his answer: contemporary society values, and is based upon, individualism (Durkheim 1973). By this Durkheim does not mean the self-centred search for individual satisfaction – what he terms 'the egoistic cult of the self' (Durkheim 1973:45) or 'egoism' (Durkheim 1952:251) – but something broader, a sense of duty to respect the dignity of each individual – what we would now term 'human rights'. Individualism means that we accept the right of each person to follow their own path and realise their desires (Durkheim 1973:45–8). Durkheim argues this form of individualism has become 'our religion ... in which man is at once the worshiper and the god' (Durkheim 1973:46). Each individual is sacred and to harm or stand in their way is a form of secular sin. The value given to this is partly due to the complexity of modern societies. Previously individuals were united by a shared religion and values while also, in a period of a low division of labour, doing similar tasks. This meant such values could unite individuals and could direct their allegiance to a shared religious creed. Now, with the different values, religious practices and high division of labour there is no shared body strong enough to generate such reverence. This means 'nothing remains which men can love and honour in common if not man himself' (Durkheim 1973:52).

It should be noted that Durkheim's use of 'men' may not just be a relic of his time. As others have argued (Witz and Marshall 2004; Cristi 2012) Durkheim's conception of individualism seemed to privilege men and their public activity. While not wishing to sideline such a valuable critique which highlights flaws in Durkheim's idea of individualism, for the rest of this chapter we can suggest that since Durkheim had no basis for such a distinction (Cristi 2012), and since his alternative did not state any particular relationship between the genders, we should imagine his conception of individualism as universal. This does not mean such a conception of individualism is impervious to further critique, rather that for this chapter we can use it as a working concept.

Therefore, following through our earlier discussion, any critique from Durkheim would be a critique concerning the *lack of individualism*. Certain social forms must be standing in the way of realising this. This is true of the malaise Durkheim discussed, which I suggest has three forms: moral, economic and political.

Moral malaise

As we saw above, Durkheim argues that morality is external to the individual; it is a social fact which creates rules. This is essential for Durkheim; humans without moral guidelines have unlimited desires, which we will return to later. Therefore, 'a moral power is required whose superiority he recognises, and which cries out "You must go no further"' (Durkheim 1959:200). Importantly, and this is often overlooked by Durkheim's critics, this does not mean every individual always follows the moral rules, or even that those who do follow them do so in the same way. Morality can be 'refracted' in different ways when people act it out (Durkheim 1982:54). To take a contemporary example, some may take the right of the individual as including prohibitions on abortion, while others will emphasise the right of the woman to choose. In such situations some compromise is possible via agreed-upon laws. But there can also be instances where the very basis of social morality seems repugnant to us, so that:

> We are not then obliged to bend our heads under the force of moral opinion. We can even in certain cases feel ourselves justified in rebelling against it ... we shall feel it out duty to combat moral ideas that we know to be out of date and nothing more than survivals. The best way of doing this may appear to be the denial of these ideas, not only theoretically but also in action. (Durkheim 1953:61)

A good case of this could be those who hid, or aided the escape of, Jews during World War II due to an overriding belief in what Durkheim would see as individualism, rather than subservience to the ideals of Nazism.

Therefore, morality as a social fact is essential but it must be directly related, and relevant, to our activities; this is what makes it normal. If it does not relate to such activity and seems immoral, we will reject that set of rules. This leads Durkheim to make a distinction between two sets of moral rules (Durkheim 1992). Firstly, there are civic morals. These are broad moral guidelines which hold for the whole of society, such as the value of individualism. The state is essential to the development of these since, as the 'social brain', it is able to develop the 'collective representations' of the values, priorities and ideals which provide the basis for civic morals (Durkheim 1992:51–3).

The second form of moral guidelines is professional ethics; these concern the division of labour. While the division of labour was an evil to be fought for Marx, Durkheim saw it as both inevitable and worthy; as knowledge increases tasks become more specific and require more training (Durkheim 1984).

The result is that we are all left doing particular, and divergent, jobs. However, no form of civic morals could account for this diversity since:

> As professors, we have duties which are not those of merchants. Those of the industrialist are quite different from those of the solider, those of the soldier from those of the priest, and so on … there are as many forms of morals as there are different callings, and since, in theory, each individual carries on only one calling, the result is that these different forms of morals apply to entirely different groups of individuals. (Durkheim 1992:5)

Professional ethics are these occupation-specific morals, not only informing us of the moral obligations of our job but also making us aware of our workplace rights (Durkheim 1992:14–27). The problem for Durkheim is that since the division of labour has expanded so quickly professional ethics have not kept up. They are currently either weak or non-existent in most professional fields. Ideals concerning the morals of the industrialist, professor or soldier are lacking, with the few that do exist being outdated.

Without such guidelines, workplace activity seeks guidance from elsewhere in the form of the 'amoral character of economic life' (Durkheim 1992:12). Making money, rather than being a means towards an end, becomes 'the supreme end of individuals and societies alike' (Durkheim 1952:216). In our professional activity we begin to only value profit generation, promotion and our own salary rather than the morality of how we should be doing our job and the wider social value of our activity. This is why, for Durkheim, the extension of the amoral character of economic life amounts to a 'public danger' (Durkheim 1992:12). More and more activities are subjected to the demands of the market and profit-making; this becomes the 'first rank' function of society (Durkheim 1992:11).

Thus a major part of our life, our time at work, is defined by a lack of morality and a resulting emphasis on money and profit. Therefore, in this area, our morality is pathological. To make matters worse, there is currently no body available which could develop and present such guidelines. The state would seem the obvious option, but this is a 'cumbersome machine' (Durkheim 1952:347) which is 'so removed from individual interests that it cannot take into account the special or local and other conditions in which they exist' (Durkheim 1992:63). Meanwhile trade unions are, for Durkheim, too sectional and focused on confrontation (Durkheim 1908). As we shall see, this inspired Durkheim to look for more specialised forms of work-based organisation. Before that, let us continue our discussion of the malaise.

Economic malaise

The moral malaise mentioned above, and the expansion of the amoral character of economic life it engenders, also has a profound economic impact. There are two factors Durkheim highlights here: just versus unjust contracts and economic anomie. Both are united by seeing inequality as a central factor. Unlike Marx, Durkheim advocates the achievement of greater economic equality as an essential goal in the here and now.

Let us begin with contracts. One thing that determines our economic activity under capitalism for Durkheim is that we are bound by contracts; most prominently, there is the contract we sign as an employee or employer. When considering contracts Durkheim argues they have undergone a historical shift. In earlier economic systems, such as feudalism, a contract was considered appropriate if it was consensual (Durkheim 1992:186). However, as time passed and capitalism emerged contracts became more numerous and important; as a result, they are regulated by laws. At this point there emerges a fundamental shift in how contracts are judged. It is not enough that they be consensual, they must also be *just*. A just contract is one in which 'things and services are exchanged at the true and normal value, in short, at the just value' (Durkheim 1992:211). So, were you tricked into buying a product at a price which you latter found out was not justified or if it was misadvertised, the fact you consented to buy it would not mean you give up your right to challenge the contract; you could challenge it because it was unjust.

Therefore, any contract we sign as an employee should be a just contract; we should be getting a just value for our labour. This is where we face a problem for Durkheim: just employment contracts are, at the best rare, at the worst impossible, under capitalism. To understand why, it is worthwhile quoting Durkheim at length:

> If, for instance, the one contracts to obtain something to live on, and the other only to obtain something to live better on, it is clear that the force of resistance of the latter will far exceed that of the former, by the fact that he can drop the idea of contracting if he fails to get the terms he wants. The other cannot do this. He is therefore obliged to yield and to submit to what is laid down for him. Now inheritance as an institution results in men being born either rich or poor; that is to say, there are two main classes in society, linked by all sorts of intermediate classes: the one which in order to live has to make its services acceptable to the other at whatever the cost; the other class which can do without these services ... Therefore as long as such sharp class differences exists in society, fairly effective palliatives may lessen the injustice of contracts; but in principle, the system operates in conditions which do not allow of justice. (Durkheim 1992:213)

Capitalism creates a system whereby one group, the employer, has the means to survive on their wealth for a period whereas the other, the worker, has no such means and must work immediately to survive. In such a situation the employer can wait until the employee accepts the wage the employer determines, even if this is below what the worker needs. As the quote also suggests, the worker is aware of this. While the 'palliatives' – or, as Durkheim (1992:11) terms them elsewhere, 'peace treaties' – such as small wage increases, more holiday days or union recognition lessen some of the injustice, they cannot remove it. The result is that 'the stronger succeed in crushing the not so strong or at any rate in reducing them to a state of subjection' creating 'ever-recurring conflicts' between employers and employees until the workers get their 'longed-for day of revenge' (Durkheim 1992:11). As this indicates, while Durkheim was reluctant to use the term 'class war' since the malaise was 'general', he certainly saw conflict between the workers and capitalists as an inherent part of the unjust system.

The above quote also suggested the cause for such injustice: inheritance. For Durkheim, as long as people were allowed to inherit wealth, gained through no effort or initiative of their own, inequality would continue. Durkheim condemns inheritance in the strongest possible terms, saying it is 'contrary to the spirit of individualism' (Durkheim 1992:217) and therefore pathological. As we shall see, his alternative attacked this head-on.

However, it is not just inheritance which is to blame for unjust contracts; were professional ethics established it seems unlikely such contracts would be so prominent. This lack of professional ethics and resulting extension of the amoral character of economic life also creates 'economic anomie'. Anomie is one of Durkheim's most used concepts and while it has become known as a sense of being detached from the norms of society, or 'normlessness', in *Suicide* Durkheim (1952:201–19) uses it in a very specific way in relation to the economy. This is based upon Durkheim's view on humans' insatiable appetites. Our idea of what it is to be comfortable has no natural limits, rather our desires for wealth, satisfaction and luxury are 'unlimited so far as they depend on the individual alone' (Durkheim 1952:208). This is especially important when it comes to wealth. Without the moral guidelines of professional ethics, having wealth simply begets the desire for more wealth as 'the more one has, the more one wants, since satisfactions received only stimulate instead of filling needs' (Durkheim 1952:209). We enter a state of economic anomie when these desires are completely free from the limits of moral authority, which, for Durkheim, was clearly present in the time of the malaise. Economic anomie was a 'chronic' occurrence (Durkheim 1952:215), as could be seen in the ruthless greed of the employer constructing unjust contracts.

The greed of the wealthy not only is self-perpetuating under a state of economic anomie but also engenders further confrontation. Wealth is, for Durkheim, a unique privilege; having more of it guarantees the opening of further possibilities and opportunities. Moreover, becoming rich is seen as an individual success story; we attribute the success of businessmen such as Steve Jobs or Bill Gates to individual triumph and hard work. As Durkheim puts it wealth 'by the power it bestows, deceives us into believing that we depend on ourselves only. Reducing the resistance we encounter from objects, it suggests the possibility of unlimited success against them' (Durkheim 1952:214). This is incorrect; producing wealth relies upon others, especially in a society with a wide division of labour. Steve Jobs did not become rich on his own; he became rich through the combined efforts of many. Nevertheless, this 'individualized' story of wealth generation leaves the wealthy feeling even more justified in their treatment of the poor since lacking wealth is clearly a result of individual failure.

Given this inequality and the corrosive effects of economic anomie there is a clear need, in Durkheim's view, for regulation to control the economy, create just contracts and limit greed. The problem is that the government is unwilling to act; the dominance of this idea of individualized success and the view of wealth generation as an end means that 'the doctrine of the most ruthless and swift progress has become an article of faith' (Durkheim 1952:218) and there is nothing preventing the wealthy from imposing their will (Durkheim 1984:xxxix). As a result.

> government, instead of regulating economic life, has become its tool and servant ... nations are declared to have the single or chief purpose of achieving industrial prosperity; such is the implication of the dogma of economic materialism ... industry, instead of being still regarded as a means to an end transcending itself, has become the supreme end of individuals and societies alike. Thereupon the appetites thus excited have become freed of any limiting authority. By sanctifying them, so to speak, this apotheosis of well-being has placed them above all human law. Their restraint seems like a sort of sacrilege ... Ultimately, this liberation of desires has been made worse by the very development of industry and the almost infinite extension of the market. (Durkheim 1952:216)

Placing limits on the expansion of the market comes to be seen as punishing the successful and limiting the potential of the nation. Therefore, without a major shift, the pathological state of economic anomie is self-perpetuating and stands in the way of individualism for all but the very rich. This impotence, or unwillingness, of governments to regulate the economy and limit the power of the rich is also a key element of the final part of the malaise: political.

Political malaise

The political malaise is linked to the aforementioned issue of the state being 'too far removed' from individuals, meaning there is a 'lack of secondary cadres to interpose between the individual and the State' (Durkheim 1992:96). The lack of more specialised forms of political expression means that all political activities are centred on the nation state. This has two negative impacts for Durkheim. The first one, suggested in the section on the moral malaise, is that the state is too remote from our individual, everyday, activity to solve the problems located there, particularly to provide moral guidelines. This is especially so when it comes to economic life. Not only does our work life become 'very special and is daily becoming increasingly specialised' (Durkheim 1984:xxxv) but, with geographical and social mobility, it is beginning to take the central place in our life once filled by family or local affairs (Durkheim 1984).

The second impact of the political malaise concerns our attitude towards collective issues. Despite his focus on individualism Durkheim was in many ways an associational thinker, concerned with how people act together since such associational activity is inevitable:

> as soon as a certain number of individuals find they hold in common ideas, interests, sentiments and occupations which the rest of the population does not share in, it is inevitable that, under the influence of these similarities, they should be attracted to one another. They will seek one another out, enter into relationships and associate together. (Durkheim 1984:xlii–iii)

Importantly, this is often engendered by a concern with collective issues. However, this urge to associate, or, as Durkheim terms it, 'the spirit of association' (Durkheim 1961), has been blunted by the centralisation of political affairs in the state. The result of this is that:

> political life is such that we take part in it only intermittently. The State is far away. We are not directly involved in its activity … We do not constantly encounter those great political causes that can excite us, to which we can give ourselves entirely. (Durkheim 1961:233)

We get what in modern terms would be called political apathy; 'politics' seems too far removed from us and irrelevant to our day-to-day activities. The result for Durkheim is that we are likely to shun collective affairs and instead develop 'the habit of acting like lone wolves' when politics and collective concerns seem irrelevant to our lives (Durkheim 1961:234). Given this we turn to our own individual interests. When combined with the moral and economic malaise we can see that Durkheim fears the selfishness and greed of egoistic individualism has been unleashed fully and we have little collective concern.

In the previous three sections we have seen the main components of Durkheim's critique: the moral, economic and political malaise. As I have noted these three combined indicate a concern about excessive egoistic individualism, which is partly explained by the weakness of morality in professional ethics, as well as economic inequality, political apathy and conflict between the rich and the poor; these are pathological social facts standing in the way of true individualism. What solution does Durkheim have?

Durkheim's alternatives

Durkheim's alternative is actually three alternatives. While he suggests all of these will occur at the same time and provides more detail than Marx, he doesn't link them together under a system such as communism. This is not to say that Durkheim is less radical than Marx. Indeed, in the short term at least, it could be argued he is *more* radical. However, it does mean we must be aware of how these alternatives operate together. These three are: the corporations, the banning of inheritance and moral education. I will discuss each in turn and highlight how they solve problems of the malaise.

The corporations

These are the most important of Durkheim's three alternatives and form the basis upon which the other two are built. Given that the lack of professional ethics is a recent occurrence, Durkheim looks to what in the past could have played this role and identifies the guilds. These, in place for most of the feudal period, were local bodies, made up of the most specialised workers. They had a certain amount of control over the workers, voluntarily agreed by its members, and were able to set common guidelines. The guilds began to disappear with the movement of workers to cities and factories plus the increased use of machine-based production (Hawkins 1994).

For Durkheim the death of the guilds was appropriate; they were too focused on locality – 'local patriotism' as he calls it – to fit the demands of modern life. However, he calls the rejection of *any* collective association like the guilds a result of 'historic prejudice' (Durkheim 1992:28) where 'because the new industry did not fit in with the [guilds], a conclusion from this was drawn that it was opposed, in principle, to every kind of organization' (Durkheim 2009:4). Nothing, for Durkheim, could be further from the truth. The lack of professional ethics and the resulting conflict between employer and employee demonstrate the need for some form of workplace organisation.

This is the role of the corporations. A corporation is a body made up of all the individuals working in a specific profession, meaning there would be a corporation for plumbers, one for computer technicians, one for teachers and so on. Importantly, this would include workers as well as managers; therefore the corporation is made up 'of all those working in the same industry, assembled together and organized in a single body' (Durkheim 1984:xxxv). This separates them from the trade unions which, as we saw above, Durkheim saw as encouraging sectional interests. Once established the corporations in effect run the industry: they determine the wages of all levels, lay down guidelines (including the rights of workers) and establish common policies, including the price of goods (Durkheim 1984:xxxi–lix). Durkheim also argued the corporations would provide non-professional activities for its members, such as education, 'drama performances, recreation and intellectual pursuits' (Durkheim 1984:liii). These corporations would be internally democratic, but, since asking all workers to meet in order to debate would be impractical, representatives would be elected. The result is the following:

> Let us imagine – spread over the whole country – the various industries grouped in separate categories based on similarity and natural affinity. An administrative council, a kind of miniature parliament, nominated by

election, would preside over each group. We go on to imagine this council or parliament as having the power ... to regulate whatever concerns the business: relations of employers and employed – conditions of labour – wages and salaries – relations of competitors with one another, and so on ... and there we have the guild restored, but in an entirely novel form. (Durkheim 1992:37)

Durkheim then extends this principle even further. Given that our professional activity is so important to our daily life all political representation, including voting for the national government, should be done there. Instead of voting in our local constituency, we would vote as part of our occupation. This would mark a fundamental change:

Society, instead of remaining what it is today – a conglomerate of land masses juxtaposed together – would become a vast system of national corporations. The demand is raised in various quarters for electoral colleges to be constituted by professions and not by territorial constituencies. Certainly in this way political assemblies would more accurately reflect the diversity of social interests and their interconnections. They would more exactly epitomise social life as a whole. (Durkheim 1984:liii)

Therefore the corporation would become the key element of our daily life. While Durkheim suggests joining our corporation would not be compulsory (Durkheim 1952:346) ultimately he believes most will join voluntarily (Durkheim 1992:39).

Why does Durkheim place such value in the corporations? Most important is their aforementioned everyday connection. Since we spend most days, and a lot of time, at work our corporation is 'always in contact' with us, due to 'the constant exercise' of our occupational activity (Durkheim 1952:346). The issues raised by the corporation are ones we have a direct connection to. While the activities of the state seemed withdrawn from us, question of our wages, working conditions and rights are very much our concern. They would also, through including all levels of the profession, lessen some of the conflict between employer and employees. By setting wage levels and conditions of employment according to principles of justice they would also prevent the extreme inequalities of pay (Durkheim 1984:xxxix).

However, their key purpose returns us to professional ethics. Corporations, as specialised bodies, are able to develop the professional ethics which are beyond the abilities of the nation state. Consequently, the guidelines of work drawn up by the corporations would be not only practical but moral guidelines. For example, the plumber's corporation would provide professional ethics by saying what is moral as a plumber, as well as highlighting the wider moral value of plumbers to society. Currently, we go about our professional work without much consideration of its value to society as a whole. This, for Durkheim, is inevitable since 'the individual can take in no more than a small stretch of the social horizon' (Durkheim 1992:15). However, once we were a member of a corporation this would be able to remind us how our work is valuable socially.

As we have seen, the corporations are a key element of Durkheim's alternative, and attempt to solve elements of the malaise. They attempt to fight the moral malaise by developing the professional ethics currently missing. By developing these, and providing democratically determined guidelines and worker rights, Durkheim claims they can lessen the amoral character of economic life. Production is no longer conducted according to the impersonal whims of the market but rather the desires of the occupation. Durkheim also argues – echoing Engels' concept of the anarchy of the production – that having such regulation would mean less of the overproduction which leads to crisis (Durkheim 1992:16).

The corporations also have positive impacts on the economic and political malaise. On the economic side the democratic determination of wages should lessen some of the inequality lying behind unjust contracts, but its main impact is on economic anomie. As we saw, this creates a situation where the rich feel comfortable in their disregard for the poor and their never-ending greed. Consequently, the poor begin to resent the rich and plot their day of revenge. The corporation has a clear purpose here:

> Whenever excited appetites tended to exceed all limits, the corporation would have to decide the share that should equitably revert to each of the cooperative parts ... By forcing the strongest to use their strength with moderation, by preventing the weakest from endlessly multiplying their protests, by recalling both to the sense of their reciprocal duties and the general interests, and by regulating production in certain cases so that it does not degenerate into a morbid fever, it would moderate one set of passions by another, and permit their appeasement by assigning them limits. (Durkheim 1952:350)

So, as we can see, the corporation, as a moral authority, limits the desires of the rich and instead creates clear reciprocal interests for all. By determining how much each person deserves in a wage it also, *inter alia*, determines the social value of their work. This new moral discipline provides what was missing during a period of economic anomie.

Finally, the corporations combat the political malaise by providing a political body in between the individual and the state, connected to our everyday activity. Not only does this lessen the level of political apathy in our daily lives, it can also provide the basis for a reinvigorated form of national government based upon occupational representation.

Despite how powerful the corporations would be they cannot combat all elements of the malaise. Notably, despite the admirable goal of a more equitable distribution of wages, they do not fully remove the economic inequality Durkheim saw as problematic to modern society. This is where the next alternative comes in.

Banning inheritance

As we saw, Durkheim condemned inheritance in the strongest words possible for him: it is contrary to the spirit of individualism. Therefore, the obvious step is to attack this. Durkheim initially considered a system of taxation on inheritance, similar to the inheritance taxes which currently operate in many countries (Durkheim 1885:94). However, these do little to remove the principle of inheritance – after all, even a tax rate of 80 per cent would still leave some- one inheriting £1,000,000 with £200,000. Therefore, the answer for Durkheim is simply to stop inheritance. Since he focuses mostly on property (Durkheim 1992:215–19) it seems small forms of inheritance, family heirlooms for exam- ple, could be continued. What should be banned is anything that gives an indi- vidual the edge in contractual negotiations since 'it is obvious that inheritance, by creating inequalities amongst men from birth, that are unrelated to merit or services, invalidates the whole contractual system at its very roots' (Durkheim 1992:213). Therefore, any property and seemingly any large amount of wealth should no longer be allowed to pass down the family tree.

This raises the question of what should be done with this property and wealth. Here, Durkheim returns to his first alternative by saying that all prop- erty should be given to the individual's corporation upon their death (Durkheim 1992:218). Individuals gain their wealth and property through their profes- sional activity, so it seems only appropriate the corporation should receive the fruits of their labour upon their death. This, being a democratic organisation, can make a decision on what to do with the inherited wealth. As Durkheim (1992:218) highlights the corporation could take account of specific concerns, perhaps in one area there is a need for housing which this inherited property could cure whereas in others it may be more fruitful to sell the property and use the proceeds to fund other activities. Such concerns are beyond the state but available to the corporations.

Therefore, the banning of inheritance is the key element in the battle against unjust economic inequality for Durkheim. He did imagine there would be some inequality in society; individuals have different 'natural talents' which enable them to do differing tasks and public opinion will determine 'the rela- tive reward' due to different occupations (Durkheim 1952:212, 210). However, to justify these small forms of inequality, which Durkheim imagines as getting as close to 'true' equality as possible (Durkheim 1952:212), it must follow this principle:

> the distribution of things amongst individuals can be just only if it be made relative to the social deserts of each one. The property of individu- als should be the counter-part of the services they have rendered in the society. (Durkheim 1992:214)

This can only be achieved by removing the inbuilt and unjust advantage some have gained through inheritance.

Whereas the two alternatives discussed thus far have been specifically economic – although with moral and political outcomes – the final one will turn our attention to a wider social issue: moral education.

Moral education

Given the fact sociology was never fully established as an academic discipline in France during Durkheim's lifetime, despite his Herculean efforts to do so, his job title did not include the word 'sociology' until 1913. This was after all his major works had been published and barely five years before his death; even then he had to settle for 'Professor of Education and Sociology'. Indeed, it was as a professor of education that Durkheim spent much of his life. This required him to research, lecture and write on a topic which he otherwise may well have avoided (Fournier 2013:417). Durkheim's nephew Marcel Mauss claimed his uncle saw his teaching on education as a 'burden' (Lukes 1973:110). However, Durkheim's personal loss is sociology's gain since his main lecture course, *Moral Education*, was eventually published (Durkheim 1961). Here Durkheim outlines a new philosophy of education which complements his other alternatives.

The idea of moral education emerges via the shift from a religious to a secular education. Without religion education required a central theme which, for Durkheim, should be morality (Durkheim 1961). As Cladis (1995) points out, 'education' for Durkheim is much broader than simply the imparting of knowledge in a classroom, being closer to 'socialisation'. Therefore, the school is to take the central role in moral socialisation which previously would have been left to the church or the family. The school is well placed to do this for Durkheim since, much like the corporations, it is an institution between the individual and the state able to take a collective view, unlike the narrow view of the family or church. As he put it, 'we have through the school the means of training the child in a collective life different from home life' (Durkheim 1961:235). This is a central task for Durkheim since, even with the best professional ethics and civic morals, if:

> beyond school age – the foundations of morality have not been laid, they never will be. From this point on, all one can do is to complete the job already begun, defining sensibilities and giving them some intellectual content, i.e., informing them increasingly with intelligence. But the groundwork must have been laid. (Durkheim 1961:18)

Therefore, for the school to perform its task correctly it must develop three key elements of morality. The first of these is discipline, whereby one must recognise that moral rules carry with them some authority. Durkheim can be very strict here, for example, claiming 'one must obey a moral precept out of respect for it and for this reason alone' (Durkheim 1961:30). The explanation for this returns us to the 'religious' nature of contemporary morality since 'a society stands in relation to its members as a god stands in relation to his followers'

(Durkheim 1995:31). The moral discipline exerted by the school is a central part of its activity; it provides an earthly authority for these moral rules. The second is 'attachment to social groups'. Here Durkheim highlights that morality is not an individual matter; rather we are moral because we are social (Durkheim 1961:64). The school is therefore tasked with developing the attachment to social groups, particularly connection to the nation and our fellow citizens. Morality only exists 'through the relationships of associated individuals' (Durkheim 1961:86) so a role of the school is to develop our connections and sense of allegiance to others. The third, and final element of morality, is autonomy. This returns us to individualism, since secular morality is one of individualism; autonomy is teaching not just respect for other individuals but also allowing the individual to question moral precepts, since 'we desire [morality] because we know the reason for its existence' (Durkheim 1961:118; Cladis 1995).

This is Durkheim's ideal: a school which teaches all three of these elements is providing a 'moral' education. While it can sound authoritarian at points it is important to remember that, as the final element of autonomy highlights, Durkheim does not expect individuals to kneel unquestionably at the feet of our current moral rules but rather to respect the need for some socially generated moral rules. Indeed, a moral education can partly be about questioning the rules we have at the moment:

A society like ours cannot, therefore, content itself with a complacent possession of moral results that have been handed down to it. It must go on to new conquests; it is necessary that the teacher prepare the children who are in his trust for those necessary advances. He must be on his guard against transmitting the moral gospel of our elders as a sort of closed book. On the contrary, he must excite in them a desire to add a few lines of their own, and give them the tools to satisfy this legitimate ambition. (Durkheim 1961:13–14)

How would such an education be produced? Here Durkheim provides some practical policies concerning punishment and rewards as well as the school environment.

Durkheim is dismissive of punishment in school, in particular corporal punishment, as 'quite a serious moral handicap. They affront a feeling that is at the bottom of all our morality, the religious respect in which the human person is held' (Durkheim 1961:182). Although he acknowledges some form of punishment may be essential he sees any teacher who resorts to it as lacking both the respect and allegiance of their students; it is a mark of failure. Therefore, Durkheim advocates a greater use of rewards (including withholding them when needed). In particular, he argues these should be administered at a class level, rather than an individual one. When breaching of the rules occurs it is breaching a collectively agreed morality, rather than an individual one, so the class should have rewards withheld from it. In order to ensure all members of the class agree to these 'each class should have its little code of precepts, worked out in the course of everyday life' (Durkheim 1961:244). Durkheim also suggests new rewards. Noting that currently there are only rewards for academic achievement, he argues there should also be one for exemplary moral activity, which he terms a 'prize for virtue' (Durkheim 1961:206).

Turning to the school environment, we saw earlier that Durkheim argued there was currently a reluctance to engage in associational activity. Therefore, in order for the corporations to have fully committed members it is important to develop the associational spirit early. Here Durkheim returns to the value of the class. Rather than just a collection of students the class should be seen by the students as having its own personality which, Durkheim suggests, many teachers already know each class has. As he puts it, 'such phrases as the *class*, the *spirit of the class*, and the *honour of the class* must become something more than abstract expressions in the student's mind' (Durkheim 1961:241). In order to achieve this Durkheim argues that groups should stay together from the beginning of school to the end and as the class progresses through the educational levels a summary of its rewards, accomplishments and work should travel with it (Durkheim 1961:244). This is intended to make the students feel like part of an association where 'the value of each is a function of the worth of all' (Durkheim 1961:245). This is another reason why Durkheim favours rewards for the class as a whole.

Therefore, as we have seen, Durkheim gives education an important role in the curing of the malaise. Its most prominent role is, by developing the components of morality in the child, lessening some of the issues of the moral malaise. However, by also developing the spirit of association – and therefore creating the conditions for the flourishing of the corporations – it has a part to play in combating its political and economic forms.

Conclusion

As the above has demonstrated, although Durkheim's three alternatives are distinct they are interlinked and, seemingly, should be implemented at the same time. The corporations are the central part of the alternative; moral education exists, at least to some extent, to provide the associational spirit necessary for these. Furthermore, without the corporations to absorb the wealth, it would not be possible to ban inheritance. This continues to be significant when inheritance is linked to a growth in inequality (Piketty 2014) and economic crises indicate the key feature of economic anomie. In this concluding section I will recap how Durkheim's alternative would cure the malaise he confronted before turning to the question of how we can categorise this alternative.

To discuss the effectiveness of Durkheim's alternative I will go through each part of the malaise one by one. The moral malaise is confronted primarily via moral education and the corporations. The former of these provides the basis for the authority of social morality and the autonomy of the individual while the latter provides the professional ethics currently lacking in the division of labour. The corporations also, by democratically determining the activity of the profession, have a role in combating the expansion of the amoral character of economic life which, without professional ethics, is an inevitable result of making more jobs respond to the needs of the market. The economic malaise also relies upon the corporations. These decide on a just distribution of wages between the different levels of the occupation as well as removing the economic anomie by putting a check on individual desires for the greater good. The banning of inheritance is also important to the lessening of economic inequality by eradicating most of the potential for unjust contracts and creating greater equality. Finally, the political malaise is combated by using the corporations as an everyday connection to political issues which matter to its members. By extending this across society we have a strong connection to politics and less apathy. Moral education is also significant here by providing an early teaching in the child's connection to social groups.

We have seen that Durkheim's sociological alternatives differ from that of Marx and Engels in many ways – most notably their fundamental disagreement on the value of the division of labour. While some have linked this to corporatism (Black 1984, Muller 1993) others have suggested that Durkheim's alternative was at least inspired by socialism (Gane 1984, Stedman Jones 2001). Indeed, rather than the negotiation under a capitalist system encouraged by corporatism, Durkheim's alternative has a striking similarity to the system of guild or libertarian socialism (Cole 1920, Dawson 2013). The focus on socialisation of the economy, distribution of property, greater economic equality and political participation is shared by many socialist doctrines.

However, more importantly for this book is the nature of Durkheim's alternative as a *sociological* alternative. He was much more willing to provide a blueprint than Marx, due to his belief that sociology is a 'practical' discipline, concerned with solving problems in the here and now, rather than leaving the impetus to a revolutionary class. Moreover, we have seen that Durkheim considered factors such as morality and greed which were somewhat neglected by Marx yet maintained a focus on property, economic socialisation and work. In the alternatives to come we will find many sociologists, socialist or not, who shared these concerns. Furthermore, as we shall see in Chapters 9 and 10 contemporary sociologists such as Levitas and Burawoy are likely to cite Durkheim, rather than Marx, as the initial impetus towards a critical sociology of alternatives.

This is a role Durkheim would, most likely, cherish. In his discussion of individualism he reminds sociologists of the need not just to value negative freedom (as in removing constraints from individuals) but positive, or political, freedom (allowing individuals the means to do what they wish). In doing so he says 'political freedom is a means, not an end; its worth lies in the manner in which it is used … it is a battle weapon' (Durkheim 1973:55). A Durkheimian sociological alternative is one which, fully aware of the power of this weapon and the value of individualism, hopes to place it in the hands of individuals.

W.E.B. Du Bois: A Black Radical Alternative

4

The alternatives considered thus far from Marx and Durkheim defined inequal ity in a particular form. For Durkheim, inequality was linked explicitly to economic means and for Marx, when inequality was a factor, it was also defined economically (as in his 'right to inequality' during the first stage of communism). In doing so, other forms of inequality have tended to be marginalised. In Chapter 7 we will turn more fully to the question of gender; this chapter instead takes racism as its focus and, in particular, the work of W.E.B. Du Bois (1868–1963).

Du Bois has had a problematic relationship to sociology throughout much of the discipline's history. He was involved in many early American sociological endeavours, such as advocating the teaching of sociology alongside publication of one of the earliest urban ethnographies in his *The Philadelphia Negro* (Du Bois 1996). However, despite such actions, which formed part of his attempt to place racism within a sociological lens, Du Bois was long marginalised as a 'forgotten black sociologist' and denied his place in the discipline's history (Rudwick 1969, Morris 2015). While it has been argued this was due to the historical 'segregation' of US sociology between white and African-American writers (Bhambra 2014) his work, with some exceptions (see Gilroy 1993), has also tended to be ignored beyond the US.

This has changed to some extent in recent years with Du Bois more readily placed alongside writers such as Marx and Durkheim as part of the 'sociological canon' (Lemert 2008). In doing so a particular type of theorist is being recognised, not just one who wrote about race but who is marked by what we shall discuss in Chapter 10 as a commitment to 'public sociology'. Like Mead, discussed in the next chapter, Du Bois' sociological alternative is defined as much by what he did as what he wrote. I have called this a 'black radical alternative' reflecting other classifications of Du Bois' work (Marable 1986). But, as we shall see, Du Bois became progressively more radical as he developed his thought. Significantly, Du Bois is marked out by a desire to link his ideas to sociological insight. Therefore, he is an ideal figure for consideration in this book.

Du Bois' early life and key concepts

Du Bois lived an eventful life, marked by its length as well as its scope. He was born three years after the end of the civil war and died the day before Martin Luther King delivered his 'I have a dream' speech. Therefore, Du Bois experienced, and participated in, a profound era for black politics in the US. He grew up in the town of Great Barrington, Massachusetts, and had a relatively secure upbringing. This was indicated by his childhood belief that success was open to all who were willing to work hard, regardless of race or class (Du Bois 1984:8–24). It was only during his later school years that Du Bois spoke of his growing recognition that 'some folks, a few, even several, actually considered my black skin a misfortune' (Du Bois 2003:40). Small instances, such as the white girl who refused his calling card (Du Bois 1984:14), added up to a realisation of his different position from others. This was only enhanced during a trip to Germany where he realised the racism he experienced in the US was specific. Here his desire to advance the position of black people in his home country was born. Upon the completion of his studies Du Bois held posts at Wilberforce College followed by Pennsylvania and Atlanta Universities. It was during these years that his critique, and the earliest form of his alternative, was developed.

To understand Du Bois' critique we must turn to his starting point: the everyday experience of racism. For Du Bois, as in his experience with the girl who refused his card, awareness of one's ethnicity occurs through everyday practices and interactions. However, this is only true of those who are not white; whiteness allows one to have the realisation that their world 'is white and by that token, wonderful!' (Du Bois 2003:56). Indeed, to be white is to be not actively aware of your race. However, if you are black, this is not possible, daily acts remind you of your race, whether it be people ignoring you, crossing the street when they saw you, addressing only your white companion or finding landlords unwilling to rent. Du Bois experienced all of these, as well as, during a summer job as a waiter, finding his well-educated black friend playing the clown for a group of white diners knowing this was likely to lead to tips (Du Bois 2003:127–8). Importantly, while such acts of racism were not necessarily a daily occurrence, Du Bois had a constant awareness that they can be. It may have been four days since a taxi driver ignored him in the rain as he waved his hand, but that doesn't mean it won't happen today. The area he lived in may be relatively free of racially motivated violence (including the lynching he would read about in the daily paper) but there's no guarantee today isn't the day where it happens. These events add up to a continual awareness of one as different, as a problem:

> They approach me in a half-hesitant sort of way, eye me curiously or compassionately, and then, instead of saying directly, How does it feel to be a problem? they say, I know an excellent coloured man in my town; or, I fought at Mechanicsville; or, Do not these Southern outrages make your blood boil? At these I smile, or am interested, or reduce the boiling to a simmer, as the occasion may require. To the real question, How does it feel to be a problem? I answer seldom a word. (Du Bois 1994:1)

Such a situation creates what Du Bois terms a 'double consciousness'. This is a 'sense of always looking at one's self through the eyes of others', thereby measuring one's self by the standards imposed by whiteness (Du Bois 1994:2). This creates a fundamental 'two-ness' of being where one is forced to ask:

> What after all, am I? Am I an American or am I a Negro? Can I be both? Or is it my duty to cease to be a Negro as soon as possible and be an American? If I strive as a Negro, am I not perpetuating the very cleft that threatens and separates Black and White America? Is not my only possible practical aim that subduction of all that is Negro in me to the American? Does my black blood place upon me any more obligation to assert my nationality than German, or Irish or Italian blood would? (Du Bois 1897:821)

This double consciousness therefore creates an impossible situation for anyone subjected to it, where recognition of one category is seen to invalidate the other. In turn, it shapes how we view the world, with life experienced from 'within the veil' (Du Bois 2003). The way in which people view the world and act is shaped by their position in relation to the veil and what Du Bois terms 'the colour-line' (Du Bois 1994:v). Therefore, racism becomes the key social dividing line in Du Bois' sociology due to its possibility to produce the double consciousness and force some to live within the veil.

There is, however, one area of social life where the colour line is, at least theoretically, removed: knowledge. While, as we shall see, Du Bois was critical of the means of education available to African-Americans, knowledge itself does not intrinsically discriminate; it can go above the veil. Du Bois' own, very intensive, education had shown this:

> I sit with Shakespeare and he winces not. Across the colour-line I move arm in arm with Balzac and Dumas, where smiling men and welcoming women glide in gilded halls. From out the caves of evening that swing between the strong-limbed earth and the tracery of the stars, I summon Aristotle and Aurelius and what I will, and they come all graciously with no scorn nor condescension. So, wed with Truth, I dwell above the Veil. (Du Bois 1994:67)

Therefore, it is perhaps unsurprising that Du Bois' earliest critique focused on the relation of race and education.

Du Bois' early critique: *The Philadelphia Negro*

Du Bois came to intellectual maturity at a significant point in the struggle for racial equality. During his early years African-American political organisation was largely dominated by Booker T. Washington. Washington had been born a slave but, with the end of slavery, had risen to the position as the dominant activist and organiser for black Americans. He had also developed an education network of black colleges centred on his own base of Tuskegee Institute in Alabama in which Robert Park, one of the key figures in early American sociology, was active (Magubane 2014). However, in reaching this position Washington has crafted a very particular political programme, of which Du Bois had two criticisms (Du Bois 1994:25–36). Firstly, Washington had framed the struggle for emancipation purely as one of uplift and education, arguing that political liberty and rights were not, at that time, the most important factor for a group who lacked basic schooling. While, as we shall see, Du Bois shared this concern with education, he argued that the sole focus on this had harmed the cause of African-Americans rights. This had included some reversal of rights post-slavery and the lack of any political action to confront lynching and other forms of violence. The second factor concerned the form of education on offer. Washington had developed Tuskegee and other institutions to focus largely on a vocational education, the reasoning behind this being that, in the short term, such teaching and the occupations it allowed were the best available option for black students. Du Bois saw such an education – which excluded the reading of Shakespeare, Balzac, Dumas and the writers he had adored 'above the Veil' – as furthering inequality by restricting African-Americans to vocational work and leaving the academic world to whites. It was not fortuitous for someone in Du Bois' position to disagree with Washington, as he later lamented (Du Bois 1984:72). Washington's dominance in the civil rights movement meant that any alternative programme, such as Du Bois', was unlikely to occur without his approval. This, as we shall see, encouraged his later move away from academia and into activism.

Before this rupture, Du Bois was busy trying to carve a space for himself, and sociology, within what was termed at the time 'the study of Negro problems' (Williams 2006). For Du Bois, sociology was the discipline that sought to understand the nature of social laws. In understanding how people work within and against these laws it is 'the science that seeks the limits of Chance in human conduct' (Du Bois 2000:44). Such a view of sociology can be found in his study on *The Philadelphia Negro* (Du Bois 1996).

This study was an early example of the kind of urban ethnography whose method was later popularised in sociology by the Chicago School. However, at the time of its publication, it was largely ignored, including at the University of Pennsylvania where Du Bois was working at the time. It would later be mentioned more frequently for its ground-breaking nature, leading Du Bois to comment that 'nobody ever reads that fat volume on "The Philadelphia Negro" but they treat it with respect, and that consoles me' (Du Bois 2003:47). At nearly 400 pages it was indeed a 'fat volume' but one with many insights into the nature of African-American life. Important for our discussion is the concluding chapter, 'A Final Word', in which Du Bois turns his focus towards the causes of racism and the possible path forward. Perhaps unsurprisingly, Du Bois blames ignorance but, importantly, places the ignorance on both sides. The whites of the city had maintained their ignorance concerning the position of their black counterparts by offering limited work opportunities and education. The legacy of slavery and the Washington schooling had given whites a (false) justification for claims of their superiority over black people. Given that, at this point and for a long time after, there was no black middle class to speak of; any change in these opportunities for African-Americans relied on white compliance and assistance, such as providing more skilled jobs. Du Bois sees such an expansion of opportunities as valuable for both black and white people. Motivated workers who believe what they are doing is worthwhile and valued, rather than something they are forced to do because of the colour of their skin, work harder.

This is also important for the question of ignorance. Whites may object to the 'ignorance' of African-Americans, but 'if by our actions we have been responsible for their ignorance and are still actively engaged in keeping them ignorant, the argument loses its moral force' (Du Bois 1996:394). For him, such ignorance was an inevitable result of the legacy of slavery and the limited education available. This had wider impacts: work, rightly seen as toil with no reward, was resented and shunned; crime increased; and a lack of pride was taken in the communities – unsurprising given the conditions in which this group was forced to live. While these conditions and attitudes could be explained socially their perpetuation harmed the African-American political cause. These everyday practices of ignorance could, and should, be changed. As he put it:

> Efforts to stop this crime must commence in the Negro homes; they must cease to be, as they often are, breeders of idleness and extravagance and complaint. Work, continuous and intensive; work, although it be menial and poorly rewarded; work, though done in travail of soul and sweat of brow, must be so impressed upon Negro children as the road to salvation, that a child would feel it a greater disgrace to be idle than to do the humblest labour. (Du Bois 1996:390)

This then links into a wider point for Du Bois: being black in America meant knowing you had been the victim of a large-scale injustice whose impact could still be felt years after its abolition. Nevertheless, this did not justify the claim that the system which for a long period had allowed such injustice should be overturned. Instead:

> Simply because the ancestors of the present white inhabitants of America went out of their way barbarously to mistreat and enslave the ancestors of the present black inhabitants gives those blacks no right to ask that the civilisation and morality of the land be seriously menaced for their benefit. Men have a right to demand that the members of a civilised community be civilised; that the fabric of human culture, so laboriously woven, be not wantonly or ignorantly destroyed. (Du Bois 1996:389)

Therefore, the goal for African-Americans was not a new civilisation but rather full inclusion in the existing one. Fortunately, in *The Philadelphia Negro* Du Bois found a group able to institute this. Here he implores that 'the better classes of the Negroes should recognise their duty toward the masses' (Du Bois 1996:392) and it is this which leads us to his first alternative.

Du Bois' first alternative: the Talented Tenth and education

These 'better classes of the Negroes' which Du Bois referred to would famously be captured in his claim for a 'Talented Tenth', at whom his first alternative was primarily aimed (Du Bois 1903). However, to appreciate the reason for this we must begin with what determined a 'race' for Du Bois.

There were, for Du Bois, many ways to determine 'race'; the most common being skin colour, hair and language. However, all of these are faulty. Skin colour varies greatly even for people who have similar backgrounds and, with the increase in mixed-race relationships, is likely to have even less importance; the same can be said for hair and language. Instead, for Du Bois, races are defined by culture, with each group having a distinctive cultural heritage and practices which help create a shared racial identity. Modern civilisation, marked by the interaction and mixture of races, is therefore shaped by the contribution of all these distinct groups to a common heritage and culture (Du Bois 1897:815–20).

In this black people had, in limited opportunities, developed their own culture and made a contribution to modern societies. As Du Bois puts it:

> We are that people whose subtle sense of song had given America its only American music, its only American fairy tales, its only touch of pathos and humour amid its made money-getting plutocracy. As such, it is our duty to conserve our physical powers, our intellectual endowments, our spiritual ideals; as a race we must strive by race organisation, by race solidarity, by race unity to the realisation of that broader humanity which freely recognises differences in men, but sternly deprecates inequality in their opportunities of development. (Du Bois 1897:822)

Therefore, there is a need for such a culture to be maintained and, importantly, developed further. It is here that the Talented Tenth are central. Such a group, the scholars, artists and leaders of any race, are the ones who develop this culture since 'was there ever a nation on God's fair earth civilised from the bottom upward? Never, it is, ever was and ever will be from the top downward that culture filters' (Du Bois 1903:847). Consequently, it is the responsibility of the whole group to provide opportunities for the Talented Tenth, a cultural elite, to develop. Without them, the group as a whole will fail as 'the Negro race, like all races, is going to be saved by its exceptional men' (Du Bois 1903:841).

It is here that Du Bois turns to the key element of his first alternative, the establishment of organisations dedicated to the development of African-American culture, of which he lists: 'Negro colleges, Negro newspapers, Negro business organisations, a Negro school of literature and art, and an intellectual clearing house, for all these products of the Negro mind, which we may call a Negro Academy' (Du Bois 1897:822). All of these organs provide training and/ or an outlet for African-American culture to be developed and expressed. In short, they provide space for the Talented Tenth to act.

Of all these institutions it is undoubtedly the 'Negro Academy' which was most important for Du Bois. Not only did these, contrary to the institutions encouraged by Washington, allow for the expanded education favoured by Du Bois but, in so doing, opened up possibilities for social mobility. This reflected a long-term concern of Du Bois, namely the lack of class differentiation within the African-American community. This potential impact of the 'Negro Academy' can be seen in the commencement speech he gave at Fisk University, an example of such an academy, in 1898. Here he encourages the graduating students that:

> For the man who will work, and dig, and starve, there is a chance to do here incalculable good for the Negro race; for the woman in whose soul the divine music of our fathers has touched some answering chord of genius, there is a chance to do more than follow the masters; to all of you in whom the tragedy of life, or its fitful comedy, has created a tale worth the telling, there is a chance to gain listeners who will know no colour line. (Du Bois 1898:838–9)

He then lists the potential paths open to graduates including 'captains of industry', 'well trained physicians', 'the Negro merchant' and 'specially trained teachers' among other professional/bourgeois occupations (Du Bois 1898:839). The claim is clear: use the education of the 'Negro Academy', an example of which existed at Fisk, as the basis for the development not of a black labouring class, but rather a new black professional class: a Talented Tenth. As Du Bois put it, 'I insist that the object of all true education is not to make men carpenters, it is to make carpenters men' (Du Bois 1903:855).

The result of this alternative then, for Du Bois, means the problems identified in the critique, the ignorance of both white and black Americans on the colour line, can be overcome with the advancement of African-American education, culture and class structure. This would then lead to the lessening of the problems found in the colour line and its attendant factors of the double consciousness and the veil. If African-Americans are part of the 'civilisation' existing in America – with their activities and class structure matching more clearly white America – then the colour line lessens and the 'twoness' of being black and American would be overcome. Resting behind this is an optimistic assumption from Du Bois concerning the role of science and education in African-American emancipation. This assumption was to be challenged by events.

Du Bois' turn to activism

Du Bois was a frequent user of autobiography in his work. This was perhaps unsurprising given how living from within the veil was an experience he knew intimately. However, while many sociologists have written autobiographies, where Du Bois differed was that his biography was often interwoven with his sociological writings. In this one particular story occurs frequently: the grue-some death of Sam Hose.

Hose was a black man who had killed his landlord's wife. While the circum-stances of the case were contested it seems the victim had been a bystander to an argument between Hose and her husband in which the former may have been trying to defend himself. Whatever the circumstances, having heard of Hose's arrest Du Bois, then working at the University of Atlanta, put together some data about the number of black men accused of murder and headed down to the local newspaper to discuss the case. He never reached the newspaper offices. On the way there he heard that Hose had been caught by a mob who tortured and then lynched him; his knuckles were on sale in a butcher's shop further down the street on which Du Bois was walking (Du Bois 1984:67). As he would later put it, 'something died in me that day' (Du Bois 1944:53). What died was his belief in the possibility of rational and reasoned argument to solve the problem of racism; when people were being tortured and their knuckles sold as meat, scientific argument was not going to convince the torturers to stop. Since 'one could not be a calm, cool, and detached scientist while Negroes were lynched, murdered and starved' (Du Bois 1984:67) a new role opened up for Du Bois, beyond science:

> I suddenly saw life, full and face to face; I began to know the problem of Negroes in the United States as a present startling reality; and moreover (and this was most upsetting) I faced situations that called – shrieked – for action, even before any detailed, scientific study could possibly be prepared. It was as though, as a bridge-builder, I was compelled to throw a bridge across a stream without waiting for the careful mathematical resting of materialism. Such testing was indispensable, but it had to be done so often in the midst of building or even after construction, and not in the calm and leisure long before. (Du Bois 1944:57)

This role was to be activism. Du Bois would become one of the first, and most successful, examples of public sociology. He would remain a sociologist, in the sense of using the tools of sociological analysis, but would do so from outside the academy and the institutions of sociology, as an activist.

Du Bois' most prominent activity concerned the National Association for the Advancement of Colored People (NAACP). This was formed in 1909 partly as an attempt to create a separate activist base away from the apparatus of Booker T. Washington. Du Bois was central to its formation, helping push for the use of the term 'coloured' rather than 'black' in order to broaden its poten-tial reach and membership. Once the organisation was formed he was given the post of director of publication and research which included being editor of the house magazine *The Crisis* (DeMarco 1983:66). Given the centrality of the written word as, at this point, the most effective means of mass com-munication, this role was central to the NAACP's advocacy goals. This also changed Du Bois' activity; while he continued to produce scholarly work his focus inevitably became one of writing for a mass audience and pushing the causes of the NAACP. It also led to his greater public prominence as a spokesman for racial equality. His activities also took on an international focus, such as helping to organise the first Pan-African Congress in 1921. This grew out of a meeting at the Paris Congress which, following World War I, had famously sidelined African voices while carving the continent up for the colonial powers (Du Bois 1984:274–8).

While Du Bois was proud of his activist work it was not a role he was comfortable with, commenting that 'of the movement I was willy-nilly leader. I hated the role' (2003:49). It also led to difficult decisions and compromises for Du Bois who was increasingly becoming influenced by Marxism (DeMarco 1983:63–78). For example, the NAACP had, as part of a general campaign against segregation, fought against this in the army. However, once that fight was lost and separate black units were formed, should the NAACP then join the demand for black officers? This would allow for training and advancement but seemed to approve of, and formalise, segregation. The organisation did eventually decide to join the successful campaign for them. As Du Bois forlornly notes, despite such advances for some African-Americans, lynchings and other forms of violence continued (Du Bois 1984:248–51).

Du Bois' encounter with Marxism, encouraged by a trip to Soviet Russia in the 1920s, which 'was and still is to my mind, the most hopeful land in the modern world' (Du Bois 1944:60), caused further problems within the NAACP. It meant that mainstream politicians were reluctant to be associated with the organisation given the fear of communism. Furthermore, his increasingly economically focused articles in *The Crisis* created disagreement with others in the organisation who did not necessarily share his analysis. As we shall see below, Du Bois also increasingly advocated a form of segregation which went against the founding mission and activities of the organisation. Therefore, while Du Bois would never give up his activism, having resigned his post with the NAACP and *The Crisis* in 1934, he returned to the University of Atlanta. Here he would develop his second critique and alternative which was based on the legacy of the civil war.

Du Bois' second critique: the legacy of the civil war

The year after returning to academia Du Bois would publish perhaps his most Marxist, and most impressive, text *Black Reconstruction in America* (Du Bois 1956). A historical study, this was concerned with the civil war and its immediate aftermath. For Du Bois, the war had quickly gained a ready story: it was a war to end slavery. He contested this, arguing that it was started primarily for economic reasons. The largely developed capitalist North took on a South which was still partly feudal in order to institute a capitalist regime. This would open up further markets and secure the cotton produced in the South which was so central to the Northern economy. These goals did include the abolition of slavery, a key tenet of capitalism being the ability to sell one's labour, but this was not central. The war also united the Southern white working class, who were unable to compete with slave labour for jobs, with the black slaves. While the entry of black soldiers into the Union army meant the war gained a moral dimension (Du Bois 1956:83), it retained its original and primary goal as an economic war for the advancement of capitalism.

Following the Northern victory reconstruction governments were imposed on the South. Largely mandated by Washington D.C. these were intended to ensure some level of black equality and political participation, alongside the shift to a capitalist market. However, for Du Bois, it is at this point that the class solidarity of the war begins to break down. Southern whites, previously tied to the idea of ending slavery in order to relieve pressure on their own wages, begin to resent the improved position of their black neighbours and the loss of their previous colour-based advantage. Even more significantly, the ending of slave labour pushes up the price of cotton. This then unites the Southern bourgeoisie (who want to push the production cost back down to increase surplus value), the Northern bourgeoisie (who wish the same) and the Northern working class (at least its white component who find it difficult to afford the increased price of goods). This ensures that the colour line between the white and black working class is more significant than their shared class position (Du Bois 1956:670–91). The result of this for Du Bois is that the Southern bourgeoisie (universally white) had *carte blanche* to attack reconstruction government for their supposed corruption. This had the added goal of seeking to control the black labouring class by presenting a simple choice: either sign labour contracts which tie you to work in conditions not far removed from slavery or be lynched. Not unsurprisingly 'from 1880 onward, in order to earn a living, the American Negro was compelled to give up his political power' culminating in the replacement of reconstruction governments with white elites (Du Bois 1956:693). This then ensured that wider policies of reconstruction, including education for the former slaves – at least beyond the vocational form conveniently supported by Booker T. Washington – were impossible. Consequently:

> It must be remembered and never forgotten that the civil war in the South [the actions of the bourgeoisie following the original 'civil war'] which overthrew Reconstruction was a determined effort to reduce black labour as nearly as possible to a condition of unlimited exploitation and build a new class of capitalists on this foundation. (Du Bois 1956:670)

Black economic inequality and ignorance is maintained post-reconstruction by limiting education, overthrowing reconstruction governments and ensuring a black labouring class working in close to slavery conditions. Therefore, for Du Bois, the position of African-Americans was fundamentally shaped by the legacy of slavery and the obstacles placed in the way of any attempt at reconstruction. The story then told about the civil war (that the Northern whites freed the slaves who had been too lazy/weak to do it themselves) had helped legitimate such inequality in what Du Bois termed the 'propaganda of history' (Du Bois 1956:711–31).

Two important points emerged from this for Du Bois. Firstly, it reasserted his earlier concern for the lack of black class differentiation. The legacy of reconstruction had assured the former slaves and their descendants the position of a labouring class – not even a full proletariat since they were not able to freely sell their labour. While there would be forms of cultural class differentiation – some African-Americans such as Du Bois gained a high education and performed some professional activity – there was to be very little economic differentiation (Du Bois 1984:184–5). Secondly, this study had placed an important qualifier on his Marxism. The class solidarity of the proletariat had been made precarious and ultimately had broken down due to the colour line. As soon as any slight division emerged between black labourers and their white companions this overrode any shared class interest. This led to an important point about future strategy, namely that 'so long as we were fighting a colour line, we must strive by colour organisation. We have no choice' (Du Bois 1984:311). Such an organisation would be found in Du Bois' second alternative.

Du Bois' second alternative: black economic cooperation

As we have seen, the nature of Du Bois' second critique concerned the economic position of African-Americans, seeing their inequality as due to the legacy of the reconstruction era following slavery. Therefore, much more than his first alternative, his second alternative has an economic focus. It also shares with Durkheim an utilisation of bodies akin to the corporations to conduct economic activity. Du Bois advocated the expansion of black-owned and run cooperatives. These would begin as cooperatives of consumption, before becoming ones of production. In doing so they are said to build upon a successful history of cooperation within the black community. Du Bois argues that most distinctively 'black' organisations in the US, churches, professional groupings, arts group and learned societies were established and continued to exist, almost solely because of investment and support from those who use them (Du Bois 1984:197–8). Therefore, economic cooperation is the next step.

Such cooperatives would open in areas with a large black population and encourage membership for all. Membership would not only allow one to shop in the cooperative but would also entail some measure of contribution of labour along with a vote in the affairs of the company (Du Bois 1984:212). For Du Bois, if such cooperatives were able to capture the majority of the black consumer market they would, especially in cities, quickly become large-scale operations with significant turnover. Such large organisations would then require some form of leadership and management which, reflecting the cooperative model, would be elected by the members.

This expansion of wealth would open possibilities for the cooperatives to move into production. Whereas previously the stores would have been reliant on outside producers (most likely members of the white bourgeoisie) for their goods, by establishing production mechanisms the whole economic process, from production to consumption, could stay within the black community. The democratic mechanisms of the cooperatives also allow for the nature of such production to change. Rather than occurring without any reference to need, the goods produced could be voted upon and decided by the membership, creating production linked to the needs of the community. Therefore, there would be a separate, but powerful, black economy run on a cooperative basis.

As DeMarco (1983:139–50) notes, Du Bois differed in his use of the cooperative idea over time. When he first began to advocate it, during his time editing *The Crisis*, they were conceived as capitalist bodies, used for profit production and developing black economic power. It was this which led to his role in establishing the Negro Co-Operative Guild, formed in his office at *The Crisis* headquarters (Du Bois 1984:280). In this period, they did not include mechanisms for democratic control and were imagined as bodies useful for developing the Talented Tenth. It was only later, with Du Bois' increased turn to Marxism, that they took on a democratic and productive basis. They became fundamentally socialist, as opposed to capitalist, organisations, not just seeking to create a segregated economy, but a different one.

This formation was no coincidence. In *Dusk of Dawn*, originally published in 1940, Du Bois argues that:

> We have reached the end of an economic era, which seemed but a few years ago omnipotent and eternal. We have lived to see the collapse of capitalism. It makes no difference what we may say, and how we may boast in the United States of the failures and changed objectives of the New Deal, and the prospective rehabilitation of the rule of finance capital; that is but wishful thinking. In Europe and in the United States as well as in Russia the whole organisation and direction of industry is changing. We are not called upon to be dogmatic as to just what the end of this change will be and what form the new organisation will take. What we are sure of is the present fundamental change. (Du Bois 1984:198–9)

Such sentiments, with the large-scale success of Roosevelt's new deal, the rapid development of the USSR under communist control and the emergence of fascism in Europe, were not uncommon at the time (Sassoon 2010). What made Du Bois' position unique was that he sought to link this collapse of capitalism to an opportunity for a marginalised group who were not a class, in this case African-Americans, to be the vanguard of this new society. As he put it 'we have a chance here to teach industrial and cultural democracy to a world that bitterly needs it' (Du Bois 1984:219). In doing so, the initial role of the cooperatives as consumer organisations is central since:

> What I propose is that into the interstices of this collapse of the industrial machine, the Negro shall search intelligently and carefully and

far-sightedly plan for his entrance into the new economic world, not as a continuing slave but as an intelligent free man with power in his hands. I see this chance for planning in the role which the Negro plays as a consumer. In the future reorganisation of industry the consumer as against the producer is going to be the key man. Industry is going to be guided according to his wants and needs and not exclusively with regard to the profit of the producers and transporters. (Du Bois 1984:208)

Therefore, the cooperatives can indicate the future path for the economy beyond capitalism. Consequently, while Du Bois' second alternative is imagined to apply initially only to African-Americans, the end goal is for it to expand over society as a whole following the end of capitalism.

In addition to this, part of the justification for the cooperatives from Du Bois is based upon the differential class positions of black and white America. There was no black bourgeoisie and the working class was split along colour lines, both politically and economically. Du Bois' first alternative had relied upon social mobility occurring along broadly cultural lines: provide an education befitting of a professional class, and you will make a professional class. Therefore, the hope was placed with a cultural elite. However, as he comments when advocating his second alternative (Du Bois 1984:217), this was a mistake. Economic inequality and power are so strong that they cannot easily be overcome by cultural means. This is why separate economic means are needed. But reflecting his shift to Marxism, for Du Bois the cooperative is not a way to create a new capitalist class for the part of America currently excluded from this. Instead cooperation provides an alternative in which the goal is to overcome such inequities. As a result, this will not be a system which allows people to become rich. Like Durkheim, Du Bois argues that having internal votes on the wages of managers in the cooperatives will keep wage differences down and ensure greater equality. He recognises that this calls for 'self-control' since his alternative will:

> eliminate the millionaire and even the rich Negro; it will put the Negro leader upon a salary which will be modest as American salaries go and yet sufficient for a life under modern standards of decency and enjoyment. It will eliminate also the pauper and the industrial derelict. (Du Bois 1984:215)

Therefore, Du Bois' second alternative aims to do three things: develop wealth, and therefore power, within the African-American community; maintain greater equality; and provide an example of industrial democracy. In this sense it hopes to build upon the history of cooperation within this community while also ensuring the improvement in their condition both within and beyond capitalism.

In this sense, Du Bois' second alternative seeks to solve the problems highlighted in his second critique by aiming to remove the forms of economic subjugation which had created a black labouring class. In doing so, the goal is not, immediately, to fight against the colour line but rather to recognise its promi-nence and seek to find mechanisms within which the conditions of African-Americans can be improved until the day, seemingly post-capitalism, in which the colour line can be overcome. Therefore, it does not seek to remove the problem of the double consciousness, at least not in the short term, but rather to resolve it in favour of one side: the black side.

This leads us to another important factor to Du Bois' second alternative: it is, as we have seen, a programme of segregation. Du Bois' move towards advocating segregation, not only within the economy, was one of the factors which led to his difficulties with the NAACP. For example, his later writings on the 'Negro College' argued that these should be segregated, unlike his 'Negro Academies' of the first alternative which, while primarily aimed at African-Americans, would not make such segregation a policy (Du Bois 1933). Du Bois increasingly faced open censure in the pages of *The Crisis* for advocating this position, which was inconsistent with his earlier focus on integration within the 'civilised' world found on the pages of *The Philadelphia Negro*. Du Bois' (1934) response to this was clear; 1934 was not 1910. In the intervening years white America had increasingly shut its doors to black America. No longer could black academics, like Du Bois, get jobs at mainstream universities, stay in some hotels, attend certain restaurants or visit various spaces. Segregation had actually increased in the first decades of the twentieth century, as the NAACP had found in its protests about the army. More problematically, lynching and other forms of violence remained a fact of life. In such situations, for Du Bois, the slogan 'no segregation' had increasingly been used as a way for more highly educated African-Americans to seek re-entry into privileged spaces rather than a wider strategy of equality (Du Bois 1934:1244). Meanwhile, white America continued to cut off interaction with their black counterparts beyond the most basic level needed. There was only one response to such behaviour:

> When my room-mate gets too noisy and dirty, I leave him; when my neighbours get too annoying and insulting I seek another home; when white Americans refuse to treat me as a man, I will cut my intercourse with white Americans to the minimum demanded by decent living. (Du Bois 1934:1248)

For Du Bois, his critics accused him of wanting to create segregation when in fact this was already there. Therefore his second alternative, while being a programme of segregation, was justified since 'we are now segregated largely without reason. Let us put reason and power beneath this segregation' (Du Bois 1984:215). It takes both sides to end segregation and, if one side was unwill-ing to do so, the only response was to seek to work within segregated barriers. This was the moral of the split in class affinities along the colour line during the reconstruction era and it was the story of the early twentieth century. While Du Bois' alternative ultimately is one for all of society – hence its 'teaching a lesson' to the world – in the interim segregated tactics were required.

Du Bois' later years and his socialism

Following the end of World War II Du Bois' thought would take a further shift. He remained a significant public figure, for example, running for the US Senate in 1950 on a Progressive Party ticket and gaining 224,599 votes (DeMarco 1983:181). He also became chairman of the Peace Information Centre (PIC), which was an organisation designed to campaign against the spread of nuclear weapons and uphold the principles of peace post-World War II. It also led Du Bois to write:

> I have faced during my life many unpleasant experiences: the growl of a mob; the personal threat of murder; the scowling distaste of an audience. But nothing has so cowed me as that day, November 8, 1951, when I took my seat in a Washington courtroom as an indicted criminal. (Du Bois 1952a:1071)

At the height of McCarthyism, the US had taken the decision to prosecute Du Bois, and four other members of PIC, on the grounds their organisation was an agent of the Soviet Union. Du Bois and his co-accused had been asked to register as foreign agents; their refusal had instigated the trial. There was no evidence to substantiate the claim and Du Bois, along with his colleagues, was acquitted. After the trial Du Bois reflected on why the government had bought such charges, and his conclusion was clear: 'to quell Communists' (Du Bois 1952b:1105). This indicates some of Du Bois' changing political relation to socialism.

While there is controversy as to when Du Bois embraced socialism, with some seeing it as part of his belief from the very start, and others only seeing it emerging during World War I, there is little doubt that Du Bois moved leftwards, and closer to socialist orthodoxy, as his life moved on (Reed 1985:443–50). For him, this was a reflection of the lifelong questions he had faced in terms of how to achieve black equality. Now, in the 1950s, the focus was on maintaining and extending the successes of the welfare state:

> Thus it is clear today that the salvation of American Negroes lies in socialism. They should support all measures and men who favour the welfare state; they should vote for government ownership of capital in industry; they should favour strict regulation of corporations or their public ownership; they should vote to prevent monopoly from controlling the press and the publishing of opinions. They should favour public ownership and control of water, electric, and atomic power; they should stand for a clean ballot, the encouragement of third parties, independent candidates, and the elimination of graft and gambling on television and even in church. (Du Bois 1958a:190–1)

His critique therefore moved increasingly towards identifying capitalism generally – not just its racist practices in the US – as a problem, since 'today we are lying, stealing and killing. We call this by finer names: Advertising, Free Enterprise, and National Defence' (Du Bois 1958b:1111). The silence of the NAACP concerning Du Bois' trial convinced him that in fact, unlike the suggestion of his second alternative, many African-Americans were invested in maintaining, rather than ending, capitalism (DeMarco 1983:160 ff.). Therefore, the 'universal class' of the proletariat who act in the interest of African-Americans by bringing socialism into being was a suitable ideal. Not only was this appealing but was inevitable. As Du Bois put it on his nineteenth birthday:

> Socialism progresses and will progress. All we can do is to silence and jail its promoters. I believe in socialism. I seek a world where the ideals of communism will triumph – to each according to his need; from each according to his ability. For this I will work as along as I live. And I still live. (Du Bois 1958b:1113)

This path would eventually lead Du Bois to becoming a member of the Communist Party of the US in 1961, just as he was to leave the country in order to live in Ghana and work on an *Encyclopedia Africana*. He would die just two years later.

Conclusion: Du Bois' alternatives

We have seen that Du Bois' critique and alternative takes ethnic inequality as its focus. For him racism plays out at the everyday level, through living 'within the veil' which ensures a double consciousness for those who live behind the colour line. In an era where forms of ethnic-based inequalities, racial violence and everyday forms of racism remain, Du Bois' work still has valuable points to make (Smith 2015). His early critique linked this to the limited vocational education available to black people at the time. The expansion of 'Negro Academies' would remove this and allow for entry into the 'civilisation' built up in America. It was events, most notably the brutal lynching of Sam Hose, which convinced Du Bois that knowledge was not enough and inspired his move into activism and, later, his emphasis on economics. Here Du Bois' critique saw the position of African-Americans as linked to the legacy of slavery and the desire to create a class of black labourers, upon which the Southern bourgeoisie could become rich. This meant racism had an economic base and, inspired by the lack of cross-ethnicity class solidarity of the reconstruction era, Du Bois advocated a form of economic segregation. Here, the formation of cooperatives would allow wealth to remain within the black community. These cooperatives were also meant to show a path beyond capitalism, which Du Bois saw as coming to an end. It was this which led to his becoming a member of the Communist Party just before his death.

Whether Du Bois' alternative would solve the problems of ethnic inequality depends on the nature of the critique offered. If we accept Du Bois' first critique that racism was due to the ignorance on both sides of the colour line, then the expanded education of the 'Negro Academies' was an effective solution. His cooperatives however were an unnecessary and potential dangerous attempt to cut off economic activity without the knowledge and wealth to sustain it. But if we accept Du Bois' second critique, that segregation was a fact of the twentieth century and was largely used to maintain a class of black labourers for capital's benefit, then his first alternative is largely pointless and instead a more socialist alternative is required. As we shall see again in chapters to come, to speak of what the alternative is for, whether that be racial equality, democracy or cosmopolitanism, is opaque without an idea of what the problem actually is. Du Bois' life, expressed in a social theory which utilises different critiques, and therefore alternatives, demonstrates this well.

George Herbert Mead and Karl Mannheim: Sociology and Democracy

The previous three chapters have outlined some of the earliest sociological alternatives provided by one theorist or, in the case of Marx and Engels, two working together. The next four chapters consider broad themes common to particular alternatives and discuss how two, or more, writers have approached them. We shall begin by considering the theme of democracy in the work of George Herbert Mead (1863–1931) and Karl Mannheim (1893–1947).

It is common to hear it argued that sociology and democracy are tied together. In Chapter 10, we shall see that this is a key justification for the idea of public sociology. Such a link can also be found in C. Wright Mills' claim that 'the political role of social science … is relevant to the extent to which democracy prevails … we are trying to make society more democratic' (Mills 1959:189). Sociology is a 'means to democracy' since it gives 'an understanding of the social forces involved in the democratizing of society' (Sanderson 1943:7). There are many explanations given for this link. A common one is akin to Bauman's claims for sociology as critical discussed in Chapter 1. Here sociology is seen to make us aware of the limits placed on our activities. By being aware of this we can critique the actions of politics: to what extent do laws prejudice against certain groups? Is it possible to have an equal say in the democratic process? Is power used legitimately? and so on. This is perhaps an explanation for why non-democratic states may greatly limit, or even ban, sociological study, such as the Communist Poland from which Bauman was exiled (Walaszek 1977). It may also help explain why, in attempting to secure government recognition and funding, sociologists emphasise their democratic credentials, as was the case in Sweden (Larsson and Magdalenić 2015).

However, 'democracy' is a very broad category with many competing conception of what its right form, and ultimate value, is (Held 2006). Our current form of representative, or liberal, democracy is different from the more direct form favoured in Du Bois' cooperatives for example. Therefore, this chapter considers in more depth how sociology has developed ways for society to become more democratic. As we shall see, the alternatives offered by Mead and Mannheim are markedly different, reflecting not only different national and historical contexts but ideas of how sociologists should offer alternatives. In doing so, they also demonstrate conflicting ideas of what it means for society to be democratic. It is these contrasting ideas which make them ideal for our discussion. This chapter could have considered further the link Mills drew between sociology and democracy, Carole Pateman's (1988) work on the 'sexual contract' at the heart of liberal democracy and therefore how new forms of participation would allow for a more democratic society or Paul Hirst's (1994) use of a sociological critique as the basis for his 'associative democracy'. But the value of discussing Mead and Mannheim is their opening up of two discussions. Firstly, they offer diametrically opposed ideas of how to develop democracy, as either a 'bottom-up' process engendered by creating everyday forms of participation and expression or a 'top-down' process in which enlightened experts create the conditions for what they conceive a democratic society to be. Secondly, and leading on from this, they demonstrate two distinct ways in which sociologists can assist in this process. Consequently, this comparison allows us to make broader points concerning the role of sociologists in offering alternatives. I will consider Mead and Mannheim separately before returning to these differences in the final section.

George Herbert Mead

Mead was born in 1863 in Massachusetts; his father was a protestant clergyman, just like his grandfather. He attended Oberlin College, which employed his father and provided training for evangelical clergymen-to-be with a strong focus on working in the community (Shalin 1988:915). Upon graduating, and having lost his faith, Mead spent a year at Harvard before travelling, primarily to do the doctorate he never completed, to Germany. Here, as we shall see below, he was inspired by the work of the German Social Democratic Party (SPD). Returning to America he was appointed to a position in the philosophy department at the University of Chicago, where he stayed until just before his death in 1931 (Joas 1997:15–32). At Chicago Mead combined with his friend and colleague John Dewey to develop American 'pragmatist' philosophy. This means that he never identified as a sociologist and, despite claims to the contrary, had very little interaction with, or impact upon, the burgeoning 'Chicago School' of sociology (Fisher and Strauss 1979) and would only come to be considered a sociologist after his death (Huebner 2014). Nevertheless, Mead's philosophy had a strong sociological focus, based within his concept of the 'social self' (Mead 1913). This would be central to the school of symbolic interactionist sociology, partly founded by one of Mead's students, Herbert Blumer (1969). It is Mead's concept of the social self from which we must begin to understand his wider critique and alternative since, as Silva puts it, Mead 'mobilizes the conceptual apparatus of his social psychology in order to put forth a scientific analysis of political and moral phenomena' (Silva 2007a:292). This concept of the social self has had a variety of readings over time (see Silva 2007b:91–115). In what follows I will utilise a sociological reading rather than the more philosophical reading of, for example, Habermas (Silva 2007b:95–101).

   Mead argues our self, our sense of who we are, is inherently social. In order to become aware of ourselves as somehow 'unique' – as Mead terms it, ourselves 'as a subject' – we need to act and think with reference to others, partly so we can differentiate ourselves from them. As he suggests:

> it is only as the individual finds himself acting with reference to himself as he acts towards others, that he becomes a subject of himself rather than an object, and only as he is affected by his social conduct in the manner in which he is affected by that of others, that he becomes an object to his own social conduct. (Mead 1913:143)

Based upon this Mead argues our self contains two components: the 'I' and the 'me'. The 'I' is made up of what Mead terms 'reflective thought' (Mead 1934:201) and is individual. This is our conception of our self and our activity – how we think about ourselves, the things we do and our individual desires. Importantly this is not done as isolated activity but rather is a 'response of the individual to the attitude of the community' (Mead 1934:196). The 'me' however is outside the individual and is part of this 'community' as the 'organized set of attitudes of others' (Mead 1934:194). This is the norms, values and social conceptions that go along with our role. Both of these, the I and the me, combine to make the self, meaning we are both aware of and react in response to social demands and interests.

To provide an example, Mead compares the I and the me to playing a team game. When we do so we act in line with a set of rules and the responses of our teammates. Therefore, the activities of the I, say in throwing the ball to my teammate, always occur with reference to the me – do the rules allow me to throw the ball, has my teammate called for it and so on (Mead 1934:173–8). As a player of the game both of these elements determine my action and demand my being aware of the expectations of others. To act purely as an 'I' would mean doing what I want without reference to the rules and my teammates. Acting purely as a me would mean I would be paralysed by inactivity, not knowing whether to throw or keep the ball; the rules allow both, but the I makes the decision. The same process for Mead can be seen in the family, the child develops their sense of self by both identifying with the family (the me) and by positioning him/herself as a unique member of that family (the I) (Mead 1934:368–73). Here, my sense of myself as the 'child' of the family is partly about my own reflection and activity, but this only occurs with reference to the expectations of others concerning what being 'the child' demands. Doing this requires us to develop a sense of what Mead terms the 'generalised other' or being able to take the position of others in our community and understand what our role commands (Mead 1934:154). What makes up this community changes (family, teammates and so on) but Mead argues this should be a broad community over the life course as we become aware of different interests and requirements (Mead 1934:202).

Therefore, our community is central, providing as it does our sense of self and directing our action through the generalised other. For this to happen we must enter into communication with others. This is where democracy is useful for Mead. Democracy contains a sense of 'universality' whereby all members of community have an opportunity to contribute towards public debate and choose rulers; indeed democracy is based upon communication for Mead (Mead 1934:284–7). Such communication is realised via what Mead terms 'government through public opinion' (Mead 2011:87) where we recognise a sense of universal connection to our fellow citizens (Mead 1934:286). The best democratically elected leaders are able to take the position of many different groups and realise their demands (Mead 1934:256). Therefore, democracy and Mead's sense of the self are tied together; democracy allows us to widen our sense of community and take account of as many different individuals and concerns as possible; in effect, it widens our 'me'. Rather than acting narrowly and in a self-centred way, we are obliged to consider others. For Mead this is inevitably a question of equality; when we understand and take the position of many, we can consider their complaints, issues and inequalities. As he puts it:

> This very attitude, however, of putting one's self in the other man's shoes brings with it not only the stimulus to assist him, but also a judgment upon that situation … One cannot assume the role of the wretched without considering under what conditions the wretchedness can or may be avoided … The step from this attitude to the idea of social conditions under which this evil would not exist is inevitable. (Mead 1930:398)

Therefore, democracy for Mead is fundamentally a process of increased communication within society so that multiple demands can be considered and, if needed, solutions found to problems and sources of inequality; the first step inevitably contains the second (Mead 1930:400). Mead terms this the 'ideal' democracy (Mead 1934:326). Alas, Mead confronted something which was not ideal and here we turn to his critique.

Mead's critique: narrow 'personality' democracy

For this ideal democracy to function its institutions must form what Mead terms 'social habits' whereby individuals will habitually and automatically take the position of the wider community (Mead 1936:33–4). This includes encouraging 'social' against 'asocial' activity. The former involves acting with reference to others and expanding our me, the latter purely with reference to our I (Mead 1934:317–28). Unfortunately, democracy as currently constituted encourages asocial against social habits thereby furthering self-interest and decreasing our sense of community. Mead provides three examples of such asocial habits. The first concerns nationalism and war. By seeing nation states as the 'external authority' over individuals (Mead 2011:87) they become the body which can legitimate war and demand obedience (Mead 2011). This for Mead was central to World War I, where the power interest of states created a situation whereby individuals were dragged into a war with an appeal to patriotic fervour; he terms this 'national mindedness' versus 'international mindedness' (Mead 1929). This is not only problematic for Mead due to the horrors of war but also because it jars with everyday life. Increasingly, nations are interdependent due to globalization, creating a global society in which 'what takes places in India, in Afghanistan, in Mesopotamia [sic], is entering into our lives' (Mead 1934:291, 270). Therefore, 'when states have appealed to the *ultima ratio* of states' (Mead 2011:88) they ignore the interdependence of nations and we are left with the potential for war. Our community is narrowed and our current partners become potential enemies.

The second example concerns immigration. The universality of democracy has notably, for Mead, been denied to immigrants. As he puts it:

> The immigrant is imported to provide that fund of unskilled labour upon which our industries may draw at will. He comes ignorant and helpless before the system of exploitation which ... may last for two generations after he enters our gates. Our government has nothing to offer him by way of protection but the doctrine of the abstract rights of man, a vote he cannot intelligently exercise, and the police to hold him in his place. (Mead 1907:123)

Despite their centrality to industry, immigrants come to be seen as a problem and are provided with little by the state, except criminalisation. They are, in effect, seen as 'outsiders' and therefore a source of trouble.

The third example for Mead concerns the relations of capital and labour. Some (Batiuk and Sacks 1981, Shalin 1988) have drawn links between Mead's condemning of capitalism turning the individual into simply 'part of a machine' (Mead as quoted by Batiuk and Sacks 1981:216) and Marx's conception of alienation. Mead differs from Marx however in seeing the conflict of capital and labour as due to a lack of forms of communication between the two sides. By saying capitalism is defined by conflict socialists have created a self-fulfilling prophecy where it will be (Mead 1987a). The same is true of capital where it has come to see workers as inevitably standing in its way. The state then takes the side of capital and becomes a 'business body operating for the benefit of those who make it up' (Mead 1899a:367). Consequently, while Mead supported trade unions he saw conflict as a result of a lack of democratic communication between labour and capital rather than an inherent element of capitalism.

The cause of these problems, and therefore the basis of Mead's critique, returns us to the un-ideal democracy. For Mead, liberal democracy as currently constituted with its reliance on national governments, political parties and presidential leaders is best seen as 'personality' democracy. The political community is brought together by allegiance to particular leaders or groups. This inevitably, for Mead (1934:313–17), creates forms of conflict (each state has its own leaders), xenophobia (immigrants come from 'outside') and class conflict (each class has its own parties and leader). It also, and this is perhaps the most important problem for Mead, limits the ability of people to take part in democracy. We are reduced simply to casting a vote every few years and following the decision of 'leaders'. Consequently, there is little possibility for us to have a direct influence on events in our daily lives. The result of this is that individuals are left to act as part of what Mead terms the 'mob'; petitions and public debates in which the target of the mob is always 'some hated object of the group', such as immigrants (Mead 1934:221). Therefore, division and a lack of communication are furthered and the problems of personality democracy are exacerbated. This then limits our opportunities to take the position of others and, following Mead's earlier comment, limits our potential to realise the 'evils' and 'wretchedness' which plague others' lives.

Mead contrasts this form of personality democracy with his alternative: rational democracy, to which we now turn.

Mead's alternative: rational democracy through scientific reform

As mentioned earlier, Mead was greatly influenced by the German SPD. One factor especially pleased Mead: the SPD had focused on the importance of, and had great success in, local politics (Joas 1997:20). Much like Durkheim, Mead saw the nation state as 'too far away from the average man' to expect it to solve everyday problems (Mead 1987b:272). Therefore, rather than focus on national politics, for Mead 'the direction in which we must work seems to me very clear. City politics' (Mead 1987b:272). By ending up in Chicago Mead had found the perfect city in which to pursue this goal. The city had swelled drastically in the latter half of the nineteenth century and, by the time of Mead's arrival, was already home to 1.2 million people, of whom more than a third were foreign born (Cook 1993:99). Like Du Bois, but to an even greater extent, Mead's sociological alternative not only concerns what he said but what he did, reflected in the fact that during his lifetime he was known more for his public rather than academic work (Huebner 2014:25–39). His alternative was in fact a career-long passion for practical social reform, with Chicago as the backdrop (Cook 1993:99–114).

As we have seen, Mead had a pragmatist sense of the self. We conceive of ourselves in relation to others; if more people become part of our community we become aware of them and, if needed, act to relieve their suffering. This was why he advocated the 'social habits' of democracy and its potential for communication between groups. Obtaining a rational democracy is therefore about finding forms of institutions which will encourage these social against asocial habits. In attempting to do this, Mead was critical of the urge, which he found in socialism, to begin with 'utopias' (Mead 1899b:409) since these are 'impotent to lead to better conditions' (Mead 1899a:367). Even that arch critic of utopias, Marx, was guilty of this for Mead by creating a theory which, being based on the irresistible laws of history, was dangerous due to its 'calls for the torch, the guillotine, and the dagger' (Mead 1899b:408). Mead was willing to accept the idea of socialism as a 'standpoint or attitude' (Mead 1899b:406) but saw changing society as something done in the here and now, based not on utopian but pragmatic grounds:

> A conception of a different world comes to us always as the result of some specific problem which involves readjustment of the world as it is, not to meet a detailed ideal of a perfect universe, but to obviate the present difficulty. (Mead 1899a:371)

Therefore, to discover what things *should* look like, it is essential to see what they *do* look like and come up with practical ideas to solve problems in the here and now. Mead encouraged those interested in social change to realise that 'there is nothing so interesting as human life if you can become an understanding part of it' (Mead 1907–8:110) and to conceive of alternatives as responses to problems of the status quo. This is what Mead terms 'scientific' or 'intelligent' reform, since science provides a clear idea of how change should be conducted: the experimental method (Mead 1938). Once the problem is identified we can develop working hypotheses as to what causes it and how changes in institutions, carried out as experiments, could remove it (Mead 1899a). Constructing such experiments was Mead's goal throughout his life. There are five particular experiments which demonstrate his goal of encouraging a rational democracy.

The first of these was Hull House. This was an example of a wider trend towards 'social settlements' in the late nineteenth/early twentieth century (Addams 1910). These settlements were founded on the idea of placing social workers within the communities they serve and Chicago was home to many. Hull House contained social workers as well as communal spaces where locals could meet and plan events or seek help. The location of the settlement was central since, as Mead put it:

> The corner stone of settlement theory has been that the residents have identified themselves with the immediate portion of the community where their work is found by making their home there. It is upon this foundation that the further characteristics of settlement theory and practice have been built. It is this foundation that makes the settlement an institution which distinguishes it from either the church or the university. (Mead 1907–8:108)

As this indicates, rather than having social workers disconnected from their client's lives, social settlements ensure they are part of their community. To put it in the terms of Mead, their 'me' is located with the people they are trying to help. This means that they do not enter the community from outside to condemn or praise but rather become fully aware of how those they help live their lives and the pressures they face. This means that Hull House was primarily concerned with 'finding out what the evils are; not in enforcing performed moral judgements' (Mead 1907–8:110). This was a central element of

Mead's conception of democracy since, as Cook puts it, it allowed the social workers to achieve 'neighbourhood consciousness' whereby 'instead of falling back upon preformed moral judgements settlement workers embraced a strategy of open-minded inquiry to arrive at new moral judgements' so that they 'might correctly identify the problems of that community' and 'work toward their solution' (Cook 1993:101). It is a localised form of the scientific reform and rational democracy Mead favoured. While Jane Addams was the main figure in establishing Hull House (Deegan 2013) Mead was for a long time the treasurer and a frequent visitor, including giving lectures. He also served on its board of directors for fourteen years, operated as chief fund-raiser and helped carry out surveys on the needs of the community (Cook 1993:99–103, Joas 1997:22).

A second activity concerned the City Club. This was a group of intellectuals and businessmen who used their influence with local politicians to advance such agendas as 'the political participation of immigrants, the democratization of urban planning, and the reform of municipal health services and of vocational training' (Joas 1997:23). Mead joined the club in 1906 and remained a member until his death, during which time he held multiple positions. Most prominently, Mead was chairman of committee of education. This meant that Mead engaged in varied activities including successfully petitioning the Chicago Board of Education to ensure better pay and conditions for teachers, securing funding for vocational education in the state and developing surveys to track variations in student achievement across the city. Mead was president of the club from 1918 to 1920 and used this position to lobby senators to support the ultimately forlorn proposal for US membership of the League of Nations (Cook 1993:105–8). Again here, we see Mead attempting to use sociological knowledge to respond to specific problems emerging in the everyday life of the city.

The third activity was the Immigrants' Protective League. As highlighted above, Mead saw the treatment of immigrants in Chicago as a major problem, which led him to co-found, and from 1909 to 1919 serve as vice-president of, this organisation. The League set up its office across the street from the train station and ensured its workers were there when immigrants arrived, helping them avoid overcharging cab drivers and getting them safely to new homes. From there, League workers maintained contact with new arrivals helping them find jobs, seek education or navigate the city's complex social welfare systems. It also attempted to protect young women who were victims of human trafficking for prostitution (Cook 1993:104). The League also, much like the City Club, lobbied local government and had some success in forcing the city to establish immigration bureaus and clamp down on unscrupulous employers (Cook 1993:104–5). Here we see an example of Mead's scientific reform where a specific issue – the condition of immigrants and how democracy had treated them as outsiders – led to conceptions of an alternative experiment. The League was an example of intelligent reform and the establishment of immigration bureaus in the state, similar to the work of the League, demonstrated its success.

The fourth activity was strike arbitration. As we saw above, Mead hypothesised that labour conflicts were due to a lack of democratic communication mechanisms, such as arbitrators, between the conflicting bodies of capital and labour (Mead 1934:323). In October 1910 he was able to test this hypothesis when a strike began at the Chicago firm of Hart, Schaffer and Marx, a clothing manufacture. Before long roughly 40,000 garment workers were on strike across the city, protesting primarily against law wages and poor working conditions. At a meeting of Hull House, Mead was made chairman of a five-person committee to seek an end to the strike. The committee interviewed workers and employers, discovering a great deal of truth to the worker's claims (for example a blacklist used by employers to discriminate against union activists). Mead then spent many weeks encouraging both sides to enter into arbitration. They were unwilling to pursue this initially but eventually agreed and in January 1911 representatives for both sides reached an agreement (Deegan and Berger 1978:365–8). As we have seen, Mead believed alternatives emerged as hypotheses for scientific reform in response to the identification of specific problems; therefore:

> In the garment workers' strike Mead addressed a specific problem that needed resolution. He and the subcommittee made an investigation of all conflicting interests with this hypothesis in mind ... Basic to Mead's work in the garment workers' strike was his conviction that the environment could be altered and that the best method to determine those changes was the application of the scientific method and reflective consciousness. (Deegan and Berger 1978:368)

The eventual arbitration was an example of intelligent reform to encourage further democratic communication.

The final activity returns us to education. For many years Mead was active in the management of the 'Hospital School' established by the University of Chicago in 1900 to provide what would now be termed 'special needs education'. Mead was the first president of the school which had an especial focus on those with hearing and speaking difficulties (Joas 1997:23). The school had a turbulent financial situation, eventually being forced to close after Mead and colleagues had tapped out all possible sources of funding including, it seems, Mead's own pockets. Regardless, Mead was quickly petitioning the University to open another school (Deegan and Berger 1978:363–5). Why did Mead involve himself so intimately in the school? The reason for Silva (2010) returns us to Mead's belief in the egalitarian view of democracy and mass participation. For those children to be full participants in society they had to have the full access to knowledge and means of communication their peers had. Since 'mainstream' schools weren't able to provide this, there was a need for a new school to be set up. This explains, for Deegan and Berger (1978:364–5), why so much emphasis was placed on those with hearing and speaking difficulties. Such a school ensured these children would have the possibility to engage in communication in the same way as their peers, it was in fact 'a pragmatic step to aid the handicapped [sic] in constructing a social self' (Deegan and Berger 1978:365).

Assessing Mead's activities as alternatives

As we have seen, Mead's alternative is particularly defined not by what he *suggested* should happen but rather by what he went out and did. He criticised the utopian tendencies of others and, unlike Marx and Engels who shared this critique, never waived from the claim that his purpose was to experiment with new ideas in the here and now, rather than wait for it to emerge. He was unashamedly an 'opportunist' (Mead 1899a:367).

All of these activities were driven by Mead's social conception of the self. We develop our sense of who we are with reference to our community. In doing so we are forced to put ourselves in the position of others, including the problems of their position. Social institutions have a key role to play here; they can expand our reference point and encourage social activities or narrow them and further asocial ones. This is why the potential to make society more democratic was so important to Mead. Ensuring that more people are socially informed, assisted and involved in democratic communication ensures all of our social selves are expanded – that our 'me' is increasingly broader – and that social activities become dominant.

This is why, when discussing Mead's activities, Joas argues they are categorised by seeing democracy 'as a form of living' (Joas 1997:23). Rather than having democracy removed to the area of personalities it is linked directly to everyday lives, whether this be the immigrants able to exercise their rights and seek out opportunities free from harassment (in the Immigrants Protective League), the workers and employers able to have a space to express their concerns (as in strike arbitration), the social workers who need to understand the pressures of their clients' lives rather than judge from the sidelines (Hull House) or the children with special educational needs who deserve to be able to access the same information as their peers (Hospital School). All of these institutions make rational democracy a part of everyday life by encouraging social activities (Mead 1934:326).

Mead would be the first to admit his experiments may not work; the history of the Hospital School for example was one of continual financial uncertainties which could have hardly helped children's education (leaving aside the controversy of inclusion versus exclusion in special needs education). Also, Cook argues it was the breaking of the strike rather than Mead's arbitration which ended the garment workers' stand-off (Cook 1993:105). Some experiments, by their nature, will fail. Nevertheless, it is the lessons from those experiments, what worked and what did not, which leads to social progress. Mead argued this 'incorporated the very process of revolution into the order of society' (Mead 1936:20).

Therefore, Mead's sociological alternative is as much about the method of testing alternatives, scientific reform, as it is in the overall goal of rational democracy. Importantly, while Mead (1936:23) thought that, as a scientist, he had a unique contribution to make to such experiments – seen in the various surveys he conducted for City Club and his philosophical interest in the mind and the Hospital School – his theory of democracy always placed 'its faith not on the skills of the professional party members, but on the wisdom of the informed layman' (Silva 2007a:307). It was only when 'any mind of any class in society' (Mead 1930:406) was part of democracy that a rational democracy could be secured. Indeed, quite often being a scientist was a hindrance since 'the academic attitude of creating problems for Doctor's theses is not favourable to the just realisation of what problems are when they are genuine' (Mead 1938:326). Therefore, democracy and its fruits must become part of everyday life; after all 'human rights are never in such danger as when their only defenders are political institutions and their officers' (Mead 1915:169). This meant:

> Whether [Mead] was marching with Jane Addams on the streets of Chicago in support of women's suffrage, surveying the homes of immigrants from eastern Europe, writing editorials on the dispute between the Board of Education and the Chicago Teachers' Federation, giving public support to the beleaguered reformers at the University of Wisconsin, or serving on the citizens' committee investigating labour grievances in the Chicago garment workers' strike he was doing exactly what he thought a member of the public should do to stay politically engaged and to further the cause of reform. (Shalin 1988:936)

It is this lesson to take from Mead's sociological alternative. His view as a sociologist led him to realise the issues in his critique more clearly, and his skills put him in a better place to conduct experiments. But his ideal rational democracy was ultimately one in which every individual 'can express himself … as the scientist does' and allow for the 'genius' in everyone to be expressed (Mead 1934:221). In short, the extension of democracy in its rational form means everyone can engage in the process of critique, hypothesis and experiment which make up Mead's sociological alternative. This is Mead's link of sociology and democracy.

We shall return to why this is so important to Mead in the conclusion. Before then, let us turn to Mannheim.

Karl Mannheim

Mannheim was born in Budapest in 1893 and was to live a life of exile. During his time at university Mannheim became friends with the Marxist Georg Lukács, even becoming part of what was informally termed the 'Lukács group' (Remmling 1975:15). This association was to prove fateful since members of the group played a key role in the Hungarian Communist party's declaration of the short-lived Hungarian Soviet Republic in 1919. Mannheim himself took no part in these events, partly due to his ambivalent relationship to Marxism (Remmling 1975:14), but became linked to them in the eyes of others (Kettler and Meja 1988:626). With the crushing of the Soviet, Mannheim was forced to flee to Germany, eventually arriving in Heidelberg. He would spend ten years here followed by three at the University of Frankfurt. This period was Mannheim's most productive, including publication of the text for which he became known, *Ideology and Utopia* (Mannheim 1936). However, despite his German mother, Mannheim was always marked as a figure of suspicion by the German authorities. He lacked German citizenship and, more significantly, was Jewish. With the rise of Nazism, Mannheim was forced to flee once more, seeking security in Britain at the London School of Economics (LSE), following an invite by the famed political scientist, Harold Laski, as a lecturer in the sociology department (Kettler et al. 1984:11). The LSE was not to be a happy home for Mannheim. Although able to write English well, his spoken English was poor (Kudomi 1996:48). He also continually clashed both intellectually and personally with the only Professor of Sociology at the time, Morris Ginsberg, so much so that their clashes were later immortalised as the 'Mannheim-Ginsberg problem' (Dahrendorf 1995:295). Relationships were so poisonous that, despite his international acclaim, Mannheim was only ever to hold a junior post at the LSE (Kudomi 1996:48, 51–2). Although physically safe Mannheim was, in effect, still exiled, this time from what he saw as the 'untheoretical empiricism' of British sociology (Kettler et al. 1984:120) so much so that in 1946 he left to become a professor at London's Institute of Education. He died less than a year later of a suspected heart attack (Kudomi 1996:52). It is a sign of the extent of the animosity between Mannheim and Ginsberg that, after Mannheim's death, his wife greeted the visiting American sociologist Edward Shils with the words 'Ginsberg killed him' (Shils 1997:217).

This life of exile is particularly relevant in the case of Mannheim since his sociological alternative, constructed during his time in London, is a direct response to the regimes which had forced him to flee. This means we need to attach an extra caveat to Mannheim's alternative as not a 'universal prescription but one of limited time and space, in this case postwar Britain' (Loader 1985:175). Nonetheless, it remains interesting as a way in which, contrary to Mead, the link of sociology and democracy can be conceived as a project of social reconstruction led not by lay actors but by intellectual elites. Sociology was helpful since the key problem was a 'lack of a comprehensive sociological orientation' (Mannheim 1943:61) held by such elites.

As Kettler et al. (1984:80–128) outline, Mannheim conceived of the sociologist as a 'socio-analyst' who, like their psychoanalyst kin, distinguishes between 'pathological and healthy states' (Kettler et al. 1984:81), with the exception that the socio-analyst is not diagnosing individuals but rather societies. While similar in language to Durkheim's work, Mannheim has a much wider conception of what happens in a pathological society since this influences the 'development of personality' (Mannheim 1938:256); a pathological society makes pathological people. Moreover, while Durkheim saw 'pathological' and 'normal' as differentiated by the common values of society – a social fact, such as crime, was normal if it advanced the values of individualism, even if we dislike it (Durkheim 1982:97–104) – Mannheim judges pathology and health according to the values of what he terms the liberal intelligentsia, namely the educated elite (Mannheim 1938:255). The role of the socio-analyst is to provide cures to such pathology based upon 'synthesis'. Many different alternatives are offered; the value of being a sociologist is being able to weigh them up, consider the positives and negatives of each and then finally come up with a synthesis of the best components of each. So Mannheim hoped to synthesise positive elements of liberal democracy and the dictatorships of Europe (Mannheim 1951:29–37). Once this synthesis was achieved Mannheim had an 'activist conception' of the role of sociologists by attempting to convert as many members of the elite as possible to his cause (Kettler et al. 1984:114).

This role can be seen well in Mannheim's opening quote to *Diagnosis of Our Time*:

> Let us take the attitude of a doctor who tries to give a scientific diagnosis of the illness from which we suffer. There is no doubt that our society has been taken ill. What is the disease, and what could be its cure? If I had to summarize the situation in a single sentence I would say: 'We are living in an age of transition from laissez-fair to a planned society. The planned society that will come may take one of two shapes: it will be ruled either by a minority in terms of a dictatorship or by a new form of government which, in spite of its increased power, will still be democratically controlled.' (Mannheim 1943:1)

It is this illness, and Mannheim's attempt to cure it, which provides the basis of his critique and alternative.

Mannheim's critique: laissez-faire mass society

As the above quote indicates, Mannheim saw a key problem of contemporary society to be the, currently expiring, period of laissez-faire. While this term is often used to describe the economy – a laissez-faire economy being one with little government intervention in the market – Mannheim uses it more broadly to refer to values. A laissez-faire society is one which holds a 'neutral attitude towards the main issues of life' or, as it may also be termed, a 'liberal' society (Mannheim 1943:7). Such a society has no shared values beyond a belief in individualism, leaving everything else up to personal choice (Mannheim 1943:16). This has emerged due to the decline of traditional values upon which everyone agreed, such as religion. Throughout most of human history religion 'was alive not only because it was a creed but also a social control inspiring patterns of behaviour and ideals of the good life' (Mannheim 1951:21). However, religion has lost its ability to do this with the shift away from small groups of homogenous feudal units to the city-based and pluralised capitalism of 'mass society'.

Mass society or, as Mannheim sometimes terms it, 'Great society' (Mannheim 1943, 1951) is any society which is large and governed as such – 'British' or 'American' society are governed by national governments rather than local groups – and in which we find a division of labour. Therefore, mass society was the kind of society which had become dominant in modern times with the increased power of nation states and the division of labour. Any mass society automatically created the need for what Mannheim termed 'social techniques' which are 'those methods which aim at influencing human behaviour and which, when in the hands of the Government, act as an especially powerful means of social control' (Mannheim 1943:1). For example, mass society must have bodies such as the police to maintain order, social workers to deal with any social problems, an education system to train people for work and communication networks to maintain contact throughout society. These not only allow society to function but also influence our behaviour and actions either directly or via socialisation. It is for this reason that Mannheim adopts a very broad definition of social techniques, including all of the above examples as well as transport networks, radio programming and the army; all of these influence our behaviour, making some actions more likely than others and change how we act (Mannheim 1943:1–4).

Therefore any mass society has social techniques at its hands, which governments can use to 'produce orderly patterns of human interaction subject to norms, codes and rules' (Mannheim 1951:48). These are 'neither good nor bad' in themselves but rather their worth depends on how they're used (Mannheim 1938:277). Social techniques will, as Mannheim puts it, 'manipulate' (Mannheim 1951:46) society automatically – education will socialise individuals into certain values, the media will reproduce such values and the police will punish with reference to laws – how this is done is decided by the priorities of governments. It is here that laissez-faire becomes problematic for Mannheim since, with its liberal ethos, such a system places its faith in the individual and their choices. This means being unwilling to outline common values due to the belief that to do so would force conformity among a diverse population (Mannheim 1943:26). This leads to what Mannheim terms a 'crisis in valuation' where, lacking common values to direct social techniques, they become 'society-blind' (Mannheim 1943:17), operating without reference to any wider conception of right and wrong. As an example, Mannheim turns to education:

> we have no agreed educational policy for our normal citizens, since the further we progress the less we know what we are educating for. On the primary levels of education we are undecided whether to aim at creating millions of rationalists who discard custom and tradition and judge each case on its merits, or whether the chief aim of education should be handing on of that social and national inheritance which is focused on religion.

> On the higher levels of education we do not know whether to educate for specialization, which is urgently needed in an industrialised society with a strict division of labour, or whether we should cater for all-round person-alities with a philosophical background. (Mannheim 1943:13)

Therefore, we have 'education for chaos' (Mannheim 1943:105) where individual desires become the thing to cultivate. This relies upon a 'compartmental' understanding of education (pass the tests and you'll be fine) against an 'integral' one which sees education as serving a wider social purpose (Mannheim 1943:54–7).

The initial temptation here may be to see Mannheim's critique as actually a positive; the virtue of liberal laissez-faire society is that it allows individuals to follow their own path and make their own choices. Mannheim however sees this as a problem since 'nobody can expect a human being to live in complete uncertainty and with unlimited choice. Neither the human body nor the human mind can bear endless variety' (Mannheim 1943:25); rather people need a form of 'spiritual power' to guide and integrate them (Mannheim 1951:312). It was this need which, for Mannheim, explains how the Fascists and Communists were so successful in taking power. These creeds were based upon spiritual calls concerning the valour of the 'race' or the proletariat. Once these groups achieved power the availability of social techniques meant they were able to propagate their values easily. Their success was due 'not so much to the changing ideas of man as to changes in social technique' (Mannheim 1938:256).

Consequently, for Mannheim, 'the indecision of the laissez-faire system represents a drifting which automatically prepares the ground for the coming dictator' (Mannheim 1943:15). A crisis of valuation means that eventually a group will emerge who provide common values and use social techniques to further this. Therefore, a form of planning – using the social techniques to forward a common goal – is inevitable (Mannheim 1938:259) and 'the question is only who shall use these means for control for what end. For used they will certainly be' (Mannheim 1951:8). This is why *laissez-faire* was doomed; left unchecked it would inevitably lead to the dictatorships of either fascism or communism. To avoid such a fate, and true to his role as a socio-analyst, Mannheim seeks an alternative in which 'the thesis of laissez-faire and the antithesis of rigid regimentation' form 'the synthesis of the Third Way' (Mannheim 1951:177). Therefore, Mannheim's alternative is an attempt to combine the positive elements of laissez-faire, that individual freedom is respected, with the centralised direction of the social techniques which the dictatorships have shown is needed.

Mannheim's alternative: The Third Way

Mannheim was not the first or only person to use the term 'The Third Way'; we shall see it again in Chapter 8 with the work of Giddens and it has a long history within sociology (Eldridge 2000). However, in Mannheim's hands, it is an especially accurate term indicating as it does the combination of the two dominant systems of liberal democracy and dictatorship. This was a system of what Mannheim termed 'planning for freedom'. Despite what happened in the dictatorships, planning 'should not necessarily mean goose-step co-ordination' (Mannheim 1943:5); it was possible to use the social techniques to propagate certain values, to plan, while ensuring individual freedom (Mannheim 1938). For example, Mannheim discusses how, without knowing any more about the games, if one were to look at the rules for football and a marathon one would be able to tell that one set of rules encourages more cooperation between teammates than the other (Mannheim 1951:192–3). Mannheim wants to do something similar at a social level by using social techniques to encourage some behaviours and discourage others. This is similar to Mead's advocacy of social against asocial institutions but, returning to the key difference between the two, Mannheim sees this as a top-down process, unlike Mead's more bottom-up focus.

The Third Way was to be a 'militant democracy' (Mannheim 1943:4–8), so called because it was clear on its central values and uses the social techniques at its disposal to develop and reproduce such values. Since 'the vital needs of the community should everywhere and always override the privileges of individuals' (Mannheim 1943:9) these are values which everyone must be made to share. Fortuitously, Mannheim suggested that Britain already had many of these values, including 'decency, mutual help, honesty and social justice' (Mannheim 1943:110) as well as 'fair play', 'community spirit' (Mannheim 1938:308) and, most importantly, a sense of cooperation (Mannheim 1951:3). Therefore, for Mannheim, Britain already embodies the values a militant democracy should uphold; the needed shift is simply to proclaim them as shared values for all.

The social techniques should be used to manipulate society in order to propagate these values (Mannheim 1951). For example, rather than the overly individualist education of laissez-faire, a militant democratic education would have two stages for Mannheim. In early-years education the goal is to teach 'basic conformity, cohesion, habit-making, emotional training, obedience' to the shared values and society as a whole. Once children are taught this then later-years education can focus on specialisation and the 'creation of independent personalities'; however this cannot be achieved until after conformity and obedience are passed on (Mannheim 1943:52). Another example concerns the media. Under laissez-faire media comes to be owned by a few large companies who 'use the most powerful apparatus for dissemination of their ideas' (Mannheim 1951:135). Instead, Mannheim argues the media should be taken into public control and be used as a form of propaganda to reproduce common values (Mannheim 1951:138).

In order to ensure such values are fully proclaimed and followed throughout society Mannheim argues militant democracy would need a 'new religion' which could create the 'spiritual integration of the members of society' (Mannheim 1943:103). Here Mannheim means religion in the sociological sense, a form of 'spiritual' rules which give people common values and beliefs; fascism and communism were religions (Mannheim 1951:312–13). Nevertheless, it is a pre-existing religion, Christianity, which Mannheim turns to. Christianity embodies the values of militant democracy and should be used as a guide as to what is the correct path to follow (Mannheim 1943:100–43). This means that while under a laissez-faire system religion was simply a private matter, in a militant democracy Christian values 'test the basic principles of social organisation' (Mannheim 1943:114). Consequently, religion becomes a public matter and Christianity will determine how social techniques are used. Mannheim does not seem to be suggesting all will be forced to be Christian or attend church. Instead Christianity would not be aligned to particular groups but rather 'carries its spirit into all' (Mannheim 1943:109), though it should keep up 'with the changing order' (Mannheim 1951:313). As we shall see further below religion is the ultimate arbitrator of values in a militant democracy.

In order to ensure this militant democracy is stable Mannheim advocates changes to the class structure. While he criticised the inequalities of capitalism (Mannheim 1951:29) his focus was on the middle and ruling classes. Taking inspiration from the revolutions of communism and fascism Mannheim argues that it is the middle class who maintain social order. Being born into neither affluence nor poverty this group has gained their relative advantage through 'social mechanisms' (education, promotion, small business and so on) and therefore is 'interested in preserving the existing order and function as a balance-wheel between the tendencies towards upper-class excess and lower-class revolution' (Mannheim 1951:79). Therefore, a militant democracy would need an expanded and emboldened middle class who have an interest in maintaining the status quo. Mannheim argues this can be achieved by ensuring that 'the differentiation of rewards and status' is based on talent and effort rather than 'privilege', thus ensuring social mobility into the middle class (Mannheim 1951:29). With regard to the ruling class, Mannheim sees the establishment of a ruling elite as inevitable. For a militant democracy to work:

> A reconstructed ruling class must first vitalize and define, at least as clearly as any totalitarian ruling class, the principles and objectives of democracy in industrial society. Secondly, it must devise practicable ways and means to attain its ends by reforms and mass consensus. (Mannheim 1951:106)

Mannheim argued that much of the current forms of training for the ruling class available in Britain (especially the leading universities of Oxford and Cambridge or 'Oxbridge') were effective. These schools were a 'skilful sociological product' which had allowed Britain to rule both an empire and its own land (Mannheim 1951:99). The only problem with the system for Mannheim was it was closed off, with only a small number of families able to send their children to Oxbridge. Therefore a militant democracy will encourage openness and recruitment to Oxbridge as well as the 'best' boarding schools. If there are too many applicants and 'dilution' becomes a problem then new boarding schools and universities should be established upon this model (Mannheim 1951:102–3). Importantly though, for Mannheim, it is better to err on the side of being too selective in admitting students since a militant democracy needs to 'preserve the highest forms of cultural achievement' rather than 'engage in sudden expansion' (Mannheim 1951:103).

This militant democracy aims to solve the problems of Mannheim's critique. Rather than the crisis in valuation created by the laissez-faire system, militant democracy is clear on its central values and uses social techniques, most notably education and the media, as a means of propaganda to spread and reproduce these views throughout society. In doing so, a new form of Christianity can help guide such values and ensure that social techniques are used for the appropriate ends. Furthermore, the expansion of the middle class ensures this system is secure and the more meritocratically selected new ruling class will mean there is a group able to use the social techniques correctly. It is this final group to which we now turn since the new ruling class are to be, in many ways, sociologists.

Sociology in a militant democracy

As we saw earlier in the chapter, Mannheim saw the problems of laissez-faire society as due to its 'society-blind' social techniques and a wider lack of social awareness. Given this, it is perhaps unsurprising that Mannheim gave sociology such a prominent role in his alternative. As a sociologist, Mannheim thought he was especially qualified to provide an alternative as 'only one who can see the important ramifications of each single step can act with responsibility required by the complexity of the modern age' (Mannheim 1951:xviii). But, even more importantly, sociology also had a key role to play in a militant democracy.

Sociology should be taught universally, from a young age, in schools (Mannheim 1943:57–69). The key reason for this is to create the awareness of social factors so that all can be aware of the need for common values. This also means the new ruling class will have the knowledge to use the social techniques appropriately. Mannheim also gives the role to sociologists of determining what should be taught throughout the school system. Sociologists, being aware of the essential needs or demands of the system, are, for Mannheim, able to determine the key things an individual must learn. Fields such as sociologies of education, culture and social structure would be the main topics (Mannheim 1943:60).

It was the role of sociology in training the new ruling class which was especially important. The only change Mannheim wanted to make to the current Oxbridge education for the elite was to make sociology the core of the curriculum since 'how can new leaders lead without an adequately informed understanding of contemporary society and its problems?' (Mannheim 1951:105). Making sure sociology is prominent in education is essential for Mannheim since:

> It is one of the achievements of modern sociology that it discovered empirically remedies for social evils which formerly were looked upon as the result of ill-will and sin. If sociology was able to assist in defining the

social causes of various types of juvenile delinquency, the roots of gang behaviour, the processes which make for race-hatred and other forms of group conflicts, it is only natural to assume that it will be possible to suggest methods which might assist people in their daily adjustments and mediate in their disagreements on valuations. (Mannheim 1943:28)

However, there is a caveat to attach to the role of sociology. For Mannheim, despite his normative claims, sociology is a value-free discipline since 'to the sociologist the social conditions which produce a gangster are as relevant as the social conditions which make for the development of a good citizen' (Mannheim 1943:136). Having the sociological knowledge to use social techniques in order to plan does not mean that one knows what we should plan; sociology gives you the means to plan but does not supply the ends. Consequently, it is the new Christianity which ultimately decides what should be planned; Mannheim argues 'a body somehow similar to the priests' should be established to aid the ruling class in making such decisions (Mannheim 1943:119). Therefore, sociology is put at the whim of religion in Mannheim's alternative since it is religion which determines what should be planned.

As we have seen Mannheim considered himself an 'intellectual activist' but, unlike Mead, he did not engage in much outside activity to make his alternative come to life. Throughout the war he gave radio addresses and wrote newspaper articles advocating his view (Mannheim 1943) and used his very modest political connections to do some lobbying around educational ideas (Whitty 1997:159). However, his prime activity was as part of 'The Moot'. This was a group of intellectuals, including the poet T.S. Elliot, who met 24 times from 1938 to 1947 to debate and 'advance the cause of a Christian society' (Kettler et al. 1984:131). Mannheim was central to this group; the fact its closure coincided with his death is no coincidence since his frequent attendance and engagement meant 'The Moot was Mannheim' (Kudomi 1996:51). This engagement included giving multiple papers for discussion at the meetings, many of which would end up in his two main books on planning (Mannheim 1943, 1951). However, The Moot was in no way a campaigning group but rather, as Kettler et al. (1984:129) put it, 'a new elite' – the socially aware intellectuals that Mannheim thought would become the new ruling class in a militant democracy. Therefore, unlike Mead, Mannheim's activity to further democracy was intellectual rather than practical; the goal was to prepare the intellectual elite to take over. It is at this point that it is worthwhile to return to a comparison of Mead and Mannheim concerning the link of sociology and democracy.

Conclusion: Mead and Mannheim on democracy

While Mead and Mannheim share the view that a goal of sociology is to make society more democratic they offer differing alternatives to obtain this. There are some similarities in how they hope to achieve this. For example, Mead's asocial institutions are not dissimilar to Mannheim's 'society-blind' social techniques and indeed Mannheim references Mead's theory of the self as a justification for his claim of the need for planning (Mannheim 1951:238–41). Nevertheless their alternatives, and justifications thereof, are fundamentally different. Whereas Mead values a form of 'everyday democracy' in which local-ised forms of debate and communication link citizens into a wider democratic sphere, Mannheim favours a top-down approach by developing common values and using the tools of government to ensure these are spread throughout society. For Mead, everyday democracy is essential to allow for a 'rational' democracy based upon collective decision making and involvement, for Mannheim the development of common collective values is essential to avoid the drift towards dictatorship. Therefore, while we have seen that Mead places his faith with the 'layman' Mannheim's response is that it more likely to be the 'mob' rather than the 'enlightened' who pose a danger to democracy (Mannheim 1951:149).

Why this difference? As mentioned earlier, it is important to remember the particular circumstances under which Mannheim constructed his alternative as a Jewish refugee living in a country at war with the Nazi Germany he had been forced to flee. It also indicates the fact that 'democracy' can include a variety of different systems and goals. However, there is a more fundamental division here concerning the ways in which sociologists offer alternatives – a distinction between what Bauman (1987) terms legislators and interpreters.

For Bauman these two concepts categorise the ways in which sociologists, and other intellectuals, offer normative claims concerning society. The legisla-tor role, particularly prominent in the modern period:

> consists of making authoritative statements which arbitrate in contro-versies of opinions and which select these opinions which, having been selected, become correct and binding. The authority to arbitrate is in this case legitimized by superior (objective) knowledge to which intellectuals have a better access than the non-intellectual part of society. (Bauman 1987:4)

This role exists due to the emergence of modern nation states committed to 'remaking' society according to particular ideals (Bauman 1987:52). Intellectu-als were to use the resources of the nation state, especially education, in order to implement such ideals. This relied upon a particular conception of individuals:

> Having been stripped of the shoddy vestments of tradition, people will ... share just one attribute: the infinite capacity to be acted upon, shaped, per-fected. Having been bared of old and shabby clothes, they will be ready to be clothed again ... The will of the designers is to be restrained by Reason only. Those who will have to wear the dress in the end are neither capable of, nor likely to be willing, to make the right choice ... Education was ... a desperate attempt to regulate the deregulated, to introduce order into social reality. (Bauman 1987:68–9)

We have seen this role perfectly in the work of Mannheim. His alternative is based on intellectuals using the nation state to create a new order. This can be achieved since it sees individuals as manipulated by social techniques, particularly education, in order to produce the ideal end state. This also assumes Mannheim, as an intellectual, has a unique and authoritative view on the world and can provide answers to its problems.

We see the opposite in the role of the interpreter. Rather than seeking to make universal statements as laws the interpreter role:

> consists of translating statements, made within one communally based tradition, so that they can be understood within the system of knowledge based on another tradition. Instead of being orientated towards selecting the best social order, this strategy is aimed at facilitating communication between autonomous (sovereign) participants. (Bauman 1987:5)

Found most prominently, though not solely, in post or liquid modern times (Bauman 1987:5) the interpreter acts as a conduit between intellectual knowledge and the lay masses. Since, unlike the legislator, the interpreter thinks that individuals are intelligent and able to change their activity freely in light of new evidence, they engage in a conversation in order to translate sociological findings into everyday concerns (Bauman and Welzer 2002:110). If these ideas then go on to change society in some way it was a result of convincing lay individuals that sociology 'renders or may render to the struggle waged by the humans to comprehend, "to make sense of", their life experience' (Bauman 2008:237–8).

Mead was effectively an early adopter of the interpreter role. The whole purpose of his alternative was to use sociological insights to allow people on an everyday level to have a wider and more social view of their self and their actions. In doing so Mead hoped to awaken the 'genius' within everyone rather than seeing one group as especially privileged in constructing democracy (Mead 1934:202–17). This inevitably led Mead out onto the streets and into collaboration with these lay members whereas Mannheim's legislator role inevitably led him to turn to the state and the hope of providing universal laws.

For Bauman, neither of these roles is intrinsically 'better' than the other; this will depend rather on one's wider sociological viewpoint and values (Bauman 1987:6), although Bauman links himself decisively to the interpreter role (Bauman 2008:237). In the 'Conclusion' I will return to this distinction and discuss how many theorists have chosen one or the other of these strategies. Perhaps unsurprisingly, just like in this discussion of democracy, such strategies produce markedly different alternatives.

Henri Lefebvre and Herbert Marcuse: Neo-Marxist Alternatives

6

As we saw in Chapter 2, Marx and Engels were dismissive of those who engaged in the 'utopian' activity of outlining alternatives, despite their own occasional dabbling in doing so. Many Marxists followed this advice, including many of the key thinkers in what would become known as 'neo' or 'Western' Marxism such as Theodor Adorno, Max Horkheimer, Georg Lukács and Louis Althusser. But some, to a certain extent, crafted sociological alternatives. There were multiple reasons for this, including the emergence of a form of socialism in the Soviet Union and elsewhere with which many Marxists disagreed. This encouraged Marxists to outline what socialism *is* if it was not that form being practised in the USSR. This was not a worry for their predecessors who could almost revel in not knowing what socialism was since it was the job of the revolutionary proletariat to figure this out (Sassoon 2010:1–30). The Marxist psychoanalyst Erich Fromm (1900–80) was an example of this with his outlining of what a 'sane' society would be (Fromm 1956, Durkin 2014).

However, in this chapter, we will discuss the work of two other prominent neo-Marxists: Henri Lefebvre (1901–91) and Herbert Marcuse (1898–1979). Both reflect a shift in twentieth-century Marxism towards a greater focus on culture alongside the materialist concerns of Marx and Engels (Adorno 1991). Nevertheless, they remain Marxists, ensuring that while there is an alternative for us to discuss, it is still one which is perhaps less specific than those which we have seen, and will see, from theorists representing other perspectives.

Lefebvre and Marcuse placed a great deal of emphasis on two changes which had emerged in the mid-twentieth century. The first of these concerned protests and, more specifically, who was protesting. Whereas classical Marxism had understood protests as related to class conflict, such as the long history of protests for citizenship rights (Giddens 1982), the 1960s saw the increased prominence of seemingly non-class-based protests. Causes included civil rights in the US, liberation movements in the Third World, environmentalism, gay pride and feminism. Some ecologically minded Marxists saw a potential for ecological movements – who recognised an innate contradiction of capitalism in its use of resources without reference to nature limits – to push forward the transition to socialism (O'Connor 1996). Others drew inspiration from the protests which erupted in May 1968 throughout Europe, most prominently in France. These were based not solely on inequality but on a broader notion of personal freedom. It was the central group behind such protests, students, who especially inspired Marcuse. Their slogans of 'give us what we want and we'll demand more' or 'be realistic, demand the impossible' were music to the ears of Marxists searching for groups who would demand an alternative and act upon such a demand, given the seeming inability or reluctance of the working class to do so. Continued forms of student protest – against tuition fees and in response to unrest with the education system and government corruption – are contemporary forms of the protests which are especially important to Marcuse.

The second factor is advertising, which is part of the wider changes in desire produced by 'advanced' capitalism (Marcuse 1964). As we saw in Chapter 2, Marx and Engels thought capitalism was wasteful since it produced without reference to need and consequently had a tendency towards overproduction. One way in which capitalism could be said to overcome this problem is via advertising and producing a desire for new goods. We may not *need* the new goods produced by capitalism but this doesn't mean we don't *want* them. Advertising helps to generate this desire and want, making it seem like a need. A good example can be seen in the advertising campaign for iPhones where the iPhone 4 arrived with the advertising slogan 'This Changes Everything. Again', while the iPhone 5 proclaimed it was 'the best thing to happen to iPhone since iPhone'. Here the features of the phone are less significant than the fact it is new and, more importantly, was replaced by an iPhone 6 which made the iPhone 5 redundant, which itself had made version 4 obsolete. As Bauman puts it, a society driven by advertising and consumption is one where 'wanting, desire and longing' become key characteristics of our daily lives (Bauman 2007a:28). It is these desires, and the way consumer capitalism produces them, which so worried, yet also inspired, Lefebvre and Marcuse.

Therefore, part of the reason this chapter is focused on Lefebvre and Marcuse is their shared historical context, as responding to the changing conditions of consumer capitalism and the 'New Left' of the 1960s. In doing so, they also highlight different conceptions of Marxism and its relation to social change. As we shall see, while Lefebvre maintains the Marxist faith in the proletariat and the Leninist creed of the state 'withering away', Marcuse turns his attention to the new political groupings created by consumer capitalism. From here they draw different images of the eventual socialist society to replace capitalism. Consequently, these writers remind us how sharing a theoretical school and intellectual project does not mean sharing the same image of the ideal society.

Henri Lefebvre

Lefebvre lived a long and eventful life. Born just outside the Pyrenees he moved to Paris to pursue his education at the Sorbonne in 1920. A period of military service and two years spent as a taxi driver gave him an unusual education which was to mark out a man who was both a philosopher concerned with the abstract and a sociologist concerned with the everyday (Harvey 1991:426). He was quickly drawn to Marxism and became a member of the French Communist Party (PCF) in 1928, a move which meant he was immediately expelled from his teaching post once France was occupied in 1941. He spent the rest of the war in the resistance, producing propaganda, sabotaging Nazi trains and discovering collaborators (Elden 2004:3). With the allied victory Lefebvre returned to work and swiftly became alienated from the Stalinism gripping the PCF before being formally expelled in 1958. This expulsion meant Lefebvre was 'liberated from Stalinist constraints' (Harvey 1991:428) and was free to pursue a unique career spanning almost 70 years as a Marxist philosopher/ sociologist. He became famous for his work on the city in *The Production of Space* (Lefebvre 1991a) but also wrote widely on the state, capitalism and a three-volume *Critique of Everyday Life* (Lefebvre 1991b, 2002, 2005). Despite his expulsion Lefebvre remained a committed Marxist and communist 'of the old school' (Trebitsch 1991:xiii). He always sought to explain how capitalism could be transcended and, following Lenin, the state could 'wither away' to be replaced by forms of cooperation between free individuals (Lefebvre 1964a). Lefebvre was eventually to find the answer in the theory of *autogestion*.

For Lefebvre, everyday life has been a neglected topic for sociology. Marxist sociologists have too often favoured the 'abstract' – the grand structures of political economy, the market, state and exploitation. While important, such discussions have marginalised the lived experience of capitalism which, for Lefebvre, was Marx's original intention with concepts such as alienation (Lefebvre 1991b:176–82). Meanwhile, the sociologists who actually studied everyday life have not been critical about it since, by simply seeking to describe everyday life, 'one records, one ratified. Knowledge and acknowledgement go hand in hand' (Lefebvre 2005:4). This is troubling for Lefebvre since everyday life should be a key topic for Marxist sociology. To demonstrate this he provides an example:

> the simplest event – a woman buying a pound of sugar, for example – must be analysed ... To understand this simple event, it is not enough merely to describe it; research will disclose a tangle or reasons and causes, of essences and 'sphere': the woman's life, her biography, her job, her family, her class, her budget, her eating habits, how she uses money, her opinions and her ideas, the state of the market, etc. Finally I will have grasped the sum total of capitalist society, the nation and its history. (Lefebvre 1991b:57)

The everyday is significant for Lefebvre since it is the 'meeting place' (Lefebvre 2002:118–25) for all the social structures and inequalities which sociologists study. While sociologists talk about 'class' or 'gender roles' as abstract things, they have their impact and are felt by individuals at an everyday level. The woman buying a bag of sugar becomes aware of her gender role when she is the one expected to do the shopping and of her class when she realises she doesn't have the money to pay for it. Outside of this, for most non-sociologists such concepts have an 'aura of technicality' (Lefebvre 1991b:89) which means they are beyond lay consideration. Therefore, studying everyday life is, for Lefebvre, to see how social processes actually 'happen'. As the final sentence of the above quote indicates, Lefebvre also wants to study everyday life in order to understand society as a whole – what sociologists would now term linking the 'micro' elements of lived experience to the 'macro' structures of society. As a Marxist, Lefebvre sees this as especially important since it allows us to grasp more fully the workings of capitalism and, therefore, to critique it.

Lefebvre's critique: everyday life as alienation

Lefebvre's critique returns us to a concept discussed in Chapter 2: alienation. Marx defined this as being removed from the things which make us fundamentally human, most notably creative activity. Lefebvre sees such alienation as occurring in two elements of everyday life: repetition and commodities.

Everyday life contains repetition; a key part of our everyday activity is repeating what we did the day before: we wake up, get ready, go to work, come home, have dinner and go to sleep ready to repeat the process the next day. For Lefebvre the original French word '*la quotidienne*' including 'that which repeats itself consistently' is more accurate than the English translation 'everyday' (Lefebvre 1988:78). Part of this repetition means that much of our daily activity is determined by the dictates of capitalism and work. This includes our non-work time since, as Lefebvre puts it, 'we work to earn our leisure, and leisure has only one meaning: to get away from work. A vicious circle' (Lefebvre 1991b:40). Therefore, our leisure time, the weekend for example, is largely orientated towards giving us the rest we need to return to work on Monday morning. The experience of this repetition is also shaped by social inequalities. For example, women, who are much more likely to be found in the private realm and to engage in domestic labour, experience this repetition in a much more profound way than men who are likely to spend more time in the public realm (Lefebvre 2002:210–12; 1971:73–4). Being in the public sphere means being tasked with being 'modern' and innovating, engaging in the excitement of what Lefebvre terms 'the triumphalist consciousness of the new' (Lefebvre 1995:2). The same can't be said of domestic labour which is mainly repetitive; once the bathroom is clean all that is left is to wait before you have to clean it again. Therefore, our everyday life is alienated because it allows no space for our creativity independent from the demands of capitalism. Most likely for Lefebvre 'the black sun of boredom' defines our routinised activities (Lefebvre 2002:75, see also Gardiner 2012).

The most profound element of alienation occurs in our relationship to consumer products. The mid-twentieth century saw an explosion of consumer products which companies needed to sell. These new consumer products (TVs, kitchen appliances, home stereos, walkmans and so on) weren't 'essential' products – they did not fulfil what Lefebvre would call 'human needs' – but were products which people had to be convinced they needed. They were what Lefebvre terms 'social needs', justified by desire and want (Lefebvre 1991b:9).

Using our earlier example, an iPhone is not a human need; one can live perfectly fine without one. But it could be said to be a social need since the role of advertising is to convince us we do 'need' it, through appealing to our desire for a new and exciting product. Therefore, advertising becomes an increasingly important part of society with more and more of our everyday lives occupied with seeing, and being the subjects of, marketing (Lefebvre 1988:79). The introduction of new technologies which come to occupy our daily lives means we are more easily reached by advertisers, from television adverts to electronic billboards through to the personalised 'just for you' promotions popularised by online retailers such as Amazon.com. We cannot escape marketing which 'surrounds' and 'besieges us' (Lefebvre 2002·41) meaning the everyday is the area in which our desires are 'manipulated' by marketing (Lefebvre 1988:79). This has a pervasive effect where, rather than think of ourselves as 'citizens' of a political community, we see ourselves as 'users' of economic services (Lefebvre 2002:78; 1990).

It is this change of the everyday that fundamentally alters the nature of capitalism for Lefebvre. Rather than produce products for exchange capitalism now means that 'the manufacturers of consumer goods do all they can to manufacture consumers. To a large extent they succeed' (Lefebvre 2002:10). Therefore, the increased opportunities to advertise and thereby manufacture desire for consumer goods means that everyday life becomes the 'base' of capitalism (Lefebvre 2005:41). To be more exact, it is everyday life which allows capitalism to reproduce itself by ensuring a constant supply of customers and therefore profit (Lefebvre 1988:79). This leads Lefebvre to categorise contemporary society as the 'Bureaucratic Society of Controlled Consumption' (Lefebvre 1971) since it is this ability to control consumption via advertising which ensures the success of capitalism. This is aided by the state which becomes the 'watchtower' of capital and ensures the 'ideology of continual growth' is secured (Lefebvre 1976a:111–20, 1995:121). Lefebvre argues this is equally true of socialist countries which increasingly focused on economic growth and consumption.

But Lefebvre is not solely a doomsayer since he argues everyday life gives everyone the opportunity to engage in 'the critique of the real by the possible' (Lefebvre 1991b:9); it allows us to realise how everyday life is being manipulated, how unequal we are and that another world is possible. There are three ways in which this manifests itself.

Firstly, inequality. As we saw with the example of the woman buying a bag of sugar, Lefebvre sees everyday life as the field in which inequality is experienced; this is especially true in the bureaucratic society of controlled consumption. Not all can purchase the wonderful consumer goods which we desire and consequently there is a strict divide in our experience. As Lefebvre puts it, 'The upper bourgeoisie lives in the supra-everyday. (Onassis directed his fleet of oil tankers from his yacht.) But hundreds of millions of poor people in the world aspire to everyday life' (Lefebvre 1988:79–80). Lefebvre terms this the 'uneven development' of everyday life and sees its most extreme manifestation in the fact that while an elite began to explore space millions were left going hungry and working infertile land by hand (Lefebvre 2002:316). Therefore, inequality expressed via class remains a central factor for Lefebvre (1968:102–3).

This then leads to the second point: inequality existing is not enough to create critique, nor is inequality itself new; it is the fact that we increasingly become aware of this inequality which is new. While the technologies of everyday life may create greater inequality, they also increase knowledge. Due to the expansion of media farmers working the land know that some fellow humans are walking on the moon. We can increasingly see the life of the rich and famous and compare it to our own, notably deprived in comparison. This is what Lefebvre sees as us becoming globalized but only 'as an eye, purely and simply' (Lefebvre 2002:89). The large majority of people are simply left watching the exploits of the rich and cannot help but realise the 'gaps' which exist between the reality we live and the possible reality we could live (Lefebvre 2002:62–3). Therefore, 'rather than suppressing criticism of everyday life, modern technological progress *realises it*' (Lefebvre 1991b:9). We immediately become aware of issues of unfairness and injustice. Although he does not use the phrase, Lefebvre's argument is that the conditions of everyday life in advanced capitalism are a spur towards class consciousness.

Finally, we do experience breaks in alienation within everyday life already, returning us to the importance of leisure. As noted by Highmore (2002), Lefebvre has a contradictory reaction to this; we have seen how he dismisses leisure as time used primarily to 'recharge our batteries' to return to work, yet he also argues that our leisure time is '*other* than everyday life' (Lefebvre 1991b:40). Leisure is the time in which we can remove ourselves from the demands, and alienation, of consumer capitalism. This was especially so in the case of the festival, or carnival. Throughout French history these involved whole towns coming together to celebrate with plentiful food, wine, dancing and sports and where, as Lefebvre matter-of-factly puts it, the days would end in 'scuffles and orgies' (Lefebvre 1991b:202). While modern-day festivals may not be as carefree as these Lefebvre sees the principle which animates them to have relevance. We still see leisure as a time for rejecting the rules which govern our everyday life; it is the time for 'putting our hair down' and trying some 'escape attempts' (Cohen and Taylor 1992), whether this be extreme sports, taking drugs, collecting stamps or reading poetry. All of these, in different ways, seek to break the routines and rules which govern our daily activity and escape from our everyday life into something more exciting or creative, the realm of the 'fabulous' (Lefebvre 1991b:40–58). Holidays also indicate this since 'the true life starts the moment we go away' (Lefebvre 1995:90). Therefore, while most of our everyday life is administered and manipulated, there are moments when we are free from such demands, times which we relish. These escapes themselves are not the alternatives but, by breaking the routines of alienated everyday life, open up the potential for us to consider alternatives.

It is these three components – inequality between our everyday experience, our increased knowledge of such inequality and the fact that we do experience alternatives in our leisure – which mean that everyone potentially has their own critique of everyday life (Lefebvre 1991b:29). We become aware of the 'gaps' between the possible and the real and, as this knowledge increases for Lefebvre, it increases the possibility of *praxis* or, in Lefebvre's terms, 'total *praxis*' which 'is nothing other than the idea of *revolution*' (Lefebvre 2005:241). This is a revolution of thought since once we begin to think of capitalism as not an inevitability but rather one option amongst many the 'veil of ideology' is removed and 'once ideology has been rendered conscious, it is powerless' (Lefebvre 1976a:119, 1995:91). Consequently, Lefebvre imagines a revolutionary alternative emerging in the gaps of everyday life – or, as John Holloway (2010) would later term them, the 'cracks of capitalism' gaps we become increasingly aware of, such as leisure spaces. It is the awareness of such gaps, rather than what we currently fill the gaps with, which provides potential for new alternatives emerging. The question for Lefebvre is 'will you try to find the crack for freedom to slip through, silently filling up the empty spaces, sliding through the interstices? Good old freedom, you know it well' (Lefebvre 1995:124). This freedom for Lefebvre can be found in his sociological alternative: *autogestion*.

Lefebvre's alternative: autogestion

Autogestion has no direct English translation. Brenner and Elden (2009:3–4) interpret it as 'grassroots democracy' but a more common translation is 'self-management' (Lefebvre 1976a:120–7), which I will use here. Lefebvre, as a Marxist, sees the issues highlighted in his critique as fundamentally linked to the private ownership of the means of production, since it is this which produces the need for marketing social needs and manipulates the everyday. However, the socialist nations which had seen the socialisation of the means of production, achieved through state ownership, were equally guilty of such flaws (Lefebvre 1964b). Therefore, self-management provides an alternative way of thinking about socialisation for Lefebvre (1976a:120). In Lefebvre's idea of self-management, neither the bourgeoisie nor the state owns property or runs organisations; rather these are owned and run by those who use them.

For Lefebvre we can see examples of self-management in what he terms the 'weak points' of society, spaces where the established ways of running society have broken down. Examples can be found in the Paris Commune, Russia, during 1917 and revolutionary Algeria of the 1950s (Lefebvre 1966:144–6). We can also locate less epoch-defining examples in times of large-scale protest, such as the events of May 1968 (Lefebvre 1976a:123), Mexican towns beyond the control of the national government (Lefebvre 1976b:160) and the aforementioned festivals. In all of these cases 'ordinary' people (neither state elites nor capitalists) take it upon themselves to run things. *Autogestion* is therefore fundamentally a form of organisation which is neither the state nor the market but is the area of spontaneous and negotiated cooperation between individuals (Elden 2004:226–31). For Lefebvre this is the way in which humans operate when not dictated to by the demands of capitalism; here we work freely with others to achieve common goals.

For Lefebvre self-management should be conducted at the level of 'enterprises, units of production and branches of industry' (Lefebvre 1976a:40). However, beyond this Lefebvre leaves what a society based upon self-management would look like unelaborated. The main reason for this is that Lefebvre sees *autoges-tion* as a 'principle' to be followed rather than a fully sketched-out alternative patiently waiting to be implemented (Lefebvre 1966:148). Indeed, he speaks of self-management as having 'nothing special about it' and that it 'has posed (and still poses) as many problems as it solves' (Lefebvre 1976a:120). Among these questions are how self-management can occur without a state, whether it will be co-opted by powerful figures (such as the Soviets after the Russian Revolution) and how this transition would occur (Lefebvre 1966). Indeed, the existing evidence for self-management is mixed, with the sometimes rosy picture drawn by some advocates complicated by the evidence (Warren 2001).

So one may ask, given this, why does Lefebvre place so much faith in *autogestion,* including calling it the 'theoretical essence of freedom' (Lefebvre 1966:149)? The reason for this is how *autogestion* would be bought into being; it is fundamentally a 'bottom-up' system (Lefebvre 1966). As we have seen, Lefebvre sees the control and administration of everyday life to be his key point of critique. Introducing self-management questions this and demonstrates that a different way is possible. For example, Lefebvre (1976a:123) discusses how institutions such as the post office are central to everyday life. These are run either by the state or private capital – either way for Lefebvre they are placed at the whim of capitalist demands for profit and the conditions of alienation. Instead, an *autogestion* post office – occurring in the weak points of history when the state or market is unable to provide (Lefebvre 1976a:123) – is based upon individuals realising their shared needs and cooperating to produce a system which allows for postal communication. Furthermore, introducing self-management not focused on generating profit but rather on realising collective needs into the post office is not simply concerned with removing alienation; it is about demonstrating a more fundamental principle: if self-management works here, it can work anywhere. If the post office can be self-managed, why not the medical system? Or large corporations? Or community centres? Once the possibility of self-management is established in areas of social life then the edifice of alienated consumer capitalism will, for Lefebvre, begin to crumble. This is due to the aforementioned piercing of the veil of ideology where, for Lefebvre, the notion of capitalist organisation is partly accepted due to its current dominance. Demonstrating the possibility of an alternative way of organising and running everyday institutions questions the need for institutions such as the nation state and private property.

Autogestion also, as Elden (2004:226–31) notes, means that what Lefebvre terms 'the right to identity within difference' as part of citizenship is accounted for (Lefebvre 1990:252). Despite all being citizens and therefore having the right to equality we also have our unique forms of difference (gender, age, ethnicity, sexuality and so on) which must be recognised and accounted for; thus we need to have equality with difference. For Lefebvre, allowing for self-management and for different groups to, if needed, manage their own affairs brings us one step closer to this.

Therefore, *autogestion* is as much a strategy to achieve an alternative as much as it is the alternative itself; the alternative is guided by the principle of *autogestion*. It also contributes to the 'withering away' of the state by demonstrating other forms of control (Lefebvre 1966:150). Consequently, *autogestion* is a theory of revolution – of individuals acting in a new way in their everyday life (Lefebvre 2002:241). This revolutionary project 'cannot just change the political personnel of institutions; it must change *la vie quotidienne*' (Lefebvre 1988:80). In doing so, it:

> is a question of a slow but profound modification of the everyday – of a new usage of the body, of time and space, of sociability; something that implies a social and political project; more enhanced forms of democracy, such as direct democracy in cities; definition of a new citizenship; decentralization; participatory self-management … that is, a project for society that is at the same time cultural, social, and political. (Lefebvre 1988:86–7)

Would Lefebvre's alternative solve the problems?

Since *autogestion* is a process and the principle which animates an alternative which is not entirely elaborated it is hard to say whether this will solve the problems of capitalism Lefebvre highlights. While it seems somewhat intuitive to say that greater self-management will stop, or at least lessen, the extent of people being dictated to in their everyday lives, beyond this Lefebvre is right to say it raises more questions initially than it answers. Later sociological alternatives based upon ideas of self-management, such as Hirst's (1994) associative democracy – albeit inspired by Durkheim and Cole rather than Lefebvre – have discussed these issues in more depth. These include whether all groups of difference should have forms of self-management: is it right for a school run by a particular religious grouping to deny education to another? Should racist groups be allowed to form? What happens if one area of the country has a self-run medical system which supplies certain forms of care not available to another part of the country? And so on. Also, there is a need to ensure such groups are democratic rather than run by an aggressive elite as suggested by the 'iron law of oligarchy' (Michels 1991). Such practical considerations on the shape of *autogestion* are not discussed by Lefebvre, making an assessment of his alternative difficult.

Here we return to the nature of Marxism and its relation to alternatives. While Lefebvre is more willing than Marx to discuss the nature of an alternative, these suggestions largely remain ways to achieve change rather than *the* change. This, after all, is to be decided by the revolutionary actors who engage in action rather than a sociologist. As indicated above, Lefebvre was aware of the difficulties here and didn't seek fully to resolve them, rather arguing that the process of creating *autogestion* will throw up challenges and potential solutions. While self-management occurs now, the fact it happens under alienated capitalism means it is not fully a guide to what could happen with a greater uptake of *autogestion* and the piercing of the veil of ideology. The 'new life' which guides such activity (Lefebvre 1995:65–94) is inevitably utopian; indeed Lefebvre defends his theory of *autogestion* in this light:

> Is this utopian? Yes, because utopian thought concerns what is and is not possible. All thinking that had to do with action has a utopian element. Ideals that stimulate action, such as liberty and happiness, must contain a utopian element. This is not a refutation of such ideals; it is, rather, a necessary condition of the project of changing life. (Lefebvre 1988:87)

Our next neo-Marxist shares similarities with this view.

Herbert Marcuse

Marcuse is united with Lefebvre not only via Marxism but also by having an eventful life. Marcuse was born in 1898 to wealthy parents who were very much of the ostentatious new bourgeoisie class; his mother's family had made their money from producing paper with gilded edges (Katz 1982:15–16). His affluent upbringing was punctured by being drafted into the German army in 1916. But poor eyesight meant he never left Berlin. During this period Marcuse joined the SDP and began his acquaintance with the work of Marx. With the end of the war Marcuse turned to academia but, with the rise of Nazism, found his academic career hindered due to his Judaism. In 1932 Marcuse joined the Institute for Social Research in Frankfurt (the famed 'Frankfurt School') and followed them into exile in the US in 1934. Marcuse spent the rest of his life in the US, gaining citizenship in 1940. He worked for the precursor to the CIA in World War II, providing intelligence on Germany and producing propaganda. After the war he settled into an academic career. It was the 1960s, and the rise of the 'New Left', which made Marcuse's name. He influenced many activists through his teaching and writing, perhaps most prominently the radical black activist Angela Davis (Hornstein 2009). In doing so, Marcuse began to achieve a certain level of fame. He was denounced publically by Pope Paul VI as opening 'the way to licence cloaked as liberty', by *Pravda* (the government-controlled newspaper of the Soviet Union) as a 'false prophet' and by Ronald Reagan as 'not qualified to teach' (Katz 1982:173–4). Indeed, things got so bad that at one point Marcuse's PhD students would guard his house at night in light of death threats addressed to 'Filthy Communist Anti-American Professor

Herbert Marcuse' (Katz 1982:175–6). Marcuse continued his public appearances at New Left events and political writings throughout this period – a book on Marcuse finds its author meeting him at an event where 'Nico and the Velvet Underground were played more or less constantly in the art school studio' (Miles 2012:8) – before dying in 1979 of a stroke.

One reason why Marcuse attracted such hatred was his continual search to find the new revolutionary agent; the group who, with the seeming decline in revolutionary power of the proletariat, would usher in the new society. As we shall see below, this led him to place his hope in the 'new sensibility' found in the movements of the New Left. But, before this, we must discuss Marcuse's critique.

Marcuse's critique: the repressive totalitarian-technological stage of capitalism

Marcuse's critique of capitalism was wide ranging and, while taking from Marx, added new elements which were not part of Lefebvre's critique. In particular, Marcuse was heavily influenced by Freud and his claim that society, or as Freud termed it 'civilization', inevitably involved repression of our most basic desires. For Freud (2002) this meant we trade the freedom of being able to follow all of our urges all of the time (for example, in constantly seeking out sexual gratification or spending all of our days satisfying our urges) for some security (in this case from unwanted sexual advances and for a job which may be dull but at least puts food in the table). Marcuse agreed with the premise here but argued that the repression found in capitalist society went beyond this basic level of security and produced 'surplus repression' (Marcuse 1956:35). Rather than simply providing security by limiting our desires, capitalist society sought to *change* our desires producing, as he put it, a 'new [capitalist] biology' (Marcuse 1969a:7–22). This was achieved through the synthesis of human and 'false' needs (Marcuse 1964).

Like Lefebvre, Marcuse argued there was a difference between our human, or as he also termed them 'true' needs, and 'false' needs (Lefebvre's social needs). However, while Lefebvre had argued only that capitalism produces desire for these false needs, Marcuse goes further and argues that we come to think of false needs as *human* needs. As he puts it, false needs are:

> superimposed upon the individual by particular social interests in his repression ... most of the prevailing needs to relax, to have fun, to behave and consume in accordance with the advertisements, to love and hate what others love and hate, belong to this category of false needs. (Marcuse 1964:7)

While we might think that relaxing and having fun are human needs, for Marcuse these reflect capitalist ends. We may relax by watching pricey DVD box-sets on an equally pricey TV or by surfing the Internet on a tablet computer. Then, to have fun, we might decide to go out on an evening (having bought appropriate 'going out' clothes) to consume further. All of these require us to aid capital accumulation. More fundamentally, for Marcuse, these consumer products begin to define who we are (Marcuse 1964:10). To return to an earlier example, it is not only that we come to desire an iPhone, it is that we also come to identify ourselves as 'Apple' rather than 'PC' people (or vice versa). As Marcuse puts it, consumer products have become 'part and parcel of people's own existence, own "actualization"' (Marcuse 1969a:12).

This transformation of false into human needs goes beyond consumer products and encroaches into how we interact with one another; a good example can be found in relation to sexuality. A visitor to the US in the mid-twentieth century, such as Marcuse, may have struggled to think of this society as in anyway repressed when it came to sex. After all, it seemed sex was readily displayed and openly discussed, whether it is used to sell products, the representation of sexy images on TV and movies or the availability of pornography. We may criticise this, as we shall see in the next chapter, but it does not seem to suggest repression. However, for Marcuse, it indicates exactly this. When sexuality is made public in capitalist society it is more susceptible to 'controlled satisfaction' (Marcuse 1964:78). Rather than sexuality being something 'beyond' the reaches of capitalism, and therefore defined by more instinctual, human, desires, it becomes a product to be sold like any other. The advert which uses an attractive half-naked woman (or man) to sell a product is not using sexuality but simply the fetish of skin to sell its wares. Furthermore, allowing for the satisfaction of sexual desires within the current system means that 'pleasure … generates submission' and therefore 'sexuality turns into a vehicle for the best-sellers of oppression' (Marcuse 1964:79, 80). Rather than sex being an act expressing our 'true' pleasures it becomes a commodified and animal activity which is done partly according to the appropriate sexual desires depicted in culture. This may be fun, but, as Marcuse puts it, driving fast or pushing a power lawnmower is also fun; instead the uniquely interactional and *human* elements of sexuality are lost in its control by capitalism; it loses its critical edge and instead becomes part and parcel of the system (Marcuse 1964:78).

As this indicates, part of the repression of capitalism for Marcuse is that it not only changes the way we act but the way we think. In particular, it produces what he calls one-dimensional man (Marcuse 1964). We become one-dimensional under capitalism due to the emergence of the 'happy consciousness' which is 'the belief that the real is rational, and that the established system, in spite of everything, delivers the goods' (Marcuse 1964:82). Rather than engaging in 'positive' (assessing reality) and 'negative' (thinking about alternatives to that reality) thought, we only engage in the positive and it seems that we can conceive of no alternative to our current social system. There is, as Marcuse puts it, a lack of 'negation' of capitalist society due to the seeming paucity of alternatives (Marcuse 1968). This is especially so given that communist societies ruled by, as Marcuse terms it, 'Soviet Marxism' seemed equally focused on economic growth and developing consumer products (Marcuse 1958). Therefore, any attempt at social change in such a situation will be ineffective since 'without an objectively justifiable goal of a better, a free human existence, all liberation must remain meaningless – at best, progress in servitude' (Marcuse 1968:175).

Like any Marxist, Marcuse sees the working class as the historical agent of revolution 'by virtue of its basic position in the production process ... its numerical weight and the weight of exploitation' (Marcuse 1969a:16). Therefore, any attempt at negation and moving beyond capitalism will require the agency of the working class. Alas, for Marcuse, the working class experience the happy consciousness more than any social group. Their increased standard of living in the post-war period, including the emergence of the welfare state (Marcuse 1968:181) and the increased availability of consumer goods and 'household gadgets' (Marcuse 1969a:12) means that the working class become invested in the current system. They have privileges which, while minor compared to the very rich, they wish to defend. Therefore, this class comes not to be a radical grouping but rather 'assumes a stabilizing, conservative function' (Marcuse 1969a:55).

All these factors lead Marcuse to claim capitalism has entered a 'totalitarian-technological' stage (Marcuse 1964) since the new technologies developed by capitalism, found in household consumer goods and advertising techniques, allow it to dominate, and fundamentally change the thought processes of, individuals.

At this stage it may seem Marcuse closes down the possibility of an alternative. However, like Lefebvre, he argues that the things he wishes to criticise capitalism for also open the possibility to change. In order to understand this, we need to return to the connection of Marxism and utopia.

Marcuse's potential liberation: the utopian potentials of capitalism

As we have seen Marx and Engels were dismissive of 'utopian socialists'. One reason for this was their view that the path to communism relied upon the means of production being sufficiently developed to allow for a society in which all could have their needs fulfilled without the need for alienated labour. For Marcuse, this was not a state to achieve but rather had already been reached, since:

> Utopian possibilities are inherent in the technical and technological forces of advanced capitalism and socialism: the rational utilization of these forces on a global scale would terminate poverty and scarcity within a very foreseeable future. (Marcuse 1969a:4)

For Marcuse we now have enough resources to feed and house everyone on the earth; they are just unevenly distributed. A distribution of resources both within (from rich to poor in the US) and between (from the US to sub-Saharan Africa for instance) countries would allow all to be adequately catered for. Therefore:

> what is denounced as 'utopian' is no longer that which has 'no place' and cannot have any place in the historical universe, but rather that which is blocked from coming about by the power of the established societies. (Marcuse 1969a:3–4)

Marcuse is also part of a trend in Marxism, found in the writings of Andre Gorz (1999), which argues that the advancement of technology will allow us all to work less (Marcuse 1967). Under capitalism, work becomes the 'introjected necessity to perform productively in order to earn a living' (Marcuse 1969a:91). Our working hours are set by our employer and we work the time needed to generate profit rather than provide for basic needs. Therefore, if the purpose of work became to provide only what was needed, and technology was used not only to regulate this production but also to perform more mundane labour, we could work less (Marcuse 1967:67). This means – akin to Marx and Engels' image of us overcoming the division of labour in order to fish in the morning and criticise in the evening – that it becomes possible to have a society where 'work becomes play, a society in which even socially necessary labour can be organised in harmony with the liberated, genuine needs of men' (Marcuse 1967:68).

Therefore, Marcuse had an unashamedly positive view of the possibilities for change made available by advanced capitalism. His optimism extended to the claim that the problems of capitalist society, being man-made and therefore not 'natural', could be transcended. To solve these problems, and provide an alternative, we must turn to politics for Marcuse.

Marcuse's transition: the Great Refusal

As we have seen, Marcuse thought the working class had become co-opted into capitalism. Therefore, the question became who would lead us beyond our current social system? To use a phrase introduced in Chapter 2, who were the universal class who, acting in their own self-interest, also acted in the interest of humanity as a whole? Here Marcuse found his answer in the groups which made up the 'Great Refusal'.

The Great Refusal was a collection of groups who emerged in the 1960s and were defined by their:

> refusal to take part in the blessings of the 'affluent society' ... the need for better television sets, better automobiles, or comfort of any sort has been cast off. What we see is rather the negation of this need. 'We don't want to have anything to do with all this crap'. (Marcuse 1967:75)

As this indicates, the Great Refusal was a movement dedicated to rejecting the basic premise of consumer capitalism by refusing to engage in consumerism. This was a movement of the 1960s, as indicated by the groups Marcuse saw as part of the Great Refusal: hippies; black activists; feminists; movements emerging from, and in support of, the Third World and student activists (Marcuse 1969a). All of these were united by their desire to 'resist and deny the massive exploitative power of corporate capitalism' (Marcuse 1969a:vii). This could be seen in the hippy desire to 'drop out'; the black activist goal of highlighting the contribution of slavery, and black oppression, to capital accumulation; feminist movements highlighting that 'the personal is political' with the private realm supporting capital accumulation (Marcuse 1974); protests against Third World exploitation and, finally, how education helps produce the happy consciousness (Marcuse 1969a). Therefore, the Great Refusal was a process of negation in rejecting consumer capitalism and consequently, for Marcuse, outlines 'the limits of the established societies' (Marcuse 1969a:viii). It also provides both the impetus and space for thinking about an alternative which, for Marcuse, will inevitably be a socialist alternative, different from its Soviet form (Marcuse 1969b:123).

However, in appealing to the Great Refusal, Marcuse quickly identifies a problem, namely that there is a split between the 'objective' and 'subjective' elements needed for it to be truly revolutionary. The objective element of any revolutionary movement is 'the human base of the process of production which reproduces the established society' (Marcuse 1969a:56), the group whose non-participation in the current system would bring it crashing down. As we have seen, this is still the working class for Marcuse. However, as we also saw, Marcuse thought there was little potential of the working class, as currently constituted, overthrowing capitalism. At the very least for Marcuse, the working class would need to not stand in the way of any revolutionary movement seeking to transcend capitalism. Unfortunately, he suggests they are more likely to defend capitalism (Marcuse 1969a:65). The reason for this is that the subjective element of the movement, the 'political consciousness' which seeks out an alternative, exists not within the working class but rather among the 'nonconformist young intelligentsia' of the Great Refusal (Marcuse 1969a:56). Therefore, the political will needed to create an alternative is not shared by the group who will be needed to make that alternative. This leaves Marcuse with a problem since:

> Radical change without a mass base seems to be unimaginable. But the outlining of a mass base – at least in this country – and in the foreseeable future – seems to be equally unimaginable. What are we going to do with this contradiction? (Marcuse 1969b:123)

The answer for him returns us to the thought process of individuals and the need for a 'new sensibility'.

The new sensibility

As we saw, Marcuse argued that consumer capitalism had changed the way in which people think and what they see as their fundamental needs. The same could be done to produce what Marcuse terms a 'biological foundation for socialism', whereby our thoughts and needs direct us towards an alternative via the creation of the new sensibility. The subjective elements of the Great Refusal take the lead here by demonstrating the possibility of living 'outside' consumer capitalism (Marcuse 1964:260). Here Marcuse argues that Marxist intellectuals, such as himself, should 'remain loyal' to those who take part in the Great Refusal (Marcuse 1964:261) and that 'the development of a true consciousness is still the professional function of the universities' (Marcuse 1969a:61). Therefore, both groups should devote their energies to producing the new sensibility. This then leaves us with a further question, what is the new sensibility?

Marcuse argues this new sensibility, as a way of seeing the world, would be based upon aesthetics and an appeal to beauty. At this point Marcuse could be accused of being a little vague and in reading what he wanted to see into forms of artistic expression (Bronner 1988). However, his fundamental point is that both capitalism and Soviet Marxism have measured progress in a purely 'quantitative' manner, the growth of the economy, without considering the 'qualitative' elements of human activity, such as play, creativity and appreciation of beauty (Marcuse 1969a:18). It was these elements which the Great Refusal appealed to with claims such as 'black is beautiful' or 'flower power' (Marcuse 1969a:41). These relate to what Marcuse terms the 'aesthetic dimension' of humanity, our appreciation for beauty and art. Appealing to this creates a 'redefinition of needs' away from the false needs of capitalism and towards our own true needs (Marcuse 1964:250). The aesthetic dimension is where free expression of human desires, freed from their commodified form in products, emerges (Marcuse 1956:191).

To be more specific, let's turn to an example from Marcuse (1964:231). Imagine you're walking through a major city. Like any city, it is loud and busy with many buildings which are grey and concrete; you would struggle to call it beautiful. Then, after turning a corner you find yourself in a park; it is quiet and peaceful, with beautiful fields, trees, plants and impressive statues. As you sit there and take it all in you might think to yourself 'it is really great that the city council maintains places like this within this busy city'. That, for Marcuse, is indicative of the sensibility found under capitalism. The assumption is that cities should be built to aid economic progress and growth; nature is an obstacle to overcome. The new sensibility would instead lead you to think, 'it is awful that amidst all this brick and metal of the city this park is the only bit of beautiful space left'. This is a thought process based upon the aesthetic dimension and one which sees our needs shift from the stimulation of consumerism to the appreciation of beauty. This beauty can then also be appreciated more broadly as of value; being in a beautiful place is invigorating for us as people, we need it. This redefinition of needs then fundamentally questions the nature of contemporary society, since:

> the aesthetic dimension can serve as a sort of gauge for a free society … the radical content of the aesthetic needs become evident as the demand for their most elementary satisfaction is translated into group action on an enlarged scale. From the harmless drive for better zoning regulations and a modicum of protection from noise and dirt to the pressure for closing of whole city areas to automobiles, prohibition of transistor radios in all public places, decommercialisation of nature, total urban reconstruction, control of the birth rate – such action would become increasingly subversive to the institutions of capitalism and of their morality. (Marcuse 1969a:27–8)

Therefore, further developing the new sensibility, based upon the aesthetic dimension, within both the subjective *and* objective elements of the Great Refusal, would inevitably for Marcuse lead to the replacement of capitalism with an alternative which was concerned with the qualitative elements of humanity. True freedom emerges when our 'sensuous energy' matches the 'aesthetic state' in which we live (Marcuse 1956:191).

Marcuse's alternative: a society based upon the new sensibility

Let us recap Marcuse's argument to this point. Contemporary capitalist society is not only repressive but produces 'surplus repression' since it goes beyond the level of repression needed to provide security. This level of repression then impacts our very thought process, with our 'true' and 'false' needs being synthesised in a way which aids consumer capitalism. Not only this, but the dominance of consumer capitalism tends to limit the possibility for 'negative' thought – ideas of alternatives to the current system – and instead produces a 'one dimensional man' who, with their 'happy consciousness', accepts and defends the current system. This was especially true of the working class who had, for Marcuse, become co-opted by the system and would fight to defend it. Nevertheless, this advanced stage of capitalism, and its Soviet Marxism sibling, did provide some potential for an alternative. Most prominently, we have finally reached a stage where we are sufficiently technologically advanced to not only produce enough for everyone but also to cut down on the amount of time spent working to do so. To move to such a society Marcuse found great hope in the groups which made up the Great Refusal, including black radical activists, hippies, feminists and students. These groups rejected the affluent society of consumer capitalism and instead based their critique on the 'aesthetic dimension' with its appeal to beauty. A greater propagation of this, along with the efforts of the radical intelligentsia, would produce a 'new sensibility' among individuals which could unite the objective (the working class) and subjective (the Great Refusal) groups needed to usher in a new socialist society.

From the above, it would seem there are some initial elements of Marcuse's alternative which we can highlight. For example, his socialist alternative would be one where, not dissimilar to that of Marx and Engels, the fruits of production were distributed according to need and where 'work becomes play' (Marcuse 1967:69). In addition, any future developments of society would be driven by the aesthetic dimension:

> socially necessary labour would be diverted to the construction of an aesthetic rather than repressive environment, to parks and gardens rather than highways and parking lots, to the creation of areas of withdrawal rather than massive fun and relaxation. (Marcuse 1969a:90)

Therefore, our very motivations, both individually and socially, would move away from progress and profit towards play and beauty. We can still have cities and all the urban institutions they include, but this is secondary to the concern for beauty.

Nevertheless, this leaves unanswered practical questions of how such a society would be organised. Careful readers will not be surprised to hear that, as a Marxist, Marcuse is reluctant to provide such a blueprint. But he is unique in his justification for not doing so, as the following indicates:

> We are still confronted with the demand to state the 'concrete alternative'. The demand is meaningless if it asks for a blueprint of the specific institutions and relationships which would be those of the new society: they cannot be determined a priori; they will develop, in trial and error, as the new society develops. If we could form a concrete concept of the alternative today, it would not be that of an alternative; the possibilities of the new society are sufficiently 'abstract', i.e., removed from and incongruous with the established universe to defy any attempt to identify them in terms of this universe. (Marcuse 1969a:86)

So Marcuse cannot state the details of his alternative since, if he could, it would not be an alternative. Our thought processes are so one dimensional that the second dimension of critique is not fully attainable. Here again we see the central importance of the dominance of positive thought for Marcuse; any attempt to conceive of alternatives under the ideological dominance of consumer capitalism is bound to be limited by consumer capitalism. It is only by changing the thought processes of individuals, allowing for negative thought, that a true 'alternative' can be conceived.

Therefore, Marcuse's alternative is the new sensibility. Since we have the technological mechanisms available for utopia and as the Great Refusal is laying the groundwork for the aesthetic dimension we know the broad parameters of what an alternative would be like; it is the goal of the new sensibility to bring it into being. Indeed, as Marcuse puts it, 'society would be rational and free to the extent to which it is organized, sustained and reproduced by an essentially new historical Subject' (Marcuse 1964:256).

Consequently, to answer our third question of whether Marcuse's alternative would solve the problems he identifies, Marcuse's answer would be that it inevitably would. Any society created by those holding the new subjectivity would, *ipso facto*, solve the problems of consumer capitalism. In this sense, as I argued earlier, Marcuse's goal was always to find the new subject who would create an alternative; as Bernstein (1988:21) put it Marcuse 'searched – in what sometimes seems like a desperate manner – for the signs of those social movements and tendencies that were progressive and liberating'. Therefore, like Lefebvre, Marcuse's alternative is more about how we create a different world rather than being the alternative itself. Where they differ is that Lefebvre looks to a mode of organisation (*autogestion*) whereas Marcuse looks to a group and its subjectivity. To conclude this chapter, I will turn to the further differences and similarities between Marcuse and Lefebvre.

Conclusion: comparing Lefebvre and Marcuse

As we have seen, Lefebvre and Marcuse share some similarities. Both start their critique with the increased dominance of consumer capitalism in the 1960s and turn to the new movements which emerge from this. Their concerns with consumerism, social/false needs, diversity, global inequality and the possibility of reduced work hours continue to be concerns of the current day. However, in this final section, I would like to discuss how the similarities and differences between their alternatives relate to the trends we've seen throughout the book.

Perhaps most significant here is that both, being Marxists, are somewhat reluctant to compose those recipes for the cook-shops of the future which Marx discussed. However, as we have also seen, both do engage in some suggestion of what the alternative will look like; if they do not compose recipes, they certainly talk about the ingredients. Whether this be the *autogestion* which will make the state disappear or the new sensibility and distribution of work which will mean we value beauty and redesign our cities, there are clear ideas here. This also indicates another similarity that each bases their hopes for the alternative on an idea of 'needs', with our social/false needs being replaced with human/true ones.

This opens up a problem. It could be argued that to talk of people's 'true' needs and to criticise the 'false' needs which occupy them is to adopt the ultimate legislative role – to provide universal statements concerning what people 'really' need but don't realise it. This means that somehow the sociologist is able to see through the fog of this repression, despite the fact that they live in the same society as everyone else. Indeed, this has been a frequent criticism made of Marcuse, given his call for the redefinition of needs. As MacIntyre puts it, 'The human nature of those who inhabit advanced industrial societies has been moulded so that their very wants, needs and aspirations have become conformist – except for a minority which includes Marcuse' (MacIntyre 1970:88). This is especially problematic given that:

> The truth is carried by the revolutionary minorities and their intellectual spokesmen, such as Marcuse, and the majority have to be liberated by being re-educated into the truth by the minority who are entitled to suppress rival and harmful opinions. This is perhaps the most dangerous of all Marcuse's doctrines, for not only is what he asserts false, but his is a doctrine which if it were widely held would be an effective barrier to any rational progress and liberation … What Marcuse invites us to repeat is part of the experience of Stalinism. (MacIntyre 1970:90, 92)

Marcuse did, of course, disassociate himself from Soviet Marxism and strongly rejected any role akin to a leader (Marcuse 1969b). And, as we saw, Lefebvre was kicked out of the PCF for opposing Stalinism but retained his Leninism. Nevertheless, it does show one of the key issues surrounding their alternatives – what are our needs?

In defence of both, they see this question as primarily not being answered by them but by revolutionary agents; as good Marxists, they see the alternative created by someone else. It is here we come to their key difference, one which Lefebvre tackled head-on:

> This is where I am against the thought and work of Herbert Marcuse. His standpoint is the theorisation of the *fait accompli* … He takes it for granted that coherence has been achieved; he demonstrates an immanent rationality at work which is ravaging but effective, which has succeeded in making 'man' one-dimensional and has enclosed the system … Instead of demonstrating the faults at the heart of this coherence, Marcuse insists on its internal logic, which is derived from the application of knowledge to the social practices of capitalism. If under such conditions the capitalist centres are solid, powerful, logical and destined to expand, where can the counter-offensive come from? The only answer then is that either it will not take place at all, or that it will come only from the peripheries. (Lefebvre 1976a:114–15)

For Lefebvre, Marcuse is too fatalistic concerning the effectiveness of capitalism in creating anything like a one-dimensional man. This is why he has to go looking elsewhere for people 'outside' the system to question it. As we saw, Lefebvre rejected this, arguing that in fact everyday individuals are potentially heavily critical of the world they inhabit; indeed, it was inevitable they would be given the unrealised promises of everyday life. Therefore, he retains a fundamental faith in the revolutionary potential of the working class, as every-day people, which Marcuse does not share.

Both are ultimately looking for the group which will, from the bottom up, create an alternative society, whether through *autogestion* or the new sensibility. What divides them is that whereas Lefebvre finds the answer in the classic Marxist group, the working class, Marcuse turns his attention and hope elsewhere. In the next chapter we shall see how one of the groups Marcuse highlighted, feminist activists, approached the question of sociological alternatives.

Selma James, Andrea Dworkin and Their Interlocutors: Feminist Alternatives

It could be argued that the alternatives discussed thus far in this book have had a flaw: they have marginalised women.

There are two ways in which this claim would seem to have some merit. Firstly, to this point, we have largely seen a 'Great Man' history of social theory. Each chapter has been devoted either to one or two men. Not only is the gender of these writers problematic but, more broadly, it could be argued that to treat these men as somehow unique or 'special' overlooks the contribution of many, including women, to their ideas and ability to express them. We may thank history for the fact that Marx devoted all his time to careful study of government reports in the British Library in order to write *Das Kapital*; however this life was only possible due to the efforts, and sacrifices in terms of lifestyle and health, of his long-suffering wife Jenny and his daughters (Wheen 1999). Furthermore, such a history marginalises prominent female sociologists of the time who are forgotten, while their male counterparts are venerated. For example, the contributions of Eleanor Marx to socialist theory and organisation are often ignored (Holmes 2014). This was the fate of many other early female theorists (McDonald 1997).

Secondly, and related to the above, the question of gender has largely been absent in previous chapters. There have been some exceptions to this; in the last chapter we saw how Lefebvre condemned the way in which the repetitive and alienating elements of everyday life fell disproportionally on women (a claim criticised as overlooking the creativity women practise at the everyday; see Felski 1999/2000). We also saw how Marcuse took inspiration from the feminist movement in his conception of the Great Refusal since this was 'perhaps the most important and potentially the most radical political movement that we have' (Marcuse 1974:165). Also, Mead was a frequent contributor to, and advocate for, female suffrage campaigns in the US, partly due to his friendship and collaboration with Jane Addams (Shalin 1988, Deegan 2007). However, beyond these isolated examples, women, and the question of gender equality, have largely been marginalised.

Part of the reason for this could be linked to the topics discussed to this point. If we were to survey the common factors such sociological alternatives hoped to change we would see factors such as paid work/labour (Marx and Engels, Durkheim, Marcuse), the economy (Marx and Engels, Du Bois, Lefebvre), politics (Durkheim, Mead, Mannheim, Marcuse), debate (Mead, Durkheim), the use of public space (Lefebvre, Marcuse) and education (Durkheim, Du Bois,

Mead, Mannheim). What marks these out is that they are public occurrences. All of our sociologists thus far, representing the dominant trend in nineteenth- and twentieth-century liberal thought and politics, saw public activity as that which needs reforming; what happened in the private realm was, both figuratively and literally, behind closed doors. It was not the role of any group, be it the state, a revolutionary class or particularly enlightened intellectuals, to intervene there. However, as we shall see in this chapter, it is often in this private realm – including the confinement to it – that women experience the most profound forms of inequality, exploitation and oppression.

Therefore, it could be argued, this book thus far has employed a particular standpoint theory, namely the standpoint of men. It may be suggested that in doing so the alternatives discussed to this point ignore a key problem with contemporary society: patriarchy.

Patriarchy can be defined as 'a system of social structures and practices in which men dominate, oppress and exploit women' (Walby 1990:20). For a society to be patriarchal it does not mean that each individual man sets out to dominate and exploit women, though many will and do, rather that the society is constructed in such a way so that the dominance of men and the masculine, whether this be in politics, business, the home or sexual relations, will reproduce itself.

Therefore, this chapter will be slightly different from those that have come before. While there are two key theorists here – Selma James (1930–) and Andrea Dworkin (1946–2005) – the following will discuss their alternatives as part of the wider feminist movement and body of thought. This is in order to recognise a key feminist claim that ideas are not products of Great Men or Great Women but rather emerge from within a particular social and political milieu. While some have suggested that contemporary feminism has lost interest in outlining alternatives (see Bergman et al. 2014) since this school has only Marxism as a competitor for its claim for most 'political' body of thought there are numerous feminist alternatives, though most have come from outside social theory (see Sargisson 1996 for an overview). Furthermore, feminist alternatives, reflecting the diversity of the field, tend to find their most perceptive critics in other feminists. In doing so such alternatives have – despite disagreement on the value of the term and resulting use of others such as 'gender regime' (Walby 2011:104) – attempted to confront patriarchy. I will begin by tracing some broad themes in feminism before turning to the specific alternatives of James and Dworkin for further discussion.

Feminist alternatives

As highlighted above, feminism is a broad school with many different streams of thought. For example, liberal feminist thought has often focused on finding ways to make the current system more just. This was a position advocated by Betty Friedan who, in her classic *Feminine Mystique*, advocated a new 'life plan for women' in which 'she must learn to compete then, not as a women, but as a human being' (Friedan 1963:328). This included greater female representation in public fields including education, law, business, politics and the media which would allow women to 'make life plans geared to their real abilities' (Friedan 1963:329). Such a view was instrumental to the passing of laws which made discrimination on the basis of gender illegal, such as the 1970 Equal Pay Act in the UK.

A further alternative offered in this field is the use of quotas, whereby a certain number of women within an organisation is set as a minimum. For example, a law drafted by the EU parliament would require 40 per cent of non-executive directors of stock-exchange-listed companies to be women (European Parliament 2013). Furthermore, the use of quotas in politics has become an increasing trend, where regulations are set down requiring the number of female MPs or where political parties use an all-women shortlist of candidates for vacant seats (Squires 2007). The UK Labour Party has been a notable supporter of this policy as a way of ensuring that 50 per cent of its candidates in winnable seats are women (Labour Women's Network 2014).

A different strategy, found more prominently within Marxist feminism, is the goal of conscious raising in order to create more feminists and ultimately a revolution. For example, Sheila Rowbotham argues:

> I consider the solution to exploitation and oppression to be communism … the cultural and economic liberation of women is inseparable from the creation of a society in which all people no longer have their lives stolen from them, and in which the conditions of their production and reproduction will no longer be distorted or held back by the subordination of sex, race, and class. (Rowbotham 1973:xvi)

Achieving this ultimately requires the expansion of 'women's consciousness' and the 'making of a revolutionary socialist organization' as 'an effective movement for the liberation of women' (Rowbotham 1973:126). In this view it is communism which will solve the question of patriarchy. We will return to a further example of this below.

Finally, a slightly different version of the above is to see the state as the key foci of female oppression. The state becomes the 'public patriarchy' of modern societies in the same way the man was the 'private patriarchy' in the family home previously (Walby 1990). For scholars such as Wendy Brown seeking salvation from the state (whether by the imposition of quotas or the collectivisation of the means of production) means feminists 'implicitly cast the state as if it were or could be a deeply democratic and nonviolent institution' (Brown 2001:36). Instead, the state increasingly dictates to women, who also become dependent upon it due to their greater representation in public services and state welfare. Taking inspiration from anarchism, Brown sees the state as increasingly becoming the 'man' in women's lives and would seek a non-, or greatly weakened, state alternative (Brown 1995).

This has been a very quick tour of some feminist alternatives. To explore this further I will now turn to two specific ideas offered by James and Dworkin respectively: wages for housework and banning pornography.

There are three reasons why I have chosen these two alternatives as my focus. Firstly, they are distinctly feminist. Looking through the above alternatives they are ones which could, conceivably, have been held by some of the sociologists we have discussed to this point. For example, Marx and Engels would certainly support Rowbotham's declaration of a socialist organisation and revolution; Lefebvre would have had few qualms signing up to Brown's views of the state and it seems that Mead would have supported Friedan's ideas on the public role of women. These two alternatives however are uniquely feminist. Secondly, reflecting my argument at the start of the chapter, in their feminist standpoint, they aim directly at the private realm and embody the key feminist claim of the personal being political. Thirdly, these are alternatives which, in the best tradition of feminism, have united sociologists with activists from outside academia, often blurring the line between the two. Therefore I will discuss each of these, including the critiques offered by other feminists, in turn.

Wages for housework

The push to make housework paid labour was a prominent cause within Marxist feminism. Therefore, it relied upon a distinctively Marxist critique of society, related to the workings of capitalism (Acker 2004). Capitalism as an economic system exacerbates and reinforces a strict divide between two realms: the public and the private. Prior to the emergence of capitalism most work was done in, or at least around, the home. Therefore, there was little to no divide between our private lives and our professional work. Capitalism however exacerbated such a division. Increasingly people went 'out' to work, partly because of the emergence of factories where work would be conducted. Therefore, the public realm, the world of work, becomes increasingly associated with productive activity.

However, this leaves behind a private realm, the world of the home. Since productive work has moved outside, this leaves the home with reproductive work. Reproductive here means not just the reproduction of the species – children are made, born and raised in the home – but more everyday forms of reproduction of people as workers. This includes cooking, cleaning, washing, providing relaxation and sleep. Since both productive and reproductive work are full-time jobs it requires two people to achieve them. It is from this that the split between housework as women's work and paid work as men's work emerges for Marxist feminists. This position was outlined in embryonic form by Engels (1978).

There are many critiques offered here, but a key one is that the public realm relies upon the private. For capitalism to generate profit, its workers must be well-fed and rested in order to return to work the next day. Also the next generation of workers must be produced in order to replace their age-ing parents. As Acker puts it, 'the rules and expectations of ordinary capitalist workplaces are built on hidden assumptions about a separation of production and reproduction' (Acker 2004:24). However, despite this reliance, capitalism claims no responsibility for the private realm. Workers are paid a wage with little reference to private needs; any home-based obstacles are cause for being fired, and housework, as unpaid labour, is not considered 'work'. Therefore, to succeed in capitalism requires being a 'Rational Economic Man' (Acker 2004:26) who seeks out their own interests and desires, moving freely without any obstacles in their private life holding them back, or, in a contemporary rephrasing, 'Davos Man' (Benería 1999:61) akin to the mostly male politicians and business leaders who meet every year in Davos, Switzerland, for the World Economic Forum.

The reader may consider this an outdated description; after all, such a strict division of public and private seems less true in many contemporary societies, especially with the increased entrance of women into the workplace and poli-tics in the last decades of the twentieth century (Walby 2000). There are two important points here. The first is that housework is still disproportionally con-ducted by women; indeed, in the UK 77 per cent of married women do more housework than their husbands, with 87 per cent doing more than 4 hours per week and 45 per cent of women doing more than 13 hours. This difference is especially pronounced for couples who have children (Lanning 2013). Moreo-ver, at least some of the 23 per cent of cases where housework is evenly split or the man does more can be explained by wealthy couples hiring someone to do this work for them; significantly this is likely to be another woman, most often an immigrant from a poorer nation (Young 2001). This then leads onto the second point that such housework will increasingly occur alongside paid work outside the home, forming what has become known as the 'double' or 'second' shift for women (Hochschild 1989). Therefore, housework remains a feminist concern, since:

> One often reads the standard, throwaway line, in feminist and non-feminist work alike: 'Women do the double shift' or 'Women retain responsibility for the home'. The very fact that it appears as a mere line of text in an article or manifesto or even a book mimics the lack of impor-tance attached to it in the world; *yet it remains one of the most important statements made about women today.* (Benn 1998:239)

It was this which led some feminist scholars to claim that the significance and extent of housework should be recognised. There are two positions here. The first is that housework should be socialised and performed collectively. The second, from James, is that it should become paid labour.

The first of these positions is represented by Margaret Benston (1980). For Benston, housework, and thereby women, occupy a unique position in a capi-talist economy. One success of capitalism was its ability to give everything a market value, to make all relations subject to 'callous "cash payment"' (Marx and Engels 1992:5). However, housework has remained outside this, being subject to no capitalist calculation. In this sense, for Benston, it is pre-capitalist, meaning each household constitutes a 'pre-industrial entity, in the same way that peasant farmers or cottage weavers constituted pre-industrial units' (Benston 1980:123). Nevertheless, as we have seen, this pre-capitalist labour remains central to capitalist profit. As a Marxist, Benston ultimately believes in the socialisation of the means of production and argues that, as part of such a process, this historical anomaly should be corrected by ensuring that housework is also socialised. Rather than individuals, most likely women, being responsible for housework, it should be done collectively. As she puts it:

> To be more specific, this means that child-rearing should no longer be the responsibility solely of the parents. Society must begin to take responsibility for children; the economic dependence of women and children on the husband-father must be ended. The other work that goes on in the home must also be changed – communal eating places and laundries for example. When such work is moved into the public sector, then the material basis for discrimination against women will be gone. (Benston 1980:126)

This means that women as a group are freed from the responsibility of doing housework, with its social value recognised. While it is likely some of these women move from a private to a communal kitchen, for Benston such work is less alienating and more social than its previous private form. Therefore, the link to dehumanising housework is broken.

A slightly different, and more prominent, idea is offered by James with her colleague Mariarosa Dalla Costa. Together they published a book entitled *The Power of Women and the Subversion of the Community* (Dalla Costa and James 1971) and in the same year James founded the International Wages for Housework campaign. They were critical of ideas, already circulating at that point, about socialising housework since this 'would regiment none other than women in some alluring work so that we will then have the possibility at lunchtime of eating shit collectively in the canteen' (Dalla Costa and James 1972: 40). This was partly due to their having a different idea of the relation of housework to capitalism from that held by Benston. Rather than seeing housework as having been left behind by capitalism, they argue women performing housework are capitalism's 'indispensable workforce, at home, cleaning, washing and ironing; making, disciplining and bringing up babies; servicing men physically, sexually and emotionally' (Dalla Costa and James 1972:3). Because women's housework is central to the surplus labour produced by capitalism, they are part of the proletariat, but their proletarian nature is 'hidden by the lack of a wage' (James 1975:27). Therefore, for James, women houseworkers are exploited like the working class but, unlike them, they are not given a wage and thereby are seen as outside the proletariat and the struggle against capitalism; they cannot be working class, they do not 'work'.

Therefore, for Dalla Costa and James, women do have a unique position within the relations of production; they produce surplus labour in the home without any monetary return. But the fact that they do produce surplus labour means they are part of the proletariat. Consequently, some of this profit should be returned to women in the form of a wage for housework, paid by the state from taxes on capital. This is the policy of wages for housework.

Dalla Costa and James argue this policy should be implemented immediately. Given that capital is being produced now and can be taxed, there are no practical issues delaying it (Dalla Costa and James 1972). If it is not brought in immediately, they encourage the enactment of a 'general strike' (Dalla Costa 1974) whereby women refuse to do housework *and* men refuse to do paid work. This would, for them, demonstrate the connection of women and men as workers producing profit for capitalism. Furthermore, elements of this strike can already be found; for example, the use of birth control by women is an indication of how the demands of housewifery are being denied (James 1975).

Would wages for housework lessen patriarchy?

Having seen the policy of wages for housework, we are left with the question of whether this would solve the critique offered by James and, importantly, whether it would lessen patriarchy. There are two justifications offered for this policy. The first is that, by giving women a wage for their labour and thus putting them in the same position as their male counterparts, it expands the number and strength of the proletariat class, with a rallying cry of 'power to the sisters and therefore to the class' (Dalla Costa and James 1972:17). It is this element of wages for housework as part of a wider campaign against capitalism which was especially important for James, as indicated in her role establishing the International Wages for Housework group. This campaign was:

> a tool to heighten the class struggle, to sharpen it, to lead it in a libertarian direction, and to gain more autonomy for women and men at the workplace and the home. If it is not with this in mind, the program is nothing more than the fight for a kinder and gentler capitalism. (Salam 2007)

Therefore, while wages for housework is an essential first step, this argument places the overall responsibility with a post-capitalist order, socialism, to remove patriarchy. This demonstrates the fundamentally Marxist nature of an argument which sees its potential success in uniting housewives and the proletariat.

The second factor would have a more immediate impact. By waging housework, it becomes a job and opens up the possibility of refusing that job. Without this it is simply assumed to be something women do naturally. Making housework a job with pay removes this natural link and sees it as a task which anyone, man or woman, can do (James 1975). The claim here is that if housework became waged, some women may well continue to do what they did before, only this time receiving a wage, while others would refuse to do it. This means others, including men, would take up the role since now it would have a monetary reward attached to it. In this sense, Fedrici (1980) is right that James' campaign was intended as one of wages *against* housework, as:

> It is the demand by which our nature ends and our struggle begins because just to want wages for housework means to refuse that work as the expression of our nature, and therefore to refuse precisely the female role that capital has invented for us. (Fedrici 1980:257)

Therefore, wages for housework could be said to lessen female exploitation and patriarchy in two ways. Firstly, it links women into the proletariat class and the struggle for communism which, as a Marxist, James sees as a positive. Secondly, in the interim it 'denaturalises' housework as a female task, by turning it into a job. By doing so, women are now able to refuse to do housework and (some) men will take it on as a paid job.

However, there are criticisms of this proposal within feminism. In what follows I will focus primarily on criticisms of the second, denaturalisation point, since they are especially important to feminist debates about patriarchy. However, the link of communism and the end of patriarchy can be greatly questioned. As we saw in Chapter 2, Marx implied communism was a world in which men worked and women stayed at home; it does not seem immediately apparent why this link would automatically be broken by a communist society. Furthermore, while some actually existing communist societies had successes in placing women in prominent public roles – often by the implementation of the aforementioned quotas (Walby 2011:61) – their record on gender equality was, to say the least, patchy (Molyneux 1991). It is for these reasons that one finds a wider literature which criticises the idea that communism is automatically a potential source of female liberation (Elshtain 1981:245–86; Segal 1991).

Turning to questions of 'denaturalisation', there are four key arguments against this in the literature. The first is that, rather than remove the link between women and housework, the wages for housework campaign would actually reinforce it. If a wage for housework is available wouldn't a woman in a heterosexual relationship be expected to take it and not seek work outside the home? As Oakley puts it, 'A system of state payment for the woman-housewife's labour in the home will recognise and perpetuate the validity of the equation "woman = housewife"' (Oakley 1974:227). This would especially be the case for working-class women who may not have the ability to refuse *any* work if it is paid (Tong 1998:111). The second point, and leading on from this, is that in reinforcing a status quo of women doing housework, such a wage may actually further essentialise women as 'caring'. Already the labour market tends to see women disproportionally represented in jobs focused on some form of care or 'emotional labour' (Hochschild 2003). Consequently, providing another job which it seems, especially in the interim, would be done mainly by women could further reinforce such a link (Tong 1998:110). In addition to this, if the state were simply taxing the husband to pay the wife, this would not change inequality between families. If, instead, the state paid it out of general revenue, it would seemingly need to tax everyone, including single parents, creating greater forms of inequality (Bergmann 1986). Therefore, others argue removing the central role given to the family under capitalism is the key point of critique rather than seeking to institutionalise a housewife role (Landes 1980).

A third criticism is that a wage would do nothing to change the nature of housework. In an echo of Lefebvre's argument in the previous chapter, it would continue to remain isolated, monotonous and alienating labour. The only exception would be that now you were being paid for it, you could not complain (Oakley 1974:230–3). Finally, it is suggested that rather than overthrow or question capitalism, as James and Dalla Costa hope, a wage for housework would actually legitimate it. Capitalism would have succeeded in sucking more activity into 'callous cash payment' and any idea of such work as loving or caring would be removed (Tong 1998:110). In addition, it would seemingly enhance capitalism's claim to being an equal and fair system which is why, Oakley notes, the policy had some support on the anti-feminist right (Oakley 1974:226). While this may not be seen as a criticism of the policy in general – making capitalism more equal may be valued – it is a criticism against James who advocates this policy precisely because she thinks it will help bring about the demise of capitalism.

As we have seen, the wages for housework alternative has attracted many detractors within feminism. However, this is not to say that the policy does not remain a live issue. James continues to advocate it, including in publications (James 2012) and in public interventions. For example, in the 2012 US presidential campaign she publically defended Ann Romney, mother of five and wife of Republican candidate Mitt Romney, against claims she had 'never worked'. Furthermore, those who may not agree with the substance of James' idea have nevertheless supported the principle of paying a wage for work currently not paid. For example, Melissa Benn advocates a 'carer's income' which:

> would reflect the active, engaged nature of bringing up a child. Both employed and unemployed men should be encouraged to claim it as much as women. It should be granted on the basis that it does not preclude its recipient from taking some work, nor from at any time going back into work for however long they want. In other words, taken with other measures that sanction and encourage paid work that women want, the risk of 'returning women to the home', the expected political charge against it, would be minimal. (Benn 1998:248–9)

Also, as we shall see in Chapter 9, those advocating a basic income have often done so partly on the basis that it would help lessen the unequal division of domestic labour. An income paid to everyone would help recognise the different life circumstances for women while also achieving equality (Lister 1999). Therefore, the principles behind wages for housework continue to live on in social theory, both within and outwith feminism, despite the criticisms offered against it. However, as we shall also see in Chapter 9, others argue this overlooks the continuing power of patriarchy to shape distinct forms of masculinity and feminity.

It is now time to turn to our second feminist alternative: banning pornography.

Banning pornography

Pornography became a key feminist issue in the 1970s/1980s with the emergence of the 'sex wars' (Bryson 1999). Few topics have managed to divide different branches of feminism as much as this one with, as we shall see, supposedly 'pro' and 'anti' positions taken not just on pornography but sex more generally (Tong 1998:65).

In what follows I will outline three broad positions taken within feminism regarding pornography. The first, radical feminist, position is held by Dworkin in collaboration with Catherine McKinnon and argues that pornography should be banned. As we shall see, Dworkin and McKinnon had some notable successes in pushing for laws against pornography. I will also highlight some recent commentators who share Dworkin's position in response to changes in the availability of pornography and its entrance into mass culture. The second, more liberal, position argues that banning it would be an authoritarian act, a limiting of free speech. Furthermore, such a potential ban overlooks the positives of pornography for female sexuality. The third position, held often, though not solely, by Marxist/socialist feminists, occupies the ground between these two. Such scholars argue that pornography is perhaps negative for women, but it does not cause patriarchy and is instead a symptom of it. Therefore, banning pornography is ultimately short-sighted and unlikely to create any change in the position of women. The reasons such positions are held reflect the differing political positions of feminists.

Before turning to such a discussion, the reader should be aware that, in what follows, there is discussion of the link between pornography and violence, particularly sexual violence. This includes some mention of such acts.

The feminist critique of pornography

We will begin with the radical feminist position of Dworkin and MacKinnon, a position put most clearly by Dworkin in her classic *Pornography: Men Possessing Women* (1989). Dworkin's argument sets out from a fundamental premise that 'pornography happens' (Dworkin 1989:xxxviii). Rather than defining pornography as a collection of videos and images Dworkin wants to see it as a *process*, something which happens or is done by men to women. Dworkin returns to the original meaning of the word 'pornography' to argue it:

> does not mean 'writing about sex' or 'depictions of the erotic' or 'depictions of sexual acts' or 'depictions of nude bodies' or 'sexual representations' or any other such euphemism. It means the graphic depiction of women as vile whores. (Dworkin 1989:200)

Therefore, pornography is defined not by the representation of nudity and sexual acts but rather the dominance of men over women; it is a 'system of dominance and submission' (Dworkin 1989:xxxviii). In such a process women are only objects for domination by men and means for them to achieve sexual gratification. Dworkin argues that even in situations where it seems a woman is the dominant partner they are only seemingly dominant since this is what the man wants; they still exist to give a man pleasure (Dworkin 1989:34–6). Therefore, 'the major theme of pornography as a genre is male power, its nature, its magnitude, its use, its meaning' (Dworkin 1989:24). As a process, this form of male power happens to women in two ways.

The first way it happens is to those who are involved in producing pornography. In 1983 Dworkin and MacKinnon were central in establishing the Meese Commission held by the state government of Minnesota. This heard from women who had worked within the pornography industry and who had been affected by it (MacKinnon and Dworkin 1997). This told the story of women forced to work in pornography, either due to a history of sexual abuse or due to coercion during production. Both elements of this can be seen in the testimony of one woman:

> As I speak about pornography, here, today ... I am talking about my life. I was raped by my uncle when I was ten, by my stepbrother and stepfather by the time I was twelve. My stepbrother was making pornography of me by the time I was fourteen. I was not even sixteen years old and my life reality consisted of sucking cocks, posing nude, performing sexual acts and actively being repeatedly raped. (Dworkin 1989:xvii)

Another example came from Linda Boreman who had achieved a certain level of fame as the star of *Deep Throat*, a popular American pornographic movie released in 1972. Boreman spoke of how she came to work on the movie due to coercion by her then husband, a pornography producer, saying 'every time someone watches that film, they are watching me being raped' (Dworkin 1989:xvi).

The second way pornography happens to women is via men who have consumed pornography seeking to 'act it out' on their sexual partners. The acts, positions and forms of contact shown in pornography, which, as we have seen, Dworkin sees as the dominance of men over women, become a guide to how sex should be conducted. As she puts it 'he comes to the pornography a believer, he goes away from it a missionary' (Dworkin 1989:202). For Dworkin, men do this without female consent, up to and including acts of rape. Such acts rely upon the idea of women being sexually available – of 'no meaning yes' – found in pornography (Dworkin 1989:xxxvi).

Therefore, pornography is a way in which male power is both expressed and reinforced. The very presence of pornography and its widespread use ensure that male power continues to be expressed via sexuality; it is 'the DNA of male dominance' (Dworkin 1989:xxxix). The effects of this are wide reaching. Male sexual violence is a continual presence and anything women achieve, such as career success, will be made 'specifically sexy, dangerous, provocative, punished, made men's in pornography' (MacKinnon 1989:327) by turning it into something else which makes women sexually appealing. Consequently, it could be said that pornography has the effect of 'sexualising hierarchy', by ensuring that male dominance is reproduced through human sexuality (MacKinnon 1989:315). This allows for the reproduction of the ideal man as the 'bad boy', someone who not only disrespects women but wins plaudits from his peers for doing so (Lynch 2012). Furthermore, black feminists have argued the portrayal of black women in pornography, either as willing participants in bondage and slavery or as having animalistic sexual desires, serves to reinforce historical ideas of black women as subhuman animals (Collins 2000:145–56). Therefore, not only can pornography be seen as central to male dominance but especially to white male dominance.

This portrayal of women in pornography as objects for male sexual gratification also ensures that women continue to be sexually objectified. This becomes such a central part of female lives that, as MacKinnon (1989:340) puts it, 'women live in sexual objectification like fish live in water'.

Contemporary anti-pornography feminism

It is on this final point that contemporary feminists have sought to expand the argument. As Phipps highlights (2014:86–8) and for reasons to be discussed further below, many feminists and activists, especially those on the Left, rejected the analysis of Dworkin and MacKinnon. Nevertheless, there has been some recent return to their critique of pornography. The main spur for this has been changes in the availability and reach of pornography. Whereas Dworkin and MacKinnon were discussing pornography primarily in terms of pornographic movies, books and magazines contemporary arguments emphasise the emergence of 'everyday pornography' (Boyle 2010a): the increased prominence of pornographic images both within and outside these 'traditional' fora. There are two elements to this. Firstly, as Dines (2010) argues, the emergence of the Internet has fundamentally changed how pornography is consumed. Not only is it more readily available but more 'extreme' forms of pornography are also easily found and become the norm for those consuming pornography (Dines 2010). These are defined by the fact that 'the man makes hate to the woman, as each sex act is designed to deliver the maximum amount of degradation' (Dines 2010:xxiv–v). The second element concerns not just the increased presence of nudity and sexual gestures in popular culture but also the elements of pornography Dworkin emphasised: male dominance and female sexual availability. This can be seen in various areas of culture: music videos; so-called lad's mags which, bordering the line of 'pornography', show women as sexually available objects; advertisements which rely upon sex to sell products; and, in the UK, page 3 models in tabloid newspapers. Writers have also highlighted the extent to which children, either wittingly or unwittingly, are exposed to pornography via the Internet (Walter 2010:106).

The sheer prominence of such material means that pornography has 'hijacked our sexuality' (Dines 2010) by increasingly subjecting all sexual interaction to its rules and commands. For such writers a particularly troubling element in this has been the role of women in 'raunch culture', reproducing the tropes of pornography by various means, for example, taking striptease classes and embodying the sexual practices of pornography (Levy 2006). These feed into a wider culture of 'porn chic' where women objectify themselves in line with the demands of the male gaze and the expectation of the dominant 'bad boy' (Lynch 2012). This can include women grooming themselves in line with male expectations and the increased use of cosmetic surgery in order to make a woman's labia fit a preconceived 'norm' as prescribed by pornography (Walter 2010:108–9). This has been made possible for Dines (2010) by pornography 'sanitising itself' and seeming more appealing to the outside world via either making mainstream stars out of pornographers (such as Jenna Jameson) or by presenting itself as playful and fun (as in the *Girls Gone Wild* series). The ubiquity of the Playboy bunny as simply another brand is one of the best examples of this (Levy 2006).

A wider critique offered by these scholars is of the nature of pornography as something produced by an industry. It is made not for sexual liberation but for profit; the increased availability of pornography therefore forces producers to find more unique, extreme, forms to carve out a niche in the market. For Boyle (2010b), sex in pornography is 'commercial sex' performed for money, with most of the profit from this sex not going to the performer but to the producer. Given the fact that most producers favour young performers, this ensures that those women who perform pornography have a relatively short shelf life, in which they encounter a high risk of STDs and personal injuries in order to ensure profit for (most likely) a male producer. This, for Boyle (2010a), means that one is not 'anti-sex' but anti-'commercial sex'.

The result of all this, for contemporary anti-pornography feminists, is that male dominance is continually reproduced and sexual violence continues to be a central part of female life. However, this is often done via new means where the portrayal of 'porn chic' is seen to be an active choice on the part of 'empowered' women. Therefore, a world without pornography would be much improved.

The alternative: 'MacDworkin' and the campaign to ban pornography

Following their involvement in the Meese Commission MacKinnon and Dworkin helped to draft a law for the state of Minnesota which, while not explicating banning pornography, had this as its end goal. The law became known as the MacKinnon-Dworkin ordinance or, simply, the MacDworkin law. This was a civil law which intended to allow those impacted by pornography – via working in the industry or through the forced re-enactment of pornography upon them – to claim compensation directly from pornographers (MacKinnon 1991). As a law, this required a definition of pornography, which was the following:

> Pornography is defined as the graphic, sexually explicit subordination of women in pictures and/or words that also includes women presented dehumanized as sexual objects, things, or commodities; or women presented as sexual objects who enjoy pain or humiliation; or women presented as sexual objects who experience sexual pleasure in being raped; or women presented as sexual objects tied up or cut up or mutilated or bruised or physically hurt; or women presented in postures or positions of sexual submission, servility, or display; or women's body parts – including but not limited to vaginas, breasts, buttocks – exhibited such that women are reduced to those parts; or women presented as whores by nature; or women presented being penetrated by objects or nature; or women presented in scenes of degradation, injury torture, shown as filthy or inferior, bleeding, bruised, or hurt in a context that makes these conditions sexual. (Dworkin 1989:xxxiii)

Dworkin and MacKinnon defended their law precisely because it did not limit its definition to 'classic' pornography but rather attacked the element outlined in their critique: male dominance and female sexual submission and availability. This could, and as we saw above does, happen outside the boundaries of traditional pornography.

So why would such a law be effective in fighting patriarchy? The answer for Dworkin is not only via the simple transfer of wealth from pornographer to claimant; instead the law has a wider impact, as she puts it:

> (1) [the law] tells the truth about what pornography is and does; (2) it tells the truth about how women are exploited and hurt by the use of pornography; (3) it seeks to expand the speech of women by taking the pornographers' gags out of our mouths; (4) it seeks to expand the speech and enhance the civil status of women by giving us the courts as a forum in which we will have standing and authority; (5) it is a mechanism for redistributing power, taking it from pimps, giving it to those they have been exploiting for profit, including for pleasure; (6) it says that women matter, including the women in pornography. (Dworkin 1989:xxxiv)

Therefore, while not directly specifying it in law, the overall goal is a world without pornography in which, as a result, women are greatly empowered.

The law had a choppy time in the US. Two Minnesota state councils passed the law before it was vetoed both times by their mayor – who, Dworkin notes sarcastically, was active in Amnesty International, 'opposing torture outside Minnesota' (Dworkin 1989:xxx). It was then passed in the city of Indianapolis in 1984 (though only in reference to violent pornography) before being ruled unconstitutional on the grounds of free speech. MacKinnon and Dworkin then sued two city councils to put it to popular vote: Cambridge, Massachusetts, in 1985 and Bellingham, Washington, in 1988. In Cambridge it received only 42 per cent of the vote but passed in Bellingham with 62 per cent of the vote before, again, being found unconstitutional (MacKinnon 1991). Despite such setbacks the law attracted a large amount of international attention and, as we shall see further below, one country did in fact pass a version of the law.

Would the MacDworkin law be successful in solving the problem identified by their critique? Below we will turn to feminist critiques which argue it would not; however at the moment we can suggest it may be successful on three grounds. Firstly, as we saw, pornography is an industry where many of those taking part do so due to a history of sexual abuse and coercion. By allowing women to claim compensation and, perhaps ultimately, remove pornography, it not only ensures the men who commit such abuse are punished but, more importantly, lessens the incentive to make pornography and therefore abuse and coerce women in the first place. Reflecting the position of Boyle (2010b), this would also mean fewer men profiting from the exploitation of female sexuality. The second way in which it may be successful is, with the lessening availability of pornography, men will be less exposed to its message and, therefore, less likely to practise it out on women. This would not only reduce the amount of unequal sex but, more importantly, lessen the amount of sexual violence carried out by men on women. It is for this reason that while some of the contemporary 'anti-pornography' scholars may not declare a belief in the value of the MacDworkin law they nevertheless support its end goal due to pornography's connection, however filtered, to sexual violence. Boyle, for instance, sees the work of Dworkin and MacKinnon as a 'starting point for political organization'; their law is not necessarily an answer to the problem but inspires feminists to fight pornography (Boyle 2010b:4). This is why, although eschewing the 'top down' regulation of the MacDworkin law, Dines had a hand in forming the Stop Porn Culture group who, through activism and 'grassroots education' (Stop Porn Culture 2014), hopes to lessen the reach and use of pornography since 'in a just society, there is no room for porn' (Dines 2010:165).

The third point is a wider one. Given the role of pornography in male dominance – recalling Dworkin, its position as the DNA of such dominance – banning it removes a key forum through which patriarchy is expressed. In particular, the space available to, as MacKinnon argued, 'sexualise' male dominance and place women in a culture of sexual domination is greatly lessened. Therefore, both are placing great hope in their alternative; while it would be inaccurate to claim that either Dworkin or MacKinnon is saying banning pornography would remove patriarchy totally, it would be accurate to say they see it as the most effective means of fighting it.

It is these three points which feminist critics of the MacDworkin law take exception to.

Feminist critics of banning pornography

Reflecting earlier claims in this chapter regarding the plurality of feminism, critics of the MacDworkin law have come from liberal and Marxist feminist voices among others. The basis of each of these critiques differs as a result of their position. I will also highlight responses to contemporary criticisms of feminism which fit less neatly into those categories. Let us begin, however, with the liberal feminist critic.

The best expression of the liberal feminist position comes from Nadine Strossen (2000) who was a prominent member and, from 1991, president of the American Civil Liberties Union which fought the MacDworkin law in court on the basis of free speech. Therefore, this position partly sets out to defend pornography on such a basis. However, Strossen provides four other points, specific to a feminist argument and not just its liberal form, about why Dworkin and MacKinnon were mistaken in their push to ban pornography.

The first of these is what the law says about women. For Strossen the MacDworkin law paints women as weak and in need of protection. Even when women may have appeared to have consented to take part in pornography or certain types of sexual practices the position of Dworkin suggests that 'women are *always* coerced in this context, whether they realise it or not' (Strossen 2000:181). This means it removes, or at least greatly downplays, the fact that women can make free choices to take part in pornography or have certain forms of sex, including those in which they are the submissive partner. Strossen also argues that laws already exist against sexual assault, violence and rape to protect women; the MacDworkin law is instead about seeing women as in need of protection as 'weak' people.

This then leads onto the second point where, for Strossen, MacKinnon and Dworkin are not anti-pornography but they're simply 'antisex' (Strossen 2000:20). This draws upon a perception of Dworkin (1987) and MacKinnon's (1997) arguments that, under the conditions of patriarchy, all forms of heterosexual sex contain at least some element of coercion. In its extreme form this is the argument that all sex is rape (Cahill 2001:15–49). While MacKinnon and Dworkin dispute this radical argument is theirs the claim that heterosexual sexual activity is fundamentally shaped by the inequalities of patriarchy is theirs. For Strossen, this paints a false picture where feminism is forced to choose between 'sexual freedom and economic, social and political freedom' (Strossen 2000:25). A more 'prosex' feminism would not paint this as a choice and instead seek to value and expand female sexual expression as a key component of social freedom.

Strossen's third point is linked to the second. Due to the antisex views of MacKinnon and Dworkin they overlook that pornography can, and does, have positive outcomes. This can be true for women seeking to discover their own sexual tastes and desires, as well as for couples seeking 'tips' on their own sex life. Furthermore, the availability of pornography means that those curious about their own sexuality can use both gay and straight forms to understand what they desire. Consequently, for Strossen, any attempt to ban pornography will simply mean that a trade in black market pornography will emerge to fill these needs and female sexuality will become an even more taboo subject (Strossen 2000:161–78).

Finally, Strossen turns the tables on MacKinnon and Dworkin. As we have seen above, one reason why the MacDworkin laws are advocated is in order to provide women protection via the laws of the state and its courts. But both MacKinnon and Dworkin believe such bodies to be patriarchal and therefore shaped by, and act in line with, the precepts of male domination (MacKinnon 1982). So why trust the patriarchal states and courts to protect women (Strossen 2000:217–18)? The result of this can be found for Strossen in the one case where the MacDworkin laws were enacted.

In the 1992 case of *R v. Butler* – concerning the prosecution of a pornographic shop owner – the Canadian Supreme Court implemented a form of the MacDworkin law into the criminal code. In effect, this made it illegal to sell pornography with the exception of some 'softer' forms. Strossen uses this as a test case for the MacDworkin laws, pointing out that rather than attack the forms of patriarchal pornography, the law was primarily used to seize, prosecute and close down those selling gay, lesbian and feminist materials (Strossen 2000:230–6). She also draws on a case where Dworkin's own *Pornography* text was seized at the Canadian border due to its explicit nature (Strossen 2000:237). This example furthers Strossen's point that if the state and law are patriarchal, giving them more power is likely to lead to the enforcement of that patriarchal order.

MacKinnon and Dworkin (1994) released a statement on this Canadian case which said four things. Firstly, that *R v. Butler* did not implement the MacDworkin law and the definition of pornography is different as are the problems it is seen to engender. Secondly, while MacKinnon participated in the case, Dworkin opposed the prosecution from the start. Thirdly, the supposed seizure of Dworkin's books was due to a routine customs check unrelated to *Butler*. Finally, while the Canadian constitution supports sexual equality and this makes the possibility of passing their civil law stronger than in the US, neither of them support a criminal law passed for this measure (MacKinnon and Dworkin 1994). This still seems problematic in line with

Strossen's reasoning; why would a criminal law reproduce patriarchy but a civil law would not?

The critique of Strossen and others was valuable in highlighting the fact that some women do enjoy watching and taking part in pornography which subsequent writers have to acknowledge. Due to this Walter (2010:105) argues that the approach of writers such as Dworkin is not appropriate. Instead, she encourages the expansion of spaces free from pornography (in the broad sense of the term), most notably by fighting the spread of everyday pornography (Walter 2010:117). However, other writers want to take the critique one step further and diverge from the liberalism in Strossen's critique. The portrayal of those working in pornography as simply making a rational and individualized choice can be said to be entwined with contemporary neoliberal ideas of individuals as simply rational economic actors (Phipps 2014). In making such a case, writers like Strossen can find themselves in unappealing company, such as Huff Hefner and Larry Flynt, who can present their businesses as helping feminism and female empowerment (Phipps 2014:88–9). Drawing her inspiration from discussion of sex workers more broadly Phipps argues it is not necessary for workers to be 'happy, empowered or to have chosen their profession in order to be able to demand rights and respect' (Phipps 2014:101). Such a position focuses the call more on the structures in which pornography is produced – notably concerning the governing of female bodies and sexuality – rather than its innate value as free speech.

It is this wider point of the context of pornography production, patriarchy and its causes which feeds into Marxist/socialist feminist critics of MacKinnon and Dworkin. For some the key point is not, unlike Strossen, to defend pornography, but rather to see this as a symptom, rather than cause, of patriarchy. Capitalism produces alienation and pornography is simply one form of this rather than, as Dworkin suggests, the key factor in reproducing patriarchy and female subjugation (McGregor 1989). Some of these writers do not deny that pornography has negative elements and perhaps is ultimately something the world would be better off without. But pornography is no more negative than forms of female representation in media or other mechanisms of female oppression (Segal 1993).

However, it is also possible to highlight another critique here: both Dworkin and Strossen present an 'ahistorical' picture of pornography as either solely male violence or stripped of any further context. For Power (2009:45–56) there is a history of pornography being used for oppositional political movements – such as during the French revolution when it was used to attack the monarchy and aristocratic values (Power 2009:47). Furthermore, the earliest forms of recorded pornography demonstrated a playful, almost slapstick, exploration of sexuality (Power 2009:51–4). All of this has been removed by the capitalist commodification of sex discussed by Marcuse in the last chapter. Therefore, to speak of pornography as 'good' or 'bad' is, for Power, to make historical point which overlooks that it can be both at varying point of history.

Such critiques also highlight a bit of a contradiction at the heart of the anti-pornography group. While radical feminists such as MacKinnon and Dworkin are central, equally active, especially in the US, are members of the religious right. This later group would seemingly not share feminism's end goal of over-throwing patriarchy. Therefore, campaigns to ban pornography, by giving strength to such groups, can actually enhance patriarchy, as:

> There certainly are formidable obstacles which continue to block wom-en's moves towards empowering political perspectives, sexual, social and economic, but anti-pornography feminism is, in my view, increasingly one of them. It accompanies, and resonates with, the rise of pre- and post feminist traditionalisms found, for example, in the assertion of Islamic fundamentalism or the recent western 'pro-family' backlash against femi-nism. (Segal 1993:94–5)

Therefore, while not necessarily sharing Strossen's view of the inherently posi-tive elements of pornography – though they do share a cynicism regarding its link to sexual violence (Segal 1990) – this group of feminists ultimately shares her conclusion. Banning pornography will simply be another way to make female sexuality an unspoken topic and the realm of sex will remain one of male desires. What is needed instead is more *feminist* pornography, more expression of female sexual desire and figures in pornography (McGregor 1989, Segal 1993). Or, as Power (2009:58) puts it, 'a re-establishment of the link between sex and politics'.

Conclusion

As the above has shown, the debates on banning pornography have been varied and vociferous. While Dworkin and MacKinnon have seen this as the key pol-icy which can be used to overcome patriarchy, others have argued either that it would be negative for women or that it misses the target and that in fact other factors, whether this be capitalism, the state or culture more generally, are to blame for patriarchy. The position one takes in this argument ultimately reflects certain theoretical assumptions which can be made about patriarchy. If this is seen as primarily expressed through sexual domination then banning pornog-raphy is a positive step. If, however, the gender representations in pornography are seen as a reflection, rather than the cause, of patriarchy, then banning it would either be short-sighted or ineffective.

It is these kinds of questions concerning the cause of patriarchy which also marked debates on wages for housework. As we saw, James and her colleagues imagined housework as the central part to the perpetuation of patriarchy; the restriction of women to the home and away from the wider class struggle removed them as a key player in producing a more just order. James' crit-ics however argued the opposite, that housework and the domestic division of labour was just one form of patriarchy. Make this paid and not only will women be expected to do it, but it will remove public opportunities for women and do nothing to lessen their daily alienation.

Therefore these alternatives are marked by the key question of where one should attack patriarchy. If housework was paid and pornography was banned, would this be removed? If not, and it seems the criticisms outlined here bring home that these policies alone may not do the job, we are left looking for further alternatives.

Anthony Giddens and Ulrich Beck: Cosmopolitan Alternatives

The alternatives considered thus far have, with some exceptions, largely been ones produced in sociology's past. We shall see in the next two chapters claims that recently sociology has neglected sociological alternatives. However, this chapter considers contemporary alternatives from two sociologists who share a research agenda with 'reflexive modernization' (Beck et al. 1994): Anthony Giddens (1938–) and Ulrich Beck (1944–2015).

Included in this joint research agenda is a focus on globalization. Many of the alternatives we have discussed to this point have seen themselves as global in scope: Marx and Engels' proletariat had been stripped 'of every trace of national character' (Marx and Engels 1992:14) and are united globally by their status as workers. For Durkheim, nation states can only claim a basis for their civic morals when they express a form of 'world patriotism' which reflects the general interests of humanity (Inglis 2014a). Finally, Lefebvre imagined his alternative of *autogestion* to incorporate an element of 'worldness' where, sharing Marx and Engels' view, the proletariat are united by their experiences and desire for self-organisation across the globe (Lefebvre 1976b:162).

However, global elements are not entirely part of the societies these writers confront and critique; rather, globality often forms part of the normative goal. For example, Lefebvre's *autogestion* helps bring this worldness into being, rather than occurring because of it. This differs from the work of Giddens and Beck, where the very existence of globalization creates the conditions and need for cosmopolitan alternatives. While, of the two, Beck is more explicit in discussing his sociology as 'cosmopolitan' (Beck 2006a), Giddens sees his alternative containing ideas which 'express and derive from this global cosmopolitanism' (Giddens 1994a:253).

Given the focus on globalization and cosmopolitanism here there were other options for consideration. For example, David Held (2000) has written of the possibility for global forms of democratic regulation, Jurgen Habermas (2000) of the possible 'post-national' public sphere developing in areas such as Europe which provides space for a new political community and Leslie Sklair (2009) has written from a Marxist perspective of the emancipatory potential in 'generic' globalization against its current capitalist form. Furthermore, writers such as David Graeber (2002) and Valentine Moghadam (2005) have written of the anarchist or feminist alternatives suggested by alter-globalization movements. Instead Giddens and Beck have been chosen for three reasons. Firstly, while in the discussion of Mannheim we have touched upon the significance of the link between sociologists and governments this has not been fully developed. Here Giddens is a useful example given that he not only developed such links to the governing party but became a parliamentarian in the UK. As we shall see, this helped shape the form of his sociological alternative. Secondly, Giddens and Beck are distinct from those mentioned above as their alternatives emerge from a sociological analysis of what they see as the emerging 'individualization' encouraged by globalization and its impact on previously stable inequalities expressed by class. Finally, neither limit their alternatives to simple global forms of regulation but seek to discuss new forms of work and ecology befitting a globalized society. Sociological attempts to create 'ecological' alternatives have been broad, including claims for the embracing of international state regulation and green political action (Martell 1994), a 'digital panopticon' which monitors and limits environmental damage (Urry 2008) or the embracing of a 'green socialism' (Benton 2002). But, as even their critics note, the strength of Giddens and Beck is their attempt to combine ecological issues and social theory, lacking in other ecological writers (Benton 2002:258). Therefore, these two are valuable to discuss for this topic due to their fitting most exactly the three-stage model of sociological alternatives and, in doing so, drawing upon distinct theoretical claims not yet covered in this book.

Before turning to their work it is necessary to define two of the key words used here: globalization and cosmopolitanism. These indicate slightly different factors which relate to the critiques and alternatives offered by Giddens and Beck. Globalization refers to a condition of the social which affects masses across the globe which:

> involves the compression of space such that distance is less of a factor than it used to be in terms of knowledge, communication and movement. Geography and territory is undermined and things start to develop at a level that is more than, and above, inter-national relations. (Martell 2010:15)

While, for many, it is important to conceive of globalization as a process rather than a state (Held et al. 1999) this does not change the fundamental point that globalization is an empirical depiction of what our social conditions are: a society or societies are either more or less globalized, alternatively, they are or are not on a process of globalization. This is different from cosmopolitanism, which instead refers to a way of viewing the world in which:

> citizenship can and ought to be founded on a worldwide community, composed of citizens of the world, or cosmopolitans. In this world-view we all have a duty to help each other or at least to be sensitive towards our respective values and ways of life, regardless of political borders and cultural differences ... moral universalism takes precedence over moral particularism. (Holton 2009:4)

Therefore, while globalized societies are more likely to generate a cosmopolitan outlook, it is not automatic that they do so. As we shall see, both Giddens and Beck are concerned with creating a world which recognises the changed conditions of globalization and therefore is fit for cosmopolitanism. We shall begin with the work of Giddens.

Anthony Giddens

Giddens was born in 1938 in Edmonton, North East London, being the first member of his family to attend university. His career began in 1961 when he joined Leicester University. The sociology department at Leicester was, along with LSE, one of the most significant in the development of sociology in Britain, helping to train a whole generation of major sociologists (Eldridge 1990). Come 1969, Giddens left Leicester to join Cambridge, where he was central to establishing sociology at a university traditionally reluctant to accept it. Indeed, it remained so, with Giddens' application for promotion to reader being rejected nine times. During this time period, Giddens' work focused primarily on two fields: the exploration and critique of the 'classics', most notably in his work on Marx, Durkheim and Weber (Giddens 1971), and the development of his own structuration theory, which attempted to combine structure and agency (Giddens 1984). He stayed at Cambridge until 1996, at which point he left to become the director of the LSE (see Bryant and Jary 2001 for a full biography). Come 2004 he entered the House of Lords as a peer for the governing Labour Party and took the title Baron Giddens of Southgate in the London Borough of Enfield.

It is this later stage of Giddens' career which will be considered in this chapter. This began in the early 1990s, with his shift in focus towards globalization, the nature of modernity, lifestyle and the changing nature of politics. Before this, Giddens did have an implicit alternative (Dawson 2013:34–41), identifying himself as a 'libertarian socialist' (Giddens 1981:175) and claiming that Marx's conception of *praxis* was 'an indispensable contribution to social theory today' (Giddens 1981:2). Here Giddens defended the emancipatory potential of a socialist project along broadly Marxist lines (Giddens et al. 1982:64–5, 72). However, come the 1990s, he argued that 'socialism is dead on both the level of theory and that of practice' (Giddens 1995:12) due to the fall of communism and the changing circumstances of the time. The new alternative Giddens developed was said to reflect these new conditions.

Giddens' late modern world

Giddens argues that we have entered a new stage of modernity, termed 'high' or 'late' modernity (Giddens 1990, 1991). This new stage is marked by three significant factors. Firstly, it is a 'post-traditional' order, where traditional ways of acting and thinking lose their appeal. This impacts all areas of social life for Giddens: traditional forms of identity (for example class) begin to lose their salience as depicters of lifestyle (Giddens 1991:82); traditional conceptions of gender roles within intimate relationships begin to decline (Giddens 1992); and, confronted with the emergence of climate change, we reconsider our relation to nature (Giddens 1994b:76–9). With the lessening ability of tradition to guide our actions, a post-traditional order is one in which choice and decisions are part of daily activity, where 'we have no choice but to choose how to be and how to act' (Giddens 1994b:75). Not only this, but, as suggested, such an order questions the nature of taken-for-granted identities such as 'working-class', 'woman' or 'socialist'. The result of which is that the choices we make in a post-traditional order reflect, and help constitute, the nature of our identity. For example, a trip to the supermarket may confront us with a variety of coffee to purchase. When confronted with such a choice our preference would not be shaped solely by taste but also by other factors: should we purchase fair trade coffee or rainforest alliance? Should we boycott certain companies? Should we purchase coffee from certain countries and not others? and so on. These questions will in turn be shaped by the ideas we have of ourselves: are we an 'ethical' shopper? Are we 'green'? Such choices reflect our sense of who we are and want to be. Consequently, in a post-traditional order:

> the question, 'How shall I live?' has to be answered in day-to-day decisions about how to behave, what to wear and what to eat – and many other things – as well as interpreted within the temporary unfolding of self-identity. (Giddens 1994a:14)

This then leads onto the second significant factor about late modernity: reflexivity. This operates at two levels. Firstly, we as individuals become more reflexive. As suggested above, late modernity forces us to consider our actions and the reasons for them. This is partly due to the increased knowledge we hold and what it means for our actions; to use Giddens' terms we increasingly engage with 'expert' or 'abstract' systems (Giddens 1990:83–91). For example, it is only by becoming aware, at least at a rudimentary level, of the science behind climate change that we begin to adjust our actions (for example, by using plastic bags less). Indeed, for Giddens, it is the fact we are increasingly knowledgeable, reflexive and questioning – as he puts it, we're increasingly 'clever people' (Giddens 1994a:7) – that tradition breaks down (Giddens 1994b:61–6).

This individual reflexivity then influences how we relate to each other, for example, our intimate relationships include a form of dialogical democracy where 'free and open communication' as part of a negotiation as equal partners concerning the status and future of a relationship becomes the expectation (Giddens 1992:194). All of these processes are, for Giddens, an attempt to obtain 'ontological security' which is 'the confidence that most human beings have in the continuity of their self-identity and in the constancy of the surrounding social and material environment of action' (Giddens 1990:92). Therefore, our individual reflexivity is concerned with obtaining, and maintaining, a sense of security in who we are and what we are doing.

The second form of reflexivity occurs at the macro level. Here societal institutions, such as the state, increasingly rely on obtaining, and developing, paths for action based on knowledge. An example of this for Giddens can be found in surveillance. The increased amount of surveillance practised by the state in late modernity influences what it can achieve and the actions it pursues as a result (Giddens 1991:149–50). Institutions are also influenced by the increased knowledge concerning their actions and therefore are forced to consider their social role, such as industry being aware of their role in climate change.

The post-traditional order and reflexivity then relate to the third key element of late modernity: globalization. For Giddens, modernity is an inevitably global order, containing the seed of universalism and expansion. While it began in the West its key features of the nation state and capitalist production are now truly global (Giddens 1990:174). The importance of this for our discussion is twofold. Firstly, globalization creates universal values and responsibilities. Giddens does not argue that globalization eradicates differences – reflecting his cosmopolitanism, he argues it is partly about the *awareness* of differences – but, the interdependence globalization creates leads to common concerns and interests, as in the example of climate change. Such common concerns are realised through the dialogue and discussion which are part of the post-traditional order, this time between nations. Secondly, the experience of globalization, and the differences which are part of a potential cosmopolitan order, exacerbates the decline of the traditional. This is done by opening up our awareness of different ways of acting and being; for example, we become aware of different ways of doing marriage across cultures (Giddens 1991:21). Once we become aware that our way of acting is just one possible tradition among many, its claim to prominence begins to decline.

Therefore, for Giddens, the post-traditional order, reflexivity and globalization all interact to create the conditions of late modernity. At this point we turn to the critique, what exactly is problematic about the way late modernity is currently formed?

Giddens' critique: the emergence of life politics

When turning to Giddens' critique we encounter somewhat of a problem in that he and Beck tend to share a flaw in their work. Namely, they collapse their normative claims of what should happen into empirical claims of what is happening (Ray 2007:52–4), making it sometimes difficult to identify (a) when a 'critique' is made if the current system is taken as the ideal and (b) when an actual 'alternative', as something currently not occurring, is being suggested. In Giddens' case, some writers have suggested this leaves him 'turning a blind eye' to forms of increasing inequality in favour of the 'post-scarcity order' we shall discuss below (Rustin 1995:21, Loyal 2003:162).

What follows therefore is an attempt to separate Giddens' critique and alternative (to the extent this is possible).

The conditions of late modernity give birth to what Giddens terms 'life politics'. This:

> is a politics, not of *life chances*, but of *life style*. It concerns disputes and struggles about how (as individuals and as collective humanity) we should live in a world where what used to be fixed either by nature of tradition is now subject to human decisions. (Giddens 1994a:14–15)

The factors discussed above, the environment, changing gender roles and the increase in expert knowledge at a daily level, all create political choices for the 'clever people' of late modernity. These are political choices not only as they concern questions of right and wrong, but also in the sense of determining what 'we' should do collectively as a society. An example of this for Giddens can be found in intimate relationships. Given the aforementioned change to relationships more marked by gender equality and democratic discussion, our daily negotiations have political connotations (such as the correct division of labour between men and women) which do not just impact us but have a wider significance. For instance, they change the way in which we educate children on sex and personal relationships (Giddens 1994a:154–5). Therefore, the increased political decisions and questions of everyday life, by encouraging debate and equality, enhance the possibility for democracy more broadly (Giddens 1992:195).

The increased prominence of life politics has come at the expense of 'emancipatory politics' which was concerned with 'liberating individuals and groups from constrains which adversely affect their life chances' (Giddens 1991:210). Shaped by the dominant political perspectives of modernity (liberalism, socialism and conservatism) this form of politics was concerned with questions of justice, equality and participation. Therefore they appealed to groups who needed assistance to achieve such goals (Giddens 1991:210–14). For example, as we have seen throughout this book, some theorists base their alternative around some connection of socialism and class, most notably for Marx and Engels but also to some extent for Du Bois, James and Lefebvre. As we also saw, it was the supposed breaking of the connection between these two which caused problems for Marcuse. For Giddens, such an emancipatory politics contained only a limited conception of freedom. It ensured some freedom from constraints but not, automatically, freedom to make choices of lifestyle (Giddens 1991:213). Emancipatory politics' contemporary appeal has also been greatly curtailed by its success; in ensuring greater levels of equality and justice, it has opened the path for life politics and its concern with how we make choices given this shared level of emancipation. Consequently, for Giddens, everyone engages in life politics; in an oft-cited claim, he argues that a poor, single, black mother is required to make life-political choices as much as anyone else (Giddens 1991:85–6).

It is here that we find Giddens' critique: while the nature of politics at the micro level has changed away from emancipatory politics and towards life-political choice politics at the macro level has remained largely stable, as seen in the welfare state. This was developed, and still largely rests upon, the model of the male full-time worker and therefore does not fully account for different types of working, whether this be part-time, flexible or temporary work as well as the increased inclusion of women in the labour market (Giddens 1994a:141). Furthermore, the welfare state continues to work largely along class lines. Imagining welfare recipients in a relatively unchanging position and location which conditions their life it seeks to achieve some level of equality through the redistribution of goods and wealth. This is flawed for Giddens when the cleavages of class are not so sharp and when people's life trajectories no longer match simple ideas of being 'working' or 'middle' class (Giddens 1994a:143–4). This reliance on redistribution has also helped to develop a 'culture of poverty' found in the underclass by not allowing such groups to make choices to escape their position (Giddens 1994a:148).

These problems of the welfare state have, for Giddens, been especially problematic for sociologists and politicians tied to a left-wing programme since socialism has increasingly become defined by its support for an outdated welfare state. Whereas conservatives have 'become radical' in their lessening attachment to tradition in favour of neoliberalism, socialists have 'become conservative' in their unthinking defence of the redistributive welfare state (Giddens 1994a:7). In turn, for Giddens, the welfare state is not aiding the complex negotiations and choices of life politics in late modernity, such as the increasing number of female divorcees who have to decide how to carry out the roles of 'mother' and 'woman' while negotiating the pressures of those roles, such as work and childcare (Giddens 1994a:91).

Therefore, Giddens' alternative is concerned with changing the nature of the welfare state. He developed this approach alongside the emergence of the New Labour project in the UK, led by the Prime Ministers Tony Blair (1997–2007) and Gordon Brown (2007–10) giving Giddens the self-declared honorific 'Blair's Guru' (Giddens 2000).

Giddens' alternative: generative politics in The Third Way

Giddens was one of the central figures in the development of 'The Third Way'. While sharing the name of Mannheim's alternative, this was a different approach which sought to utilise social democratic values in a globalized capitalist society. While Giddens was one of the key players in the debate, publishing a book laying out Third Way philosophy (Giddens 1998a) he was not alone. Blair published his own views (Blair 1998) as part of a wider global debate (see Giddens 2001). While politicians would claim they were inspired by, or even applying, Giddens' ideas, there were notable differences between Blair's Third Way and that of Giddens (Leggett 2005). However, it should also be noted that Giddens has downplayed such differences by claiming New Labour were broadly faithful to his work (Giddens 2004).

The Third Way defines its goal as helping citizens negotiate the changes of late modernity since 'the overall aim of third way politics should be to help citizens pilot their way through the major revolutions of our time: *globalization, transformations in personal life* and our *relationship to nature*' (Giddens 1998a:64). The major idea Giddens outlines to allow this to happen is 'positive welfare'. For Giddens, the problem with the current welfare state is that it works 'negatively' since it seeks to solve problems after they have occurred (for example by providing healthcare for people who are already sick). This was acceptable when the welfare state was dealing primarily with the structural flaws coming from class inequality and emancipatory politics; you could, for example, redistribute wealth to lessen already existing poverty (Giddens 1998a:10). However, in a life-political system, this is no longer feasible. Instead, positive welfare, 'the mobilizing of life-political measures, aimed once more at connecting autonomy with personal and collective responsibilities' (Giddens 1994a:18), is the appropriate path. Positive welfare measures are concerned with empowering people to make certain choices or to avoid certain risks. Giddens provides examples of such policies including encouraging lifestyles which lessen the risk of cancer, making cars safer, lowering speed limits to avoid road accidents, providing relationship training and therapy to avoid unnecessarily acrimonious break-ups and/or domestic violence and stigmatising smoking to remove its link with masculinity (Giddens 1994a:153–5). Also, this would allow individuals to pursue more ecologically friendly lives (Giddens 1994a:247).

These are examples of what Giddens sees as a wider change to the nature of the welfare state towards allowing life-political choices. He terms this a politics of 'second chances', where we change our identity and activity at various points across our life (Giddens 1994a:172). The possibility for such a politics is partly based upon what he terms a 'post-scarcity society'. While this is yet to come into existence, it is possible that the conditions of reflexivity and our awareness of the environmental damage of industrialisation will encourage an economy where economic growth is no longer our central concern. Rather than focusing on the 'bads' of capitalism, we should use the 'goods' of capitalism to orientate economic production towards life politics (Giddens 1994a:100–2). This requires adjusting our understanding of work; for example, rather than set a mandatory retirement age, we should create the possibilities of moving in and out of the labour market across the life course (Giddens 1994a:183–4). It also requires a different conception of equality, from a purely material focus towards the equality of 'human capital' (Diamond and Giddens 2005). All of these changes are united by intending to allow life-political choices to be made freely and a move away from a 'welfare' state to a 'social investment' state (Giddens 1998a:117).

While Giddens places a large degree of emphasis on reflexive actors mandating such changes to welfare via their engagement in life politics – the demand for 'democratizing democracy' (Giddens 1998a:71) central to contemporary social movements (Giddens 1994a:87) – The Third Way is ultimately a set of policies for a governing party. This party is seen to implicitly create the conditions for life politics rather than respond to them. This is done by embracing the idea of 'generative politics' which 'seeks to allow individuals and groups to *make things happen*' (Giddens 1994a:15). Therefore, positive welfare occurs when a Third Way party wins power and enacts generative politics. Through doing this government can develop the autonomy and trust which allows individuals to make life-political claims. For example, it would allow people to make informed consumer choices (Giddens 1994a:95) and relationship training would help develop the negotiated and equal relationships we all crave. As Giddens puts it, the goal is to allow people to take 'an active orientation to their lives' (Giddens 1998b:33). Such a party would also need to fight against social exclusion at 'the bottom' experienced by the 'underclass' (Giddens 1994a:148) as well as 'at the top'. For Giddens, a major reason for tax avoidance/evasion is the rich not feeling they are linked into the rest of the social system. This needs to be avoided by making people pay their taxes and, in return, ensuring they receive something from the welfare state (Diamond and Giddens 2005:112).

Such changes to politics occur alongside the recognition of 'cosmopolitan nations' (Giddens 1998a). Given the increasingly global links (such as immigration) and shared concerns (climate change) of nations there is a requirement to develop two factors. Firstly, we must have for Giddens a form of 'cosmopolitanism nationalism' which recognises the pluralism of multicultural societies where a national identity includes a reference to its plurality both historically and currently (Giddens 1998a:134–7). Secondly, forms of 'cosmopolitan democracy' should be established which allow for nations to not only share forms of representation but also for transnational collaboration and regulation. For Giddens the EU, and its efforts to fight climate change, is an example of such a system (Giddens 1998a:138–53; 2013).

Giddens' solution and being a public intellectual

As we have seen, Giddens' critique rests upon the idea that while life politics has become an increasingly central part of the reflexive late modern order, welfare states and political parties have not kept up with these changes. In order to overcome this Giddens argues we should engage in constructing forms of 'positive welfare' which allow for life-political claims to be made. This is part of a wider strategy of 'generative politics' which helps bring conditions which allow for life-political claims into being.

Giddens defends his alternative as based upon an idea of 'utopian realism' whereby utopian conceptions of the good society are tempered by and adjusted to what is possible in the here and now (Giddens 1990:154–8). In this sense, he claims that his alternative would solve his critique by allowing for life-political actors to make the reflexive choices which mark out a late modern society where emerging post-scarcity has moved us away from the concerns of emancipatory politics. As we have seen, there is some difficulty here in that Giddens seems to claim that generative politics requires political parties to create life politics rather than simply respond to them.

This brings us to a wider element of Giddens' alternative: his role as a public intellectual. In many ways, and as we shall discuss further in Chapter 10, all of the theorists in this book have been 'public' intellectuals in the sense that they have used public mechanisms, beyond the realm of academia, to advocate their alternative. What marks out Giddens is that his public advocacy of an alternative was so closely linked to the agenda of a particular person and party: Tony Blair and New Labour. Indeed, Giddens would fall fail of Durkheim's dictum that sociology should 'liberate us from all parties' (Durkheim 1982:161).

Giddens has tried at some points to distance himself from this association, claiming that while 'I feel close to and comfortable with the framework of policy of the Blair government. I'm an intellectual rather than a politician' (Giddens et al. 2001:256). However, as we have seen he also defends the legacy of New Labour as inspired by his Third Way (Giddens 2004) and wrote books with titles such as *Where Now for New Labour?* (Giddens 2002) and *Over to You, Mr. Brown: How Labour Can Win Again* (Giddens 2007a). Perhaps most significantly, he now sits in the House of Lords as a Labour peer meaning that he is indeed a Labour politician. This fundamentally changes his orientation and mode of writing; to use the terms of Lefebvre, Giddens stops being a 'statesman' who seeks to understand and critique the nature of political institutions in order to institute social change and becomes a 'man of the state', who accepts and defends the reality of what already exists in order to reform it (Lefebvre 1964b:54–6). Or, as Bourdieu more caustically put it, Giddens becomes the 'globe-trotting apostle of The Third Way' who allows 'The masters of the economy' to 'sleep in peace: they have found their Pangloss' (Bourdieu and Wacquant 2001:5). He identifies Giddens and Beck as disciples to 'the intellectually degraded and vulgarised version of the thinking – already vulgar' found in politicians such as Blair (Bourdieu 2008:385).

While not as dismissive as Bourdieu, others have argued that publication of *The Third Way* was the beginning of the end for Giddens' time as a critical sociologist. Instead he becomes a 'policy entrepreneur' (Castree 2010) – or a 'sociologist without sociology' (Garrett 2008:241) – seeking to find influence and an audience in the changing circumstances at the end of the New Labour project. As some have argued this requires him to change his focus, for example, by supporting much of the neoliberalism he previously dismissed (Giddens 1994a). This includes advocating the right of universities in the UK to charge their students unlimited tuition fees or for introducing charges into the National Health Service (Giddens 2007a:82, 84; Garrett 2008). Furthermore, in these writings, and his later work on climate change and the EU, Giddens doesn't maintain any conception of life politics and instead favours a 'technocratic mode of simple rather than reflexive modernization' (Thorpe and Jacobsen 2013:99). While, as indicated above, some sociologists have emphasised state action to tackle climate change, the difference with Giddens' later work is that the political movements, such as the Green movement, are not considered part of this.

Giddens has defended himself against such charges, arguing that being 'an intellectual in politics' ultimately means you will be attacked from both sides. Nevertheless, communicating academic ideas to a wider audience is important enough to overcome such criticisms (Giddens 2007b). This indicates an important component of sociological alternatives. Resting as they do on a critique, being in the position of Giddens – being part of the ruling institutions of society – makes such critique more challenging, as we saw from Dorothy Smith in Chapter 1. Indeed, it can lead you to claim that Muammar Gaddafi was a leader who could create a 'Norway of North Africa' and who presided over a state which was 'not especially repressive' (Giddens 2007c). Furthermore, seeking to obtain influence with a political party may go hand in hand with overlooking some things about that party with which one disagrees. Such tensions led Edward Said to recommend:

> keep reminding yourself that as an intellectual you are the one who can choose between actively representing the truth to the best of your ability and passively allowing a patron or an authority to direct you. For the secular intellectual, *those* gods always fail. (Said 1994:121)

We will now turn to Ulrich Beck who, while having some links to government in Germany, maintained his position as an intellectual much more securely than Giddens.

Ulrich Beck

Beck was born in 1944 in the town of Stolp in Germany (now Słupsk in Poland). He initially enrolled to study law and philosophy in Frieburg but ended up in Munich studying sociology, where he would spend much of his professional life. While Beck began his career writing on the sociologies of work, knowledge and the Frankfurt School he became 'simply sociologically famous' (Sørenson and Christiansen 2013:xix), with the publication of his *Risk Society: Towards a New Modernity* in 1986. From here his work began to move into areas such as climate change, politics and, increasingly, globalization. It was this that led Beck into a wider project concerning cosmopolitanism. As we shall see, this had two goals: firstly the empirical one of seeking to understand the nature of an increasingly cosmopolitan world and secondly, attempting to create the cosmopolitan sociology which Beck saw as lacking. The second of these concerns kept Beck, unlike Giddens, much more based within academia and the circles of sociology. However, he did engage in some public activities. For instance, he served on the review group which put an end to Germany's policy of building nuclear power stations and was part of the Spinelli group, a collection of politicians and academics who campaign for a federalised European state. Beck died unexpectedly in January 2015 of a heart attack.

When asked about the links between his work and that of Beck, Giddens replied, 'I've become so close to Ulrich Beck over the past few years that I can no longer easily disentangle which ideas are his and which mine' (Giddens et al. 2001:247). While this can downplay the differences between the two, as we shall see, they do share a common concern with the emergence of late, or in Beck's terms, 'second' modernity.

Beck's second modern risk society

Beck, like Giddens, believes we have entered a new stage of modernity, which is marked by a process of 'reflexive modernization' (Beck et al. 1994). This involves 'a *radicalisation* of modernity which *breaks up* the premises and contours of industrial society and opens paths to new modernities or counter-modernities' (Beck 1997:17). As this indicates, modernity becomes reflexive in the sense that it begins to question its basic premises, achievements and goals. We become aware of the successes of modernity, but also with the unintended consequences and side effects of those successes. As with Giddens, climate change is a key example here. On the one hand this is a marker of the successes of modernity – industrialisation has expanded and increased the standard of living for many around the world – but, on the other hand, this had the unintended consequence of warming the planet and potentially causing drastic environmental damage (Beck 1995).

This is where we encounter Beck's most famous concept: the risk society. For Beck, this concept is not meant to say that society is now more risky; instead we now become more concerned with identifying and calculating risk, thereby hoping to avoid the catastrophes which would occur if a risk was not identified and stopped (Beck 1992). There are three reasons why this happens. Firstly, as we have seen, we become aware of the unintended consequences of modern advances, whether this is climate change (Beck 1992:74), the nuclear fallout at Chernobyl (Beck 2006b:341) or forms of international terrorism, such as the events of 9/11 (Beck 2002). Such occurrences for Beck mean that risk calculation has become one of the key elements of reflexive modernisation (Beck 1992:22). Secondly, as the above examples indicate, such risks are global and through their impacts 'undermine the borders of nation states' (Beck 1992:47). This fundamentally changes the international order of nations who are forced to interact and collaborate since 'no nation can cope with its problems alone' (Beck 2006b:342). Finally, for Beck risks are 'social constructions based upon corresponding relations of definition' (Beck 2009:30), meaning they are defined by what we socially consider important. Therefore, like wealth, risks are distributed throughout society with different groups encountering different risks/impacts of risks (Beck 1992:19). However, unlike wealth, they are something we all inevitably confront in some form since risks come to be ascribed with citizenship and cannot be avoided. As Beck famously put it, 'poverty is hierarchic, smog is democratic' (Beck 1992:36). In a 'class society', only some are impacted by its negative elements, such as poverty; in a 'risk society', all are impacted by risk; climate change will not stop at the borders of rich nations or the houses of the wealthy.

Such changes alter the nature of contemporary societies and political formations. The failure of science to predict these side effects and its contradictory messages – is this food 'good' or 'bad' for you? – means that for Beck we come to be distrusting of its findings and consequently 'there is no expert on risk' (Beck 1992:29). Furthermore, since risks don't impact identifiable groups in the same way as class inequalities we no longer have protests where a group claims 'we're angry' but instead have lots of claims that 'I'm afraid' (Beck 1992:43); for instance different groups come together to protest against climate change. These individualized forms of political protest exacerbate another key part of second modernity: individualization.

For Beck and Beck-Gernsheim (2002:203) individualization occurs 'when the individual is removed from traditional commitments and support'. Like Giddens, and for broadly the same reasons, they believe we are living in a posttraditional order. This order shapes individualization since:

> On the one hand, individualization means the disintegration of previously existing social forms – for example, the increasing fragility of such categories as class and social status, gender roles, family, neighbourhood etc. ... [On the other hand] in modern societies new demands, controls and constraints are being imposed on individuals. (Beck and Beck-Gernsheim, 2002:2)

The traditional categories which described inequalities, most notably class, come to be 'zombie categories', alive within sociology but empirically dead. This is especially the case when inequalities operate at a transnational level. For example, it is more accurate to speak of 'European inequalities' between and within nations rather than classes within each country (Beck 2005a).

Individualization has also been exacerbated by the 'institutionalised individualism' of modernity whereby 'basic civil, political and social rights ... are geared to the individual and not to the group' (Beck and Beck-Gernsheim 2002:xxi–ii). Consequently, individualization is another instance of the unintended consequences of modern institutions, such as the welfare state which made us all individuals with rights. At the same time, individuals also encounter the increased choice and responsibilities which Giddens spoke of in a posttraditional order.

This has occurred alongside a change in the form of work. First modernity saw a 'work society' as the ideal, in the sense that not only did it claim to guarantee full employment (even if it did not deliver) but also saw work as a central part of identity and integration (Beck 2000b:10–16). This is no longer the case when work is more likely to take place on insecure and part-time contracts. Beck terms such a change the 'Brazilisation of the West': the system of 'nomadic multi-activity' where 'people are travelling vendors, small retailers or craftworkers, offer all kinds of personal service, or shuttle back and forth between different fields of activity' found in developing nations such as Brazil and now spreading to 'developed' nations (Beck 2000b:1–2). This has been encouraged by the changing gender regimes of work away from the male-only form of work society towards the mixed employment of risk society.

This brings us to the nature of society as cosmopolitan for Beck. As we have seen, cosmopolitanism is ultimately a way of viewing the world which Beck terms 'the recognition of difference, both internally and externally' (Beck 2006a:57). As we also saw, this is often conceived as a goal to be achieved and here Beck both agrees and disagrees with such a definition. His claim is that 'we do not live in an age of cosmopolitanism but in an age of cosmopolitanization' (Beck and Grande 2010:417). There are certain factors, which I will outline below, which mean that we have achieved a state of 'banal cosmopolitanism' whereby, at the everyday level, 'the differentiations between us and them are becoming confused, both at the national and at international level' (Beck 2006a:10). Not only have the boundaries separating people of different nations become less sharp but, for Beck, we have become aware of this, leading to lessening xenophobia (Beck 1997:75) and, in the most radical reading, meaning there is 'no other any more' (Beck 2012a:9).

We have already seen some of the factors which create this banal cosmopolitanism for Beck, such as climate change, global terrorism, nuclear fallout and transnational inequalities. There are others including 'world families' where the members of the family come from different regions of the globe and often live apart (Beck and Beck-Gernsheim 2014); the 'place polygamy' created when members of such families have multiple homes and relatives in different countries (Beck 2000a:72–7); awareness of global diseases, potential or not, such as the BSE (so-called 'Mad Cow disease') crisis over tainted beef (Beck 2006b); transnational political groupings such as the World Bank and NATO (Beck 2006a:85–7) and, of course, global capitalism. Though we may be critical of the operating of global capitalism each nation is required to bend to its demands since 'there is only one thing worse than being overrun by big multinationals: not being overrun by multinationals' (Beck 2005b:150).

Therefore, as we have seen, second modernity for Beck is a society with many new challenges and formations. These include the expansion of risk calculation due to reflexive modernisation, individualization and its role in limiting the importance of 'traditional' inequalities which are reduced to 'zombie categories'; changing forms of work; and an emerging 'banal cosmopolitanism'. We have also seen that resting behind all of these factors is a conception of a global society which allows them to occur. It should be noted that to this point we have not encountered Beck's critique. All of the above are empirical descriptions of changes that have happened. In what follows, we shall see this critique.

Summary

Beck's critique: methodological nationalist sociology and society

Somewhat uniquely for the writers considered in this book, Beck's critique is as much a critique of sociology as of what is happening in society. However, as we shall see, for Beck, sociology is a case, albeit an especially egregious one, of problematic trends found in second modernity.

In short, sociology has not kept up with the changes in contemporary society and has maintained a 'methodological nationalist' position (a term coined by Hermínio Martins; see Chernilo 2006). This perspective:

> equates society with nation-state societies, and sees states and their governments as the cornerstones of a social sciences analysis. It assumes that humanity is naturally divided into a limited number of nations, which on the inside, organize themselves as nation-states, and on the outside, set boundaries to distinguish themselves from other nation-states … Indeed, the social science stance is rooted in the concept of the nation-state. It is a nation-state outlook on society and politics, law, justice and history, that governs the sociological imagination. And it is exactly this methodological nationalism that prevents the social science from getting at the heart of the dynamics of modernization and globalization. (Beck 2007:287)

For Beck, this use of methodological nationalism also relies upon what he terms a 'container theory of society' whereby sociology 'aligns itself with the regulatory authority or power of the nation state' (Beck 2000a:23). So part of Beck's critique would be that many of the alternatives discussed thus far – such as those from Mannheim, Durkheim and James – utilise a container model of society by seeing their alternative as enacted by a nation-state. Such an assumption, for Beck, rests upon the idea that the nation state has complete control over what happens within that territory. Beck terms this a 'clinical loss of reality' (Beck 2006a:25) and argues sociology has maintained a focus on social stability at the expense of social change – or, as he prefers, social 'metamorphosis' (Beck 2015) – in an era of globalization.

We have seen above some of the factors Beck believes sociology fails to account for due to its methodological nationalism (such as global families, climate change and terrorism). This also returns us to class. For him, 'classes' only makes sense in a national context (such as the 'English' working class or the 'French' bourgeoisie). A cosmopolitan perspective finds this problematic in two ways. Firstly, class tends to emphasise the 'small inequalities' found between people of the same nationality at the expense of the 'large inequalities' between nations (Beck 2005c:339). This is especially problematic when these large inequalities may be played out in the same nation, for example, by the migration of poor workers to rich nations (Beck and Levy 2013:15). This also makes any cross-national comparison of countries difficult in light of the fact that they may have different forms of inequality (Beck 2005c:341). The second cosmopolitan critique of such a perspective for Beck is that it helps legitimise such global inequalities by seeing them as beyond the reach and relevance of particular nations (Beck 2013a). By defining inequality nationally it means:

> these 'external' effects find expression in a pre-determined unreality, that is, electoral irrelevance. By talking about social inequalities exclusively as 'home grown' inequalities, it becomes possible to pursue a global politics of redistribution in which the risks are externalised and passed on to weaker Third World countries, while any benefits are maximised within the national context. (Beck 2005c:342)

Therefore, the national outlook found in sociology is partly a reflection of a wider national outlook found outside the discipline. While banal cosmopolitanism has expanded we have not fully adjusted our views and expectations meaning that, at the everyday level, we tend to maintain a national outlook, especially when it comes to solving social problems. This is best found in the continuation of the 'nation-state principle', in which the people of the world are divided into, and governed by, national governments. Such a principle – much like the methodological nationalism of sociology – 'legitimises global inequality' (Beck 2010a:167). National interest comes to be seen as most important and global forms of inequality are marginalised. Furthermore, such a national outlook, linked to the welfare state, has helped to maintain an outdated model of the work society (Beck 2000b).

Instead of such a perspective Beck advocates a 'critical theory with cosmopolitan intent':

> This is a new variant of critical theory, which does not set the normative horizon itself but takes it from empirical analyses. Hence, it is an empirical analysis of the normative horizon of the self-critical world risk society. (Beck 2015:83)

For Beck, the goal of such a cosmopolitan sociology is to open up new ideas of the path we should follow based upon an assessment of our emerging cosmopolitanism. It seeks to replace the 'methodological nationalism' of sociology and society with a 'methodological cosmopolitanism' in which we become aware of, and further develop, cosmopolitanisation. This is Beck's alternative to which we now turn.

Beck's alternative: a cosmopolitan world

Beck, like Giddens, has often been accused of taking his normative visions of what should happen as empirical description of what is happening. He has been accused of engaging in 'rhetorical special pleading' by presenting cosmopolitanism as an empirical inevitability (Holton 2009:82). Such a tendency is exacerbated by, as we have already seen, Beck's claim that those who deny cosmopolitanism experience a 'clinical loss of reality' (Beck 2006a:26, 117).

However, also like Giddens, it is possible to identify some gap between empirical description and normative claims if you look closely enough. These centre around the desire to develop methodological cosmopolitanism which involves the awareness and recognition of the shared global nature of contemporary society and its problems. Beck terms this a 'compulsory re-education programme in openness to the world' (Beck 2006a:102) which has four components: the end of the nation-state principle, cosmopolitan states, a 'Green Modernity' and civil labour. I will discuss these in turn.

As we saw, for Beck the nation-state principle was responsible for legitimising global inequalities. Therefore, the adoption of a cosmopolitan perspective is central for Beck. While, as we shall see below, the institutions of governments should be changed this is also a process which occurs from the bottom-up. 'Sub-politics' is the name Beck gives to something akin to Giddens' life politics but much more focused on movements rather than individuals. When these movements respond to everyday issues (the placing of a nuclear plant, the wages of workers), they also respond to global concerns (fears of nuclear fallout, the global division of labour) and therefore, by forcing governments to answer their concerns, encourage a cosmopolitan view (Beck 1997:97–109). Such movements were central to governmental action over climate change (Beck 1995). Therefore, such sub-political action should continue and expand for Beck; this is especially the case in Europe where the European Union requires a collection of movements forming a 'Europe from below' which proclaims the shared interests of European citizens (Beck 2013b:83–6).

This then brings us to the second part of Beck's alternative: cosmopolitan states. The end of the nation-state principle will require the end of the nation-state as the primary mode of governance in society. Nation-states remain but these must become part of 'cosmopolitan states' who are, and conceive themselves as, part of a global order (Beck and Levy 2013). The European Union (EU) is in many ways a model of the cosmopolitan state Beck favours, developing via shared concerns and identity as European. While this involves recognition of European diversity it also requires some taming of such diversity to achieve union (Beck 2005a:156). In doing so, for Beck, as a condition of entry to the EU democracy and human rights are placed 'above autocracy and nationalism' and the cosmopolitan order affirmed (Beck 2005a:156).

The problem is that the EU has increasingly become a 'European Empire', or a 'German Europe', under the control of a particular group of politicians and bureaucrats (Beck 2013b). Therefore, Beck argues we need to develop the 'Europe of citizens' by instituting mechanisms which allow its citizens to engage in Europe from below (Beck 2012b:111–18). These include a European constitution (Beck and Grande 2007:228), Europe-wide referenda and elections (Beck and Grande 2007:235), something akin to the Peace Corps where the EU funds the civic activity of the unemployed youth of the continent (Beck 2012b:118) and a 'European year' which would fund everyone to spend a year living in another European nation (Beck 2013b:76–7). These changes from below would then be combined with a greater use of 'cosmopolitan realpolitik' whereby the nations of Europe engage in the EU on the basis that it is in their individual interest to do so (Beck 2007). For example, it is in the interest of each nation to engage in finding a collective solution to climate change. This, for Beck, creates the optimistic potential within a cosmopolitan order. While it would be easy to see the global challenges of the era as impossible to overcome, the fact they make combined action in everyone's interest is 'cause for hope' (Beck and Grande 2010:433).

As indicated above, this ending of the nation-state principle and embracing of cosmopolitan realpolitik is central to the third part of Beck's alternative; the development of a 'Green Modernity' (Beck 2010b). As we have seen, for Beck, climate change is caused via the successes of simple modernity, which reflexive modernisation comes to accept. Beck encourages the full realisation of this responsibility via a move away from 'consumer and voter-friendly' policies towards ones which encourage a 'political paradigm shift' (Beck 2008:80). Whereas a simple modern logic would conceive of the awareness of climate change imposing 'limits' on activity, a 'Green Modernity' realises the new potential ways of life opened by a methodological cosmopolitanism aware of climate change (Beck 2009:205). To achieve this Beck advocates two paths of action. Firstly, while sub-politics has been successful in making climate change a 'political' issue, Beck argues this should go further; for him there should be a 'storming of the Bastile … [or] Red October of ecology' (Beck 2010:254). The European year mentioned above, and civil labour discussed below, would be important ways of encouraging people to engage in further environmental activism at a transnational level. The second policy is the 'reinvention' of how we conceive of evolution (Beck 2010b). Here Beck is somewhat vague on the content of such an idea. However, he seems to echo the writings of some 'degrowth' advocates who suggest a move away from an economy and society which measures progress in terms of economic growth and towards measurements which include environmental health. For Jackson (2009:173–84) such a system would include caps on emissions, taxes on environmental damaging actions, investment in ecologically friendly development and infrastructure, lessening the time individuals spend working, 'eco-villages' and lessening encouragement to consume. While Beck doesn't outline such a detailed list, this seems to chime with his depiction of the Green Modernity as a 'greening of societies' where actors work together through a 'cosmopolitan solidarity across boundaries' (Beck 2010b:255). However, Beck does not seem to agree with some of the more radical degrowth advocates, such as the economist Serge Latouche who seeks to 'relocalise' communities, revitalise peasant agriculture, impose financial penalties on advertising (which, as discussed in the previous chapter, is seen to encourage the wastefulness of capitalism) and declare a moratorium on technological innovation (Latouche 2009:68–72). As we have seen, some of these actions would go against Beck's methodological cosmopolitan goals.

This optimistic reading of action across borders and the 'Europe from below' also feed into the fourth part of Beck's alternative which concerns work. As we have seen, Beck argues the era of full work has ended and been replaced with flexible work in which we change our professions and working conditions on a regular basis. This, in and of itself, is not negative; what is negative is that it has been enforced and not chosen. Instead, what we should do is to make this a choice since:

> Only if the insecure new forms of paid employment are converted into a right to multiple work, a right to discontinuity, a right to choose working hours, a right to sovereignty over working time enshrined in collective-bargaining agreements – only then can new free spaces be secured in the coordination of work, life and political activity. Every person would thus be enabled to plan his or her own life over a period of one or more years, in its transitions between family, paid employment, leisure and political involvement, and to harmonize this with the claims and demands of others. (Beck 2000b:7)

Therefore, we should choose how we work and when we do and do not work. The periods in which we are not working are when we can engage in 'civil labour', which would include the European year but would also include volunteering work for civic and political causes, such as climate change. In return for this civil labour we would receive 'civil money' which includes free access to services and/or a say in running them (Beck 2000b:121–49). This system for Beck would further the potential for a Europe from below by giving people the time and resources to engage in European civil society (Beck 2000c). Beck also argues that offers of new jobs, especially when these involve moving home, should come with the expectation that the spouse be offered a job as well. This ensures the possibility for the mobility of global families within the nuclear family format, which Beck and Beck-Gernsheim see as somewhat inevitable as well as ecologically friendly (Beck and Beck-Gernsheim 1995:163–7). Therefore, the expectations regarding work should be changed to achieve three things: allow flexibility to be a choice, ensure people have the time for the civic activity required for a European from below and lessen the pressures on global families.

Does Beck's alternative solve his critique? If we accept his claim that we have a form of banal cosmopolitanism and that we need to adopt a methodological cosmopolitanism to match this then his alternative does four things. Firstly, by ending the nation-state principle it changes the way we view the world and our relation to others and their problems (for example, no longer do we consider inequality at the national, but rather at the global, level). Secondly, by strengthening the EU we achieve a working model of a cosmopolitan state, both at the macro level (through cosmopolitan realpolitik) and the micro level (through Europe from below). Thirdly, the development of a Green Modernity means we reorientate our actions and societies towards environmental protection. Finally, the changes to work ensure that the flexibility of second modern work regimes is a choice and means we have the time to engage in the activities of Europe from below while maintaining our global families. Of course, it is not clear to what extent this is a European solution; if cosmopolitanism is truly global, how does the rest of the world get included? Beck's solution seems to be effectively an expansion of bodies like the EU (for example, the African Union should more fully fit this model) alongside the further expansion and consolidation of bodies such as the United Nations to help build the 'global republic' (Beck 2006a:160). Therefore, the cosmopolitan world is made up of cosmopolitan nations who, engaging in cosmopolitan realpolitik, realise their need to coop- erate with regional partners in bodies like the EU while at the global level institutions such as the UN ensure that global standards of human rights law are followed. Contrary to today, these bodies have more power and democratic legitimacy from below. This ensures, for Beck, that the globalized world has a cosmopolitan regime to match it.

Conclusion: the alternatives of Giddens and Beck

As we have seen, Giddens and Beck are united in seeing the changes of a glo- balized world as requiring a different perspective from sociologists and society and, therefore, different alternatives. For both, such alternatives emerge from, and hope to develop, the incipient or 'banal' cosmopolitanism of late modern society. In doing so, they draw upon ideas of a post-traditional order and the need to move beyond traditional political ways of solving issues whether this be the traditional welfare state or methodological nationalism. Instead, both favour an alternative which allows groups to make active choices (through positive welfare or civic labour) and increases the forms of global govern- ments by developing cosmopolitan states, of which they see the EU as a shining example. In doing so, both see potential for more ecological societies through either state action (Giddens) or the development of a broader 'Green Moder- nity' (Beck).

Despite such similarities, there is one contradiction between their alternatives which means they are not entirely compatible. As we have seen, Giddens main- tains a largely national focus for his alternative. His concern is primarily the welfare state of Britain; this, as we saw, was somewhat encouraged to his con- nection to a political party fighting for national power and then his elevation to the national legislator. Nevertheless, he does see such 'cosmopolitan nations' as responding to the demands of globalization and helping bring cosmopolitan- ism into being. Beck, however, largely rejects the possibility of any alternative at just a national level. While he does not see nation states dying out, he does see them as subsumed into, and castrated by, the new cosmopolitan regime. The potential to think in such a way is perhaps enhanced by the relative lack of con- nection Beck had to mechanisms of government. In Chapter 5 we introduced the distinction of legislator and interpreter; the case of Giddens and Beck shows there are different types of legislator. Some, like Beck, seek to legislate outside parties/forms of government while others, such as Giddens, seek a strong link to a political party. This helps shape their alternative.

However, there is a further common element of both, which is that it is some-times hard to see the line between their empirical description (life politics/cos-mopolitanisation is happening) and their alternative (we need to allow for life politics/create cosmopolitanism). Instead, their claims are often for more of what is already happening: more positive welfare, more Europe. As one of the writers we will consider in the next chapter argues, the positions of Giddens and Beck 'do not move nearly far enough from a pro-capitalist ideological posi-tion. They are too cautious, insufficiently utopian' (Levitas 2000b:198). So let us turn to what it means to be utopian.

Sociology and Utopia

> I wish to defend that 'unrealistic', 'irrational', 'naïve', 'self-indulgent', 'unscientific', 'escapist', 'élitist', activity known as utopianism.
>
> (Geoghegan 1987:1)

The above in many ways reflects the attitude of sociology, as well as society more broadly, to utopia. Indeed, the term 'utopian' has increasingly become an insult, used to dismiss schemes which seem fanciful and/or dangerous. Utopians, it is argued, are those seeking to implement their vision of a perfect society. Not only is such a 'perfect' society impossible but any attempt to implement it will inevitably mean un-enticing side effects (such as the removal of those who don't fit within the utopia).

Why would sociology want any part of this? Not only do such schemes seem dangerous, but they are also fanciful. As we saw in Chapter 2, for Marx and Engels, utopians are to be dismissed due to their reliance on 'the individual man of genius' who somehow has unique insight into the needs of humanity. Instead, Marx and Engels favoured their 'scientific' approach, namely the careful study of what actually does exist, and the potential for alternatives within this. Following this, it could also be argued the use of utopianism directs attention away from what I have presented in this book as the first step of sociological alternatives: a critique of society as it is. Marx and Engels have not been alone in their dismissal of utopianism; as we also saw, Mead was critical of the utopian urges of socialist and Giddens argues utopianism is useless without the realism to make alternatives plausible.

This chapter will suggest these claims rely upon a limited definition of both utopia and sociology. For now, the literal definition of utopia as 'the good place which is no place', the good society which doesn't exist, is a useful guide. As we shall see, once you broaden the definition of utopianism, it is something sociology has always done, continues to do and, it could be said, will inevitably do.

The two theorists to be discussed here are Ruth Levitas and Erik Olin Wright who approach utopianism in slightly different ways. Whereas Levitas sees it as a method of sociological analysis, Wright tries to extract utopian potentials from existing social practices. However, both are united in the idea that being utopianism is a central part of social theory. Therefore, this chapter, and the one which follows, moves away from the focus of Chapters 2–8 since, rather than applying the threefold definition on sociological alternatives, the focus here is on *how* sociologists can offer alternatives. While, as we shall see, both

Levitas and Wright do offer some elements of an alternative – I will discuss the basic income as a key element of this – this discussion of utopianism primarily concerns the question of how sociologists offer alternatives. In doing so, I will refer back to the alternatives outlined thus far.

The history of sociology and utopianism

Utopian writing has a long history, occurring primarily in literature as well as political philosophy (see Kumar 1991). For our purpose, there are two ways in which sociology can discuss utopia. The first is as a topic, which involves looking at the conditions which lead to the production of utopias, their changing form and social function. The second is the value of a utopian perspective to sociology and its offering of alternatives. Both can be found in the history of the discipline.

While Marx and Engels were dismissive of the role of utopianism to social theory, other writers were less critical; a good example of this is H.G. Wells. Primarily thought of as a novelist Wells was actively involved in the circles of early British sociology and, for a short period at least, thought of himself as a sociologist. Indeed, he was one of the candidates for the first professorship in sociology in the UK: the Martin White chair at the LSE eventually given to L.T. Hobhouse in 1907 (Levitas 2010). Wells' lasting contribution to sociology comes in the form of a paper entitled 'The So-Called Science of Sociology' (Wells 1907) in which he condemns the 'scientific pretensions' of the discipline and argues that 'there is no such thing in sociology as dispassionately considering what *is*, without considering what is *intended to be*' (Wells 1907:366–7). To study social institutions, whether it is the state, capitalism, the family and so on, is inevitably to discuss their overall purpose and goal, akin to how Durkheim defined the study of normal and pathological social facts. For Wells, societies form based upon a 'Social Ideal' or image of what we hope to achieve; it is impossible for sociology not to pass some form of judgement on both the ideal and the institutions it shapes. If sociologists do not form such judgements then, as Wells (1907:368) puts it, 'their very silences shape utopia' by not questioning, and thereby accepting, the ideal of what exists. Therefore, Wells advocates a sociology committed to the creation and 'exhaustive criticism' of utopias, culminating in a master text which contains the utopian visions of others, critiqued and enhanced by the tools of sociology (Wells 1907:368).

Wells didn't get his professorship and his vision of utopian sociology was sidelined in favour of the more scientific and value-free forms discussed in Chapter 1. Consequently, sociological attention turned towards discussing utopias purely as a topic even from those offering alternatives. The most prominent example of this came from Mannheim, who contrasted utopias, as ideas which challenged the status quo and lead to social change, with ideologies which uphold it (Mannheim 1936). This moved the focus of utopia away from sociology to outside the discipline; social movements, novels and ideas are utopian, sociologists are not. Indeed, in Mannheim's discussions of his own alternative of planned democracy, which seemingly if it were adopted would become a utopia, he is dismissive of 'utopian' ideas (Mannheim 1951:77).

Later, Bauman (1976b) spoke of socialism as an 'active utopia'. For Bauman, any capitalist society will inevitably contain a socialist critique as its opposite. This is a utopia since it presents an idea of the good society which does not yet exist; it is an 'active' utopia since, by existing, it encourages the critique of capitalism. As soon as socialism exists, as in the USSR, it gives up its utopian form since this must 'remain in the realm of the possible' (Bauman 1976:112). A similar view is expressed in Ernest Bloch's classic three-volume text *The Principle of Hope* (1986). Here Bloch defends the idea of utopianism as an inevitable part of human everyday activity. We will, as part of our experience in the world, conjure up images of the good life/society; these utopian images then impact our engagement with the world. Even an image of what our weekend will look like, as an image of the good life and the conditions which allow it to occur, is constructed to guide our action and is our own utopia. For Bloch, such utopias indicate the 'not yet' element of human culture, that society is always an unfinished project in which utopian visions guide our activity.

For Levitas this shift in how sociologists discussed utopia is a notable trend:

> Sociology is comfortable with utopia only as an element in the social imaginary that is the object of explanation. It repeatedly approaches utopia and retreats from it. And yet the impulse towards social transformation, there at the origin of the discipline, does not go away. The warm stream runs underground … the parallels between sociology and utopia (in Wells's sense) would lead us to expect this. For the excitement and promise of sociology lies in this presence; the disappointment lies in its recurrent repression and denial. (Levitas 2013:101–2)

Here Levitas highlights a theme we have seen throughout the book; social transformation, the offering of alternatives, has remained part of the discipline. Yet, despite this, utopianism has often been rejected as for Marx and Engels, Mead, Mannheim and Giddens. For Levitas, such a dismissal is a mistake.

Ruth Levitas: utopia as the imaginary reconstruction of society

Levitas has perhaps been most influential in sociology for her work on poverty and the discourses around social exclusion (Levitas 2005b). However, she has, throughout her career, conducted research into utopianism, reflected in her long-term involvement with both the utopian studies and William Morris societies. To understand Levitas' engagement we have to begin with her definition of utopianism as 'the expression of the desire for a better way of being or of living' (Levitas 2013:xii). Influenced by Bloch, not only does this make utopias, as these ideas of better ways of being/living, an inevitable part of human practice, but also moves the focus away from utopias as blueprints of alternative worlds and towards them as concerning the process of building a new world. Consequently, for Levitas, utopias have three functions: compensation, critique and change (Levitas 2000a:28). While utopias, as in Mannheim's work, have too often been seen as fundamentally oppositional and ascribed to 'the agents of terror' (Levitas 2007:299) they can in fact be used to justify what already exists. A conception of the good society may act as 'compensation' for the status quo, including its inequalities. A good example of this can be found in the concept of 'meritocracy'. For Levitas, this concept is fundamentally utopian; it suggests a world where social position and advantage is purely due to individual merit and work, a goal towards which we currently move. However, the idea we all desire and are working towards a meritocracy is used to justify 'the position of winners in an unequal society' by presenting success as a result of individual merit and thereby excluding critique (Levitas 2001:459); the presence of the utopian ideal creates the justification for contemporary 'meritocratic' inequalities (see Saunders 1995 for such a justification). It is perhaps unsurprising that the term 'meritocracy' was actually first used by a sociologist, Michael Young, in a book which portrayed a truly meritocratic society as dystopian (Young 1961).

While, as we will see, Levitas sees utopianism as compensation for neoliberalism, it is the other two functions, critique and change, which are especially important to the relation of sociology and utopia. Given Levitas' definition of utopianism as the longing for a better way of being or of living it is clear that, much like the sociological alternatives discussed in this book, this must start with some form of critique. This is why literary utopias inevitably make use of some form of sociological analysis (Levitas 2013:74). Levitas terms this the need for utopias to begin by 'looking for the blue': the offering of a critique. The colour blue has, historically, been associated with notions of possibility, hope and spiritual uplift, most notably in music, as in the hopes of 'the blues' (Levitas 2007). The next step from here is 'looking for the green', developing ideas of what a better society based upon this critique would be. It is here that utopias make use of what Levitas terms the Imaginary Reconstruction of Society (IROS). To be utopian is to engage in some sort of exercise where society is reimagined and a better form put in its place. An example of this can be found in William Morris' classic utopian novel, *News from Nowhere* (Morris 2004). Here Morris imagines a new socialist England in which the use of machinery is reduced, work becomes a pleasure, art and beauty are a key concern of production and participatory democracy is the governing system. Not only was Morris making use of Marxist arguments about the impacts of capitalism and the alienation of work in this text but was also critiquing the changes in the environment, and poverty, around him (Levitas 2005c).

There are two important points to note from Levitas' definition of utopia. Firstly, like other writers on utopianism (Sargisson 2012), for Levitas this does not imply a 'perfect' and 'final' state. Utopia is instead a process, driven by working towards an alternative – which, although not perfect, is better – rather than having it realised in totality. The idea of utopias as perfect is another way of dismissing the exercise as redundant and potentially dangerous. Much utopian writing in fact recognises the contradictions and problems of an alternative state which, in the round, is still better than current society. An example of this can be found in contemporary feminist utopias which often highlight the contradictions involved in developing a more gender-equal society (Sargisson 1996). Indeed, for Sargisson, 'Utopias will always fail … They need to. They are no places' (Sargisson 2012:39). But it is this 'failure', the fact that they may not be realised in total despite their desirability, which demonstrates the limitations and problems of our current society and mode of thinking (Levitas 2013:201). If we cannot have this then what is the obstacle in the way of doing so? Should we seek to overcome it? The second important factor about Levitas' conception of utopianism is its totality; to engage in utopianism is to think about, and reconstruct, society as a whole. We shall see how Levitas imagines this in the following section.

Sociology as utopia and utopia as sociology

Utopias are inevitably shaped by the social context in which they are expressed, to imagine a utopian state relies on being able to conceive of an alternative and envisioning how it may be plausible. For Levitas (1979), this inevitably creates two forms of utopias. In times when individuals have the hope of being able to influence society, and are open to alternatives – for example in democracies with high levels of party membership and political groups such as trade unions – utopias may be quite practical, based upon actions which can be performed in the here and now. However, in times when achieving such change seems more difficult or even impossible – such as in life under a dictatorship or at times of hardship – then utopias are more likely to occur elsewhere and have come about via the intervention of an outside force, such as God. Therefore, for Levitas, each social epoch will not lack utopias but may lack hope that such utopias are plausible.

It is the latter condition which we find ourselves in for Levitas. The increased dominance of capitalism around the globe and the supposed 'end of history' (Fukuyama 1992) means that capitalism is increasingly taken as inevitable. Its current neoliberal form comes to be justified since 'there is no alternative' (Bauman 2007b). This means that utopias which suggest an alternative social form are seen to match the definition of 'fanciful' and 'dangerous' (Levitas 2000a). Consequently, utopias take another form; they increasingly become individualized, reflecting quests for individual happiness or interests rather than societal transformation (Kumar 1987, Levitas 2003). As Bauman (2003) has put it, we currently have 'utopia with no topos', conceptions of the good life which don't rely on the imaginary reconstruction of society which unites groups.

It is here that sociology can fill this gap for Levitas. Sociologists, perhaps more than anyone else, take a holistic view of society and engage in critique. As we have seen throughout this book being critical and arguing certain things are negative implies some idea of a good society. The result is that much critical sociology, including for Levitas almost all the thinkers we have considered in this book, should be considered 'utopian'. Their work expresses a longing for a better way of being/living though it will not necessarily recognise this as a 'utopia' due to the incorrect assigning of this to the impossible or fanciful. Furthermore, even before questions of alternatives enter into sociology to be 'critical' involves some utopianism. For example:

> Durkheim's book [*The Division of Labour in Society*], a founding classic of sociology, is deeply utopian both in intent and content. For the last section reads the *actual* state of the world as pathological, contrasted with a benign normality which *should have* happened, and which must and will. (Levitas 2005a:13)

Therefore, the idea of a better world is central to critique despite much 'critical' sociology being reluctant to speak of utopia. Yet, for Levitas:

> Wells is surely right that sociologists carry silent utopias in their work, both as inspiration and substance. Most sociologists who work in fields of social inequality – economic inequality, class, gender, ethnicity – are driven by a critical conviction that these inequalities are damaging and wrong. Somewhere underpinning this is an implicit idea of a good society in which such inequalities are absent. (Levitas 2010:538)

There is a simple explanation why sociologists have foregone utopia: the battle for scientific recognition made it unattractive. From when Marx and Engels separated their socialism from its utopian sibling social theory has sought to claim a scientific basis for its claims, including its alternatives, echoed in some of the claims discussed in this book. However, for Levitas, utopian literature, such as Morris, continued to make use of sociological claims for their work and sociologists continued to carry their 'silent utopias' of worlds without class/race/gender inequality and so on. This means that, even if sociologists do not offer utopias, 'sociology foregrounds what utopia backgrounds, while utopia foregrounds what sociology represses'. More simply, we can see 'sociology as utopia and utopia as sociology' (Levitas 2013:84, 91).

In order to bring this into the open and incorporate utopianism further into sociology Levitas argues we should think of utopia as method (Levitas 2013). This method allows us to both critique ideals which currently exist and offer our own alternatives. This has three steps:

1. Utopia as archaeology – this requires excavating the ideas of what makes a good society from the proclamations of the particular group we are

interested in. What are the ideas of a good society we find in the advocates of meritocracy? From the bourgeoisie? From Occupy Wall Street? From a political party? In doing this we can begin to point out problems; maybe some claims contradict others or, perhaps, these ideas rely upon other more unattractive factors (for example, they require high levels of inequality).

2. Utopia as ontology – this comprises two factors. The first is how human nature is conceived of in these images of the good society. If you conceive of humans as fundamentally selfish your conception of a 'good' society will be different to if you conceive of them as altruistic. The second factor is what Bloch termed the 'education of desire'; that is, many utopias may involve people's nature being changed in reaching that end goal. An example of this would be Marx's claim that it is only in the second stage of communism that inequality could be lessened since people would need to lose their capitalist ways of thinking during the first stage. Again, here there is space for criticism for how humans are imagined or the steps suggested for how they will change. We may indeed here find some 'dangerous fools' who believe that a perfect society can be implemented against the desires of others (Sargisson 2012:243).

3. Utopia as architecture – finally, we can construct the utopian world offered in these visions by using IROS. Here a final stage of criticism can occur by pointing out flaws in such visions, as well as allowing us to offer our own alternatives.

Therefore, these three steps allow sociology to reclaim the ideals offered by Wells as a discipline involving critique and the offering of utopian alternatives. IROS is both a method of critique and of offering utopian alternatives. This is something Levitas has attempted to do in her own discussion of neoliberalism.

Levitas' utopian reading of government discourse under neoliberalism

As already suggested, one conclusion from Levitas' definition of utopia is that these are much more widespread than it may initially seem. Neoliberalism, as an economic system which imagines an end goal of economic actors making rational market-based choices free from direction by state powers (Harvey 2005), ultimately is utopian. For Levitas, the governments which have sought to implement it express this utopia in their own specific ways. In what follows I draw primarily from Levitas' writings on the British New Labour governments of 1997–2010 (Levitas 2001) and the succeeding coalition government of Conservative and Liberal Democrats from 2010 to 2015 (Levitas 2012). However, as she has argued elsewhere (Levitas 1986) these ideologies are shared across parties of the 'New Right' and would also apply to other neoliberal governments such as those of George W. Bush and Barack Obama in the US, Tony Abbott of Australia, Chancellor Merkel of Germany and so on.

The first step is the archaeological; what visions of the good society are offered by these governments? There are five common factors here. The first is the importance of work, through which individuals are seen as socially valuable and making a contribution. As an example, for the British Conservative government, society can be divided into 'strivers' (those who work hard and are deserving of help) and 'shirkers' (those who avoid work and do not deserve such help). This then leads to the second factor; 'work' in these ideals is only activity for which one is paid. Taking care of children is not work, unless you are hired to do it and receive a wage in return. Thirdly, such ideas emphasise the family. This is seen as not just as a moral good but also in making us who we are. Importantly, with the introduction of same-sex marriage, while such ideas increasingly no longer rely upon a heterosexual couple, it remains a married couple heading a nuclear family. Fourthly, community is also seen as valued. A good society is one in which we contribute towards our local community and know our neighbours. Finally, some, though not all, increasingly draw upon ideas of being 'green'; a good society makes use of renewable energy and has 'sustainable' growth to ensure climate change is not exacerbated.

With the archaeological mode complete we can already highlight some issues here, such as the restriction of work – you are not contributing by taking care of your own children, but if you leave the house and take care of other people's children for pay then you are – as well as contradictions – family and community are central, but you need to be working full time. This also means we can discuss the ontological mode. For Levitas, such ideals imagine individuals as driven by a work ethic who, while remaining work-driven, are transformed into community-focused, family-orientated and active volunteers. If the contradictions weren't already clear, they become so in the architectural element when the utopian world is constructed, as in the following:

In Blair's fantasy land, the rich deserve their wealth and are not resented. The poor have presumably abolished themselves through the saving grace of working in McDonald's and call centres, ventures indirectly subsidised through tax credits. Children have stopped playing truant partly through fear of police sweeps, and partly because they understand the consequences of educational failure. Teenagers do not have unprotected sex. People accept their obligation to maintain their employability, so that they can exploit the changing opportunities provided by markets, make individual provision against risk, discharge their obligations as parents and active citizens when they have done earning a living. (They are too tired to protest on May Day, and know anyway that all demonstrators are anarchists, meaning mindless thugs, or anti-capitalists, meaning much the same.) Continuing growth ensures a rising tax take without increased tax rates. Public funds can thus be used to underwrite essential services, mainly contracted out to the private sector where successful businesses (or, increasingly, multi-national concerns) make profits subsidised out of taxation. (Levitas 2001:458–9)

This process of IROS begins to show the problems inherent in the utopias of neoliberalism for Levitas. The utopian method provides a distinct critique, one focused on the end goals of such policies, rather than on their impact in the here and now. Therefore, it can lead sociologists to claim that 'the promotion of post-material values and well-being is utterly ideological unless they are intrinsically linked to distributive and gender justice and a reorientation of the economy to need rather than profit' (Levitas 2012:338). It leads to an alternative utopia.

This of course raises the question of what exactly this alternative would be and what the architectural vision of utopia Levitas would like to draw is. I will return to Levitas' utopia later in this chapter; before that let us turn to our second utopian thinker, Erik Olin Wright.

Erik Olin Wright: Marxist utopianism

Wright is well known for his work on class, where he has developed Marxian class analysis to incorporate the complex relations of production found in a contemporary capitalist economy (Wright 1985, 1997). This work has made notable contributions to what is called 'open' or 'analytical' Marxism which seeks to develop Marxist thought through the use of large-scale empirical, often quantitative, analysis. More importantly for this chapter he has, since the early 1990s, been involved in the 'real utopias' project. Across a series of books Wright and his collaborators have sought out examples of current practices which suggest the potential for an alternative world, including democratic associations (Cohen and Rogers 1995), radical democracy (Fung and Wright 2003) and gender equality (Gornick and Meyers 2009). These are 'real utopias', examples of a better world whose potential can be seen in the current day.

Before that, we need to confront a seeming contradiction: is it possible to be Marxist and utopian? As discussed, Marx and Engels dismissed utopian socialism in favour of their materially grounded, scientific form. Furthermore, as noted in Chapter 6, many contemporary Marxists have shared this aversion to utopian speculation, the exception to this being Marcuse. However, his utopianism was limited since he argued we were at the 'end of utopia' (Marcuse 1967); we no longer had to be utopian in thought since the conditions for a utopian transformation (abundance and technological means) were now at our disposal. Hence his embrace was the also the rejection of utopianism as an alternative to come.

Wright differentiates himself from this anti-utopian tradition of Marxism. He does so by turning to first principles. What defines Marxism for Wright is not its anti-utopianism but the fact that it is an 'emancipatory social science', in which:

> The word *emancipatory* identifies a central moral purpose in the production of knowledge – the elimination of oppression and the creation of the conditions for human flourishing. And the word *social* implies the belief

that human emancipation depends upon the transformation of the social world, not just the inner life of persons. (Wright 2010:10)

This emancipatory social science relies on an idea of justice; for full emancipation a society must be both socially and politically just. Social justice requires that everyone has 'equal access to the necessary material and social means to live flourishing lives' implying some form of economic equality (Wright 2010:12). Political justice focuses more on how decisions are made and requires that individuals have the opportunity to 'make choices that affect their lives as separate persons' and 'to participate in collective choices that affect them because of the society in which they live' (Wright 2010:18). Any social science which holds this principle must then, for Wright, be critical of capitalism along the broadly Marxist lines outlined in Chapters 2 and 6. Consequently, an emancipatory social science is concerned with alternatives.

However, we don't, and can't, know when such alternatives will come into being; Wright's (2010:22) example here is the USSR in 1987. At this point it seemed incomprehensible that communism would fall and be replaced with capitalism. Yet, only two years later, exactly that process had begun. Had consideration of alternatives to communism began earlier, despite their seemingly implausibility, the transition may have been smoother and there would have been guiding ideas for a more just alternative. Therefore, it behoves us to consider what alternatives are desirable and how they may work.

As a result, for Wright, any Marxist sociology which believes in the necessity and inevitably of social change but does not pretend to know when this will happen is required to consider alternatives (Wright 2000:155). When doing so we can use the ideas of socialism as a 'compass' (Wright 2006). This compass will lead us to social and political justice through its central values, which are (Wright 2010:129):

1. Social empowerment over the way state power affects economic activity.
2. Social empowerment over the way economic power shapes economic activity.
3. Social empowerment directly over economic activity.

In following these three compass points we can assess how enticing certain alternatives are to our capitalist order. Therefore, Wright seeks to ground the offering of utopian alternatives in a Marxist analysis.

Real utopias

As we have seen throughout this book, Marxist alternatives will emphasise tendencies which already exist and suggest an alternative beyond capitalism. This is true both in the sense of groups which will help destroy capitalism (the proletariat, the Great Refusal) and the means needed to create socialism (technology, self-management). Such a conception is contained in Wright's definition of 'real utopias' as:

> Utopian ideals that are grounded in the real potentials of humanity, utopian destinations that have accessible waystations, utopian designs of institutions that can inform our practical tasks of navigating a world of imperfect conditions for social change. (Wright 2010:6)

Therefore, a real utopia has some form of expression in the current day (the 'accessible waystations') and thereby gives us a path to follow to a better world ('inform our practical tasks'). In short, we are looking for things which exist today which, were they expanded, suggest a more socially and politically just society. What makes these utopian for Wright is that their existence suggests the potential for a better world while – here he shares with Levitas a belief in utopias as processes – inspiring people to act (Wright 2010:1–9).

During the course of the real utopias project Wright has considered many different examples. However, he has increasingly aligned on four: participatory city planning, Wikipedia, Mondragón and the basic income. Below, I will discuss the first three of these and how they fit Wright's conception of real utopias. After this will follow an expanded discussion concerning the basic income, a popular idea in sociology.

Participatory city planning involves a shift in how a city's budget is decided. Whereas currently city spending is decided by councillors, under this model, citizens come together to debate and submit their own spending plans. Such a system has been in place in the Brazilian city of Porto Alegre since 1989 and forms the basis of Wright's advocacy. Although interested parties (such as local businesses) have the opportunity to attend debates it is only the local citizens who can vote on how money is spent. This fulfils both political and social justice since not only does it mean citizens have a say in decisions affecting their activity but also, Wright argues, has resulted in a more progressive distribution of funds towards the poorer parts of the city. Furthermore, the meetings themselves have remained popular with sustainable turnout and engagement (Wright 2010:155–60).

The next real utopia is Wikipedia. For Wright Wikipedia is an 'anti-capitalist' way of organising information. Since it is free to access and allows anyone to contribute it is 'based upon the principle "to each according to need, from each according to ability"' (Wright 2010:3) which, as we saw in Chapter 2, was Marx's definition of the higher stage of communism. Therefore, for Wright, Wikipedia includes many of the principles of political justice, not only in terms of open access and contribution but also in the fact it encourages debate among its members and users, utilising democratic mechanisms to solve any disagreement (Wright 2010:194–9). While, as Wright (2010:200–4) notes, there is some controversy over the extent to which Wikipedia was founded as an anti-capitalist rather than a libertarian basis, he argues that the intention is less important than what he sees as its socialist operation now. It is also effective, not just in terms of popularity but also in reporting as few mistakes as the Encyclopaedia Britannica.

The third real utopia are cooperatives which, as we saw in Chapter 4, also inspired Du Bois' Marxist alternative. Here Wright is especially interested in worker cooperatives. These are organisations where the workers effectively own the organisation, determining how it is run and its priorities; the best example for Wright is Mondragón. This began as a single cooperative in the Basque region of Spain in 1956 producing paraffin heaters but has since expanded to be the largest company in that region. It is now a conglomerate of 257 companies, employing 74,060 people in 41 countries working in finance, industry, knowledge and retail (Mondragón 2015). Each of these companies has its own internal mechanisms of government in addition to general assemblies for all Mondragón workers. The appeal of such a system is clear for Wright (2010:240–6); not only does it assure political justice by giving an outlet for a say in our daily activity but it can also assure some social justice by allowing for a more just distribution within the organisation. For example, it can assure that growth in pay for managers doesn't outstrip that of non-managers, which has caused some of the growth of inequality in contemporary capitalism (Piketty 2014).

However, as Wright (2010:244) notes – especially in its expansion overseas – Mondragón has decreased the number of workers who have voting rights and has increasingly emphasised the production of profit while downplaying the democratic ethos (Cheney 1999). For Wright, this indicates that Mondragón, like all cooperatives, operates in a capitalist market which encourages it to produce profit and engage in continuous growth. Therefore, a more substantial change is needed through the combination of all of the real utopias Wright mentions. It is here that his fourth real utopia, the basic income, is central.

The basic income

The basic income, alternatively known as the citizen's or universal income, is a policy whereby all citizens are paid a wage, regardless of any work performed or other circumstances. In order to pay for this all, or almost all, of the other welfare benefits paid by the state are eliminated. There are no longer specific benefits such as unemployment pay, disability, childcare or pensions; instead everyone receives the basic income. While this has not yet been implemented on a large scale it has had some scale pilots, most notably in Namibia (Wright 2010:5).

Not only is the basic income Wright's fourth real utopia but it is also an increasingly popular alternative drawn up by social theorists. Initially developed by Tom Paine, it has since been advocated by Bauman (1999:180–90), G.D.H. Cole (1935:253), Beck before turning to the concept of civil money (1992:149), Andre Gorz (1999), Erich Fromm (1981) and Guy Standing (2011:171–8) among others. This also reflects the appeal of the basic income across the political spectrum, having gained support from the Left, such as the Green Party in the UK, and the Right, with the Nixon administration having given serious thought to introducing a version of the scheme (Fitzpatrick 1999:92–3). As we shall see, there are disagreements concerning the level at which the basic income should be set, but there is general agreement it should be enough to sustain a 'culturally defined respectable standard of living' which, for Wright, would be 125 per cent of the poverty line (Wright 2000:149).

The basic income also forms a key part of Levitas' utopian ideas and alternative architecture. As we have seen, Levitas imagines the utopian method as creating a process towards an end goal. She shares with Wright the commitment to ultimate values we would want to realise but differs in not relying on things already in existence which embody such values. The utopian method for Levitas requires we 'stop and think about where we are trying to get to' (Levitas 2001:459). This requires an alternative architecture in which:

> The good society has equality at its core. It demands the public ownership and control of assets currently in private hands. It requires more than that. The way we measure wealth and growth is irrational, and undervalues human activities of care and nurture. The forms of work generated by capitalism do not cultivate craftsmanship in the deepest sense. A radically different form of economy and society orientated to human need rather than profit is the starting point for fuller, freer, more satisfying human relationships. (Levitas 2013:215)

This conception of a society based upon equality emerges from Levitas' emphasis on the human qualities (the utopia as ontology element) of dignity and grace which, for her, are central to a utopian vision. Dignity involves a conception of humans as social – we gain dignity through our social relations and positions, which allow us to feel recognised and valued – and also requires everyone to have a certain standard of living in order to live a life worthwhile (Levitas 2013:200–2). Grace however implies something more fundamentally human: the ability of humans to act, have their actions realised and seek out good in the world (Levitas 2013:194–7). Although she does not make a link, dignity is akin to Wright's social justice, with its emphasis on access to materials to live a full life, and grace to his political justice given its focus on the need to have our desires heard and recognised. In this sense, she and Wright share an emphasis on the alternative society as a socialist society (Levitas 2013:217).

With the ontology in place, what is the archaeology? What type of good society is valued here? A good society, for Levitas, based upon equality, calls for a reconsideration of work (Levitas 2001). Levitas shares Marx's concern that work under capitalism is alienating (Levitas 2013:12) but has a more fundamental concern with the way that work is conceived. As we saw in her critique this is too readily conceived of as only 'paid work'. Also problematic here is the primacy given to the 'work ethic', where work is seen as an end which relies upon, and reproduces, a capitalist idea of how people act and are accorded dignity (Levitas 2001:462). The good society is one in which this is removed and the opportunity for different forms of work is accorded to individuals.

Given this, the basic income is afforded a central place in Levitas' utopia, as it is in Wright's real utopia. Their justification for this can be broken down into four categories, which share the claims offered by many other advocates of the basic income (Fitzpatrick 1999). Firstly, the basic income makes all forms of work equally possible. Since the wage should be enough to live on, it allows us to perform other activities which currently have to be sidelined in favour of paid work, such as volunteering (Levitas 2012) and care work (Levitas 2001) in the 'non-market' areas of the economy (Wright 2010:220). Secondly, and linked to this, it enhances gender equality (Pateman 2004). In a way akin to the wages for housework policy outlined in Chapter 7 it is suggested to give recognition to our care-giving activities and provide greater impetus for, and lessen the excuses against, men taking part in such activity (Wright 2000:150). Thirdly, it provides a sense of commonality and universality in its provision. Since everyone receives the basic income, they are invested in maintaining it. This provides, as Levitas puts it, 'the means by which collective provision can be made' against common social ills (Levitas 2001:463). Finally, it is seen to develop some form of equality and reduce poverty. By placing the level above the poverty line, the basic income eradicates poverty. Moreover, by being paid from taxes it ensures that any surplus value is returned to workers and society, making it 'a mechanism to transfer part of the social surplus from the capitalist market sector to the social economy' (Wright 2010:220).

More than this, and what makes the basic income a utopian alternative for these writers, is that it suggests a break with capitalism towards a different system. We have seen how, for Levitas, the basic income undermines the work ethic central to capitalism and how, as Wright emphasises, it returns much of the surplus value to society. Therefore, for both, the basic income is a stepping stone towards a more socialist society (Wright 2006; Levitas 2013:217). It is this alternative conception, and the way in which it forces us to question which already exists, which is important for Levitas since:

> The answer to any claim that an alternative will not work must, surely, invite the rejoinder that global capitalism does not work either, at least if by 'work' you mean meet the minimal conditions of being ecologically sustainable and delivering decent conditions of life to the vast majority of the world's population. (Levitas 2012:335)

But what of the role of the basic income in this alternative? This is not without its critics, to whom we now turn.

Criticisms of the basic income

Despite its wide support, the basic income has had a number of critics, a complete catalogue of which is impossible here (see Fitzpatrick 1999). Instead, I will highlight five criticisms which are especially relevant to the idea of the basic income as a utopian proposal for helping to create a better world.

The first of these concerns affordability. The basic income stands out amidst Wright's real utopias since, beyond limited pilots, it is an idea rather than an actuality. This has led some to question whether the money needed to finance it is readily available (Levine 1995). As we have seen, advocates of the basic income say it is affordable if we replace all, or at least most, state benefits with the basic income and use this money, along with the savings from less bureaucracy, to finance it (Wright 2004). But, as Fitzpatrick (1999:39) highlights, disagreements on the income occur once we go beyond a 'minimal model' (of say, £20 a week) which would make no difference to one which actually would be enough to live on. Not all agree with Wright that it should be 125 per cent of the poverty line, but this seems a roughly useful guide (Hirst 1994:179), suggesting about £10,000 in the UK (depending on what measure is used). However, immediately questions can be raised with that number; that figure is based upon single persons living alone. What if they have children? Does each child get the same number? Would there be regional differences (in parts of the UK that amount of money would be useful; in London, much less)? What if people spent all their basic income in one week or had particular needs (such as disability) which outstrip the amount of the basic income (White 2004)? Therefore, the basic income may call for both much higher taxes on capital and income – Fitzpatrick (1999:40) suggests rates of 65–80 per cent at the top end – along with the maintenance of some welfare state benefits. Some have seen this combination as unattainable given the overall cost and need for political consensus (Ackerman and Alstott 2004).

The second criticism concerns what is often termed the 'free-loader' problem (Bergmann 2004): if people can receive this wage for doing nothing, will a significant number do nothing? For Levitas, this is exactly its value since:

> 'Doing nothing' is here intended as a positive proposal ... We need to do less, and we need to do it more slowly. Doing a lot more nothing, including sleeping, would reduce resource consumption, lower stress levels and enable social relations more conducive to dignity and grace. (Levitas 2013:203)

We currently do too much work and therefore the opportunity to do nothing would be beneficial overall. This is true not only for us as individuals, but also by cutting down on the amount of resources used; this is why some of the 'degrowth' advocates mentioned in the previous chapter see their project as utopian (Latouche 2009:31–66). However, those who highlight the freeloader problem argue this is likely to be more pervasive than Levitas suggests; people simply will not reduce their work; they will do nothing at all. The concern here is that if the basic income is paid from taxes, it will quickly become unaffordable. For advocates such as Levitas and Wright, such claims are overblown and reflect the highly questionable, but long-lasting, claims that people currently 'freeload' from the welfare state (Morris 1994). However, as Wright notes, since this has not been tried on a large scale yet, the outcomes are difficult to predict (Wright 2010:222).

The third criticism hits at the heart of the basic income as a utopian alternative. Rather than, as Wright and Levitas claim, being one of many factors which lead us beyond capitalism, it is instead one of the best ways to justify, and maintain, capitalism. Liberal supporters of the basic income have often justified it on this basis (Van Parijs 1995) and its supporters include one of the 'fathers' of neoliberalism, Milton Friedman (2013). Indeed, as already mentioned, the one time the basic income came close to being attempted on a large scale was when a slightly altered version was considered by the Nixon administration in the US. Two arguments are made for the capitalist value of the basic income (Fitzpatrick 1999:75–99). The first is that by providing some level of security it allows for entrepreneurs to take risks and create new businesses. The second is that, in lessening inequality, it not only removes one key critique of the system but also ensures that people are able to consume and thereby maintain profit for capital. If we add to this the fact that the sheer cost of the basic income may well require a significant level of tax revenue to maintain, it seems questionable to what extent it will lead to a post-capitalist order.

The fourth criticism actually reverses the above, rather than justify capitalism; the sheer amount of resources required to implement the basic income would mean it would have to come after the end of capitalism rather than help usher this in (Levine 1995). Providing a basic income may require the state to own and control all the resources in a society, needing something akin to socialism. The state would need to have all these resources directly to hand and would be able to direct them rather than rely upon accessing them via taxes and depending on the business cycle. While, for socialist advocates of the scheme, this is not necessarily a problem and indeed some have advocated the basic income on exactly this basis (Cole 1929:187–9), it would seem to question its potential as one of Wright's real utopias.

Finally, as with wages for housework, some have questioned the potential of the basic income to overcome inequalities of gender. For Fraser (1997), such an idea rests upon what she terms the 'caregiver parity' model. This emphasises providing mechanisms for some parity of domestic labour and then allowing families and couples to negotiate how this is divided up. This is likely only to continue the inequality as men will refuse to take on their share. Instead, Fraser advocates a 'universal carer model' which must 'ensure that men do the same, while redesigning institutions so as to eliminate the difficulty and strain' (Fraser 1997:61). The emphasis should be on 'deconstructing gender' (Fraser 1997:62) to ensure that men are part of the caregiver model. While a basic income may create the material conditions for this it will not, in and of itself, engage in the deconstruction of gender.

Therefore, as we have seen, the basic income has its share of supporters and critics. However, perhaps getting lost in the practicalities of the policy is not a useful exercise. Using Levitas' utopia as method, we can think about the basic income as a utopian orientation point. We may like the type of society in which a basic income is in place. However, in the process of creating a better world we may not be able to realise this fully at that specific time. Perhaps, along the way, we only implement parts of it, such as a partial basic income or a negative income tax, both of which are not universal but, in different ways, ensure that no one falls below a certain level of income. Or we may postpone it due to other options being more attractive at that point. Nevertheless, what is important here is that 'thinking of universal basic security is to shift the mind away from pity to social solidarity and compassion' (Standing 2011:174). In short, the basic income inspires something central to utopianism: imagination. This imagination is then used for IROS and conceiving of a better world

Conclusion: the relationship between sociology and utopia

As we have seen in this chapter, sociology has a long and complex relationship to utopianism. While many sociologists have been willing to study utopia as a topic, the idea of sociology itself being utopian, despite early support from writers such as Wells, never attained much support, even among many of the advocates of sociological alternatives discussed in this book. However, contemporary writers such as Levitas and Wright have encouraged sociology to rediscover these utopian elements as part of a normative project of outlining a better society. For Levitas utopia is a method which allows us to both criticise the proclamations of others and construct ideals we progress towards. Conversely, for Wright, we can find things existing in the here and now which indicate a possible utopian future; the role of sociology is to highlight these. Each, in doing so, offers a distinct way of thinking about the role of utopianism in offering sociological alternatives.

These differences between the two bring us closer to the question of the relationship between sociology and utopia. Levitas has made some critical comments about Wright's utopianism, most notably its lack of 'holism' (Levitas 2013:144). For her, Wright's emphasis on real utopias implies an emphasis to 'scale up' – take these instances which already exist and expand them in number and reach. But is it that simple? Can we just multiply Mondragóns? Since Wright admits that for cooperatives like Mondragón to succeed we need a more fundamental change; what is that change (Levitas 2013:146)? To answer this, we need that key part of utopianism: imagination. For Levitas, imagination allows us to conceive how things we value, such as cooperatives and participatory city planning, can be realised. This requires some element of holism; it requires IROS. But:

> Wright's mode of argument blocks off the Imaginary Reconstitution of Society when it cannot lay claim to legitimacy in existing accepted 'scientific' knowledge. It also fails to recognise what is generated through the holistic modelling of alternative institutions – the utopian method – as knowledge, despite the fact that much scientific knowledge depends

on modelling possible scenarios. 'Scientific' knowledge, or the lack of it, becomes a criterion for limiting the utopian hypothesis, binding 'real' or 'viable' utopias closely to the present, and reproducing the opposition between science and utopia that has haunted sociology since its inception. (Levitas 2013:148)

Therefore, we can see a key difference here between Wright and Levitas concerning the role of sociology. For Levitas, one of the reasons why sociology has such a close link to utopia is that, more than any other discipline, it is concerned with society as a whole. To close this imagination off is actually to deny utopianism and return to the 'scientific pretensions' of the discipline Wells decried. Unfortunately, this is what much sociology has done; even if it has suggested some alternatives, these are often justified by reference to science, as we have seen. There is also the tendency we saw in Chapter 1, to deny offering alternatives on such grounds. The result of this is that:

The suppression of normativity and utopianism in sociology is, arguably, due to this quest for respectability through recognition as a science. It is also one of the reasons sociology is so boring: knowledge rendered unimaginatively may result from deep self-censorship. (Levitas 2010:538)

Instead, Levitas advocates a separate path for sociology:

Sociology must reclaim utopia, those normative, prescriptive, future-oriented elements that have suffused the discipline from the beginning, but are too often a cause of embarrassment rather than celebration. It needs to be released from damaging self-censorship, and turn to the vision of a better world that is so often what draws people to the discipline in the first place. If sociologists have no claim to superior imagination or ethical competence, they are no less capable of or responsible for this than anyone else. They should have something to contribute to understanding systemic connections and thus mapping alternatives. If sociology has nothing to offer here, I really don't know quite what it is for. (Levitas 2013:217)

As have seen in this book, sociologists have frequently engaged in offering alternatives, indicating the 'subterranean utopian currents' which have run through sociology's history (Levitas 2013:85). Levitas' advice here, that we should be open in our utopianism since this is a way to conceive of, and offer, alternatives, reflects the kind of social theory covered in this book.

Public Sociology

10

This final chapter considers something which has increasingly acquired all the elements of a buzzword: public sociology. Throughout this book there has been an implicit assumption that the things sociologists research, write and teach should, and do, have an impact beyond the world of universities and other sociologists. This was indicated in Chapter 1 via Weber and Gouldner's disagreement on the split between a professional scientist and a public citizen.

Public sociology argues that sociology should have a wide public impact and influence; it shouldn't simply produce obtuse books and articles that only a few people can understand and read. Such an idea can be seen in many of the key texts of sociology, such as C. Wright Mills' *The Sociological Imagination* (1959). Published at the height of the fame of the American structural functionalist thinker Talcott Parsons, Mills set out to defend a different image of sociology, one which allowed anyone practising the sociological imagination to connect 'personal troubles' to 'public issues' (Mills 1959:8). Sociology has the ability to state how a multitude of personal troubles (unemployment, divorce, city living, war and so on) reflect wider issues, be it the nature of the economy, gender relations, industrialisation or the functions of nation-states; this is the 'promise' of sociology (Mills 1959:3–24). However, too many sociologists had become obsessed with writing books of 'grand theory' which were lost in the 'Byzantine oddity of associated and disassociated Concepts, the mannerism of verbiage' (Mills 1959:224). Instead Mills encouraged the 'simplicity of the clear statement' (Mills 1959:224) so that all could engage with sociology and realise its promise. Mills himself attempted this in books such as *The Power Elite* (1956) and *Blue Collar* (1951) which attempted to link everyday problems such as unemployment, inequality and workplace conditions to the wider structure of American society at the time. Mills' conception of sociology remains influential, as seen in Les Back's argument that a key element of sociology is its ability to listen to and connect the stories of everyday people to wider social issues (Back 2007, Gane and Back 2012).

Therefore, the idea of sociology as public is one which has a long history. But the term 'public sociology' is a relatively recent one, mainly associated with the work of the 'sociological Marxist' (Burawoy and Wright 2001) Michael Burawoy. As we shall see, Burawoy not only defends the idea of sociology being a public discipline but also argues that this is, and should be, an increasingly prominent element of sociology. Therefore, as in the previous chapter, our concern here is with how sociologists, including the ones discussed in this book, can offer, and have offered, alternatives. This chapter will begin by outlining Burawoy's concept before relating it to the sociologists discussed in previous chapters. Following this I will discuss the wider argument inspired by Burawoy's intervention. While many have welcomed Burawoy's claim, some have seen it as problematic due to it being unoriginal, unnecessarily politicising sociology or exaggerating its potential impact beyond the university. I will conclude by applying these arguments to the case study of Pierre Bourdieu.

Burawoy's case for public sociology

In 2004 Burawoy was president of the American Sociological Association (ASA) and used the occasion of the association's annual conference to make the case 'For Public Sociology' (Burawoy 2005a). Burawoy started out with a key claim that 'if our predecessors set out to change the world we have too often ended up conserving it' (Burawoy 2005a:5). As we have seen throughout this book many early sociologists hoped to change the world – to develop and implement an alternative. This, for Burawoy, is no longer the case, reflecting what he terms sociology's 'stages'. Each of the three stages of sociology was produced by and mirrors the sociopolitical conditions of the times in which they emerged (Burawoy 2007a). For Burawoy, sociology originally emerged in the late nineteenth/early twentieth century as 'utopian sociology'. In this period the earliest sociologists, among whom Burawoy cites Marx, Durkheim and Du Bois, set out to construct new utopias which rejected the ravages of laissez-faire capitalism in order to imagine new industrial societies. Therefore, sociology was born as a quest for reform or reconstruction, as we also saw in the work of Mead and as found in sociologists of the period, such as Jane Addams (Deegan 2007, 2013) and the Scottish duo of Patrick Geddes and Victor Branford (Scott and Bromley 2013).

This form of sociology, reflecting arguments in the last chapter, disappeared once we reached the 1930s and onwards where a new type of sociology, policy sociology, emerged. This form was different since it:

> wanted to expel moral questions to a completely different sphere, anti-thetical to science. If the first wave of sociology was utopian, the second policy wave tended to think that utopia had already arrived and mistook it for reality. It was riveted to the present, concerned only with ironing out its small irrationalities. (Burawoy 2007a: 364–5)

Rather than the theoretical nature of the earlier utopians, policy sociologists were heavily empirical, mostly using quantitative methods. They focused on studying and 'solving' social problems. There were two pressures which led to the birth of this type of sociology. Firstly, the emergence, especially from the 1940s onwards, of the welfare state provided employment and resources to sociologists seeking to provide expert advice on how to solve problems, as seen in Gouldner's fears discussed in Chapter 1. This was especially true in countries with strong welfare states, such as Sweden (Larsson and Magdalenić 2015). If sociologists were not directly employed by the state in understanding things like crime in the inner city, they could be confident their own research on this topic would be taken up, and hopefully their recommendations put into practice, by policy makers. To return to a concept from an earlier chapter, this was the time of Bauman's legislators of sociologists collaborating with the state to 'remake' society (Bauman 1987). Therefore, as Burawoy's quote suggests, this is not a time of sociologists hoping to create a 'new' society but rather trying to improve the one which already exists.

The second pressure was that sociology at this point is still trying to establish itself as a science and shed its 'outlaw' status (Cole 1947:23). To do this, as we discussed in Chapter 1, sociologists adopted the myth of 'value freedom' which was said to differentiate them from groups working on similar topics, such as journalists (Gouldner 1962). They also changed their methods with a much greater use of statistics which seemed to give 'scientific' backing to their claims. This, in turn, convinced welfare state officials of the 'expertness' of sociologists (Halsey 2004:29–44). Such a shift also had the side effect, intended or not, of making sociology less accessible for those without statistical knowledge (Bauman 2011:160–72).

Therefore, policy sociology marked the shift away from a largely accessible subject concerned with social reform and towards an increasingly inaccessible, statistical, discipline focused on providing scientific advice to welfare state managers. This shift was especially notable in Burawoy's case study of the US. This was partly due to the prominence of early scholars such as Mead and Addams who were so committed to reform and the latter pressure for 'scientific' prestige in universities being so strong (Turner 2014). However, such a shift was shared around the globe (Burawoy 2010) and, in cases such as Britain, happened early in the history of the discipline (Renwick 2012).

This form of policy sociology has decreased in influence from the 1980s onwards to be replaced by a new type of sociology: public sociology. Public sociology, for Burawoy, involves many of the elements mentioned at the start of the chapter – making sociology accessible and available to people beyond the academy and ensuring that it speaks to everyday concerns. As he puts it, public sociology 'strikes up a dialogic relation between sociologist and public' in which the goal 'is to make visible the invisible, to make the private public' (Burawoy 2005a: 9, 8). So the question may be asked: why is this so important in the current era? Here Burawoy returns to the wider social setting in which sociologists work. Whereas earlier sociologists aimed their findings at the welfare state in the hope of remaking the world, that is no longer possible, welfare states throughout the world have had their budgets cut and many of their services (healthcare, education, punishment and so on) privatised as part of the emergence of neoliberalism (Hall 2011).

This, for Burawoy, leaves sociology in a unique position; while other social science subjects can maintain their key point of focus under neoliberalism – economists still have markets to analyse and political scientists still have nation-states to understand – sociology has a totally different area of interest: civil society. As we saw in Chapter 5, many have argued sociology is linked to democracy, and here Burawoy is making a similar point that sociology succeeds when it is able to raise democratic questions within a strong civil society. This is no longer the case when in an era of increased marketisation and inequality 'market and state have collaborated against humanity in what has commonly come to be known as neoliberalism' (Burawoy 2005a:7). Rather than raising questions such as 'is our society equal enough', 'do we punish crime fairly', 'is the government representing us correctly' in publically available spheres, increasingly key social functions are left to markets and their 'success' judged by whether they make a profit or not. This is where sociology is useful, for Burawoy, by connecting those personal troubles to public issues and making sure society continues to question itself.

Therefore, sociology has increasingly become a form of opposition to wider society. As Burawoy puts it 'in times of market tyranny and state despotism, sociology – and in particular its public face – defends the interests of humanity' (Burawoy 2005a:24) in what he terms the 'scissors movement' (Burawoy 2005a:6). While sociology always had a mixture of left-wing and right-wing voices (Strasser 1976), it has increasingly become a left-wing discipline – which some conservative sociologists have criticised it for (Saunders 2011) – while society more broadly, with the drift to marketisation, has become more right wing.

The result of all this is that, for Burawoy, practising public sociology is not something one may or may not choose to do, but rather is essential to the future of the discipline since 'sociology depends on civil society with an interest in the expansion of the social' (Burawoy 2005a:24). This then leaves two questions: how should public sociology be done? And, how does it relate to the other things sociologists do?

Doing public sociology

Before turning to how public sociology should be, and is, done, we need to discuss the question of what sociologists do. This is what Burawoy terms the 'division of sociological labour' in which there are four types of sociology, each dealing with different audiences and types of knowledge (Burawoy 2005a:9–10). These are:

1. Professional sociology – this is the research projects conducted by sociologists, with all their requirements of methods, ethics and the use of theories and concepts. Professional sociology requires a certain form of training (degrees in sociology, courses on research methods and so on) and is not available to everyone. Consequently, its main audience is other sociologists and deals in what Burawoy terms 'instrumental' knowledge. Such

knowledge is primarily concerned with obtaining findings and facts in order to engage in 'puzzle solving', for example, conducting research in order to understand the causes of poverty (Burawoy 2005a:11). Such a form of sociology is partly justified by the idea of 'knowledge for knowledge's sake'; that is, it is simply good to know more things (Burawoy 2005a:10, 2007b).

2. Policy sociology – as discussed above, this is sociology which aims to identify, and solve, problems for governments. Therefore it has an audience beyond other sociologists but a limited one. It also deals in instrumental knowledge in its aim to solve these problems. As mentioned above, with the decline in welfare state spending this form of sociology has decreased in scope but still exists.

3. Critical sociology – this is different from the critical sociology discussed in Chapter 1. Instead it shares with its professional kin a focus on the audience of other sociologists but deals in 'reflexive' knowledge since it 'interrogates the value premises' of sociology (Burawoy 2005a:11). This involves questioning the assumptions and claims of professional sociology – for example feminists such as Dorothy Smith critiquing 'malestream' sociology and post-colonial scholars criticising the lack of discussion of 'race'. Furthermore, critical sociologists question the overall values which drive sociologists: is studying poverty in order simply to understand poverty right? Should not sociology think about how that research will help the poor?

4. Public sociology – this also deals in reflexive knowledge but is aimed at an audience beyond both sociologists and policy makers.

For Burawoy each of these is important, but, as we saw above, it is public sociology which comes to play an increasingly significant role in what sociologists do.

How is public sociology done? Here Burawoy provides two possible paths. The first one is 'traditional public sociology', where the goal is to generate public debate by presenting sociological arguments in public fora. This can include writing 'popular' books/newspapers, appearing on radio/TV, producing blogs and using social media (Burawoy 2005a:7). These all rely on a 'top-down' model whereby sociologists are hoping to take the results from their professional sociological activity beyond the academy. This also means it can be quite 'one-way' with sociologists not engaging with publics beyond writing their pieces or appearing on a TV show. This is different from the second type, 'organic public sociology' where:

> The sociologist works in close connection with a visible, thick, active, local and often counterpublic...sociologists working with a labour movement, neighbourhood associations, communities of faith, immigrant rights groups, human rights organizations. Between the organic public sociologist and a public is a dialogue, a process of mutual education. (Burawoy 2005a:7–8)

Therefore, organic public sociology favours a 'bottom-up' approach, in which sociologists bring their critical skills to bear in assisting social movements and local communities in their goals. Consequently this is a more two-way process in which sociologists actively engage with groups on the ground. Indeed, while Burawoy sees the two forms as complementary many who practise organic public sociology are critical of their traditional public sociology colleagues, since:

> This is not armchair sociology in which self-proclaimed public sociologists just write articles suggesting what governments, corporations, communities, or others 'ought to do'. We are interested in the *active* connections to publics and users of the research, not a passive research process. (Nyden et al. 2012:8)

For Burawoy, the organic form of public sociology has long been overlooked and it is only with the emergence of a group of critical sociologists educated in the charged political atmosphere of the 1960s that it has become a widespread occurrence (Burawoy 2005b).

There is one type of public sociology which straddles the boundary between these two categories: teaching. Burawoy does acknowledge the role of teaching in public sociology, since:

> Every year we create approximately 25,000 new BAs, who have majored in sociology. What does it mean to think of them as a potential public? It surely does not mean we should treat them as empty vessels into which we pour our mature wine, nor blank slates upon which we inscribe our profound knowledge. Rather we must think of them as carriers of a rich lived experience that we elaborate into a deeper self-understanding of the historical and social contexts that have made them who they are...Education becomes a series of dialogues on the terrain of sociology that we foster – a dialogue between ourselves and students, between students and their own experiences, among students themselves, and finally a dialogue of students with publics beyond the university... As teachers we are all potentially public sociologists. (Burawoy 2005a:9)

Therefore, teaching is both traditional and organic public sociology, though Burawoy tends to link it more to the organic form (Burawoy 2007b:254). Furthermore, it is the promise of public sociology, of making a difference in the world, which leads many students to sociology. This is something which the dictates of professional sociology often end up pushing aside in its teaching:

> A typical graduate student, perhaps inspired by an undergraduate teacher or burnt out from a draining social movement – enters graduate school with a critical disposition, wanting to learn more about the possibilities of social change...There she confronts a succession of required courses, each

with its own abstruse texts to be mastered or abstract techniques to be acquired. ...The whole process can take anything from 5 years up. It is as if graduate school is organized to winnow away at the moral commitments that inspired the interest in sociology in the first place. (Burawoy 2005a:14)

While training in professional sociology is essential for Burawoy (2005c), there should also be space for expanding the time and teaching devoted to public sociology. Some have taken Burawoy's lead by including community service, community-based arts exhibition, working with poverty reduction movements or forming an anti-hate crime group in course assessment (see Korgen et al. 2011 for examples).

As we have seen, Burawoy claims public sociology is both old and new. From the start of the discipline sociologists have been public, notably in the 'traditional' form, but the conditions of neoliberalism and change in the political position of sociology mean even more are now public, notably in a largely new organic form. So, to explore this, let us look at how the sociologists discussed in this book have been 'public'.

Public sociology in sociological alternatives

In some ways, all of the sociologists discussed in this book have been 'public sociologists'. They have shared Burawoy's belief that sociology is greater than 'knowledge for knowledge's sake' and, for some, sociologists must live up to their 'moral convictions' (Burawoy 2005d). In doing this, as has been indicated at points throughout, sociologists have attempted to reach audiences beyond other academics in a variety of ways.

As Burawoy notes, traditional public sociology has been a particularly followed path here. This could be found in the earliest sociologists we have discussed, as in Marx's frequent contributions (some actually ghost-written by Engels) to the *New York Tribune* on topics such as British politics, finance and slavery (Marx 2007). Many of Marx and Engel's other texts were also written for a wide audience, such as the *Communist Manifesto* which aimed at a universal (or at least, universal proletariat) audience (Hobsbawm 1998) and *The Civil War in France* which was Marx's attempt to make his views public in light of his reputation as the 'Red Professor' behind the scenes of the Paris Commune (Horne 2007:430).

A trend towards traditional public sociology could also be found in the work of Durkheim. Chapter 3 opened with Durkheim's claim that sociologists should 'make a reality of the famous precept: to each according to his labour' and closed with his reminder that such 'political freedom' was a 'battle weapon'. Both of these claims come from a text entitled 'Individualism and the Intellectuals' (Durkheim 1973) which was originally published in 1898 at the height of the Dreyfus Affair. This concerned a French army captain named Alfred Dreyfus who, in 1894, was convicted of treason. It was claimed that Dreyfus had passed military secrets to the Germans; however, evidence came to light that another officer, Ferdinand Walsin Esterhazy, was the real culprit. Dreyfus was prosecuted and convicted not on the basis of evidence but because of his Judaism. When Esterhazy was acquitted at trial (partly because the French military concealed evidence) it sparked a national outcry from many who took up Dreyfus' cause, quickly becoming known as Dreyfusards. Their cause was sparked by Emile Zola's famous *J'Accuse,* an open letter published on the front page of a major French newspaper accusing the country of anti-Semitism.

Durkheim was quick to join the Dreyfusards. He became secretary of a local chapter of the Dreyfusian League for the Defence of the Rights of Human Rights (which still exists today) and was a signatory of public letters taking up Dreyfus' cause (Fournier 2013:285–308). However, the affair quickly became about more than one army captain. The anti-Dreyfusards attacked their rivals not just for their religion (many, like Durkheim, shared Dreyfus' Jewish ancestry) but for their wider world view, seeing them as advocates of a individualism which rejected religion in favour of self-interest and a lack of morality.

This claim struck at the very heart of Durkheim's sociology; as we saw in Chapter 3, his claim was that modern societies were based on individualism, which provided our shared moral values. So, in defence of himself, the body of sociology he was helping bring into being, Dreyfus and the debate about what type of country France should be Durkheim penned 'Individualism and the Intellectuals' which, written for a mass audience, appeared in *Revue Bleue* a weekly political and literary journal after the intended publisher, the widely read *Revue de Paris*, had refused it due to not wishing to pick sides (Fournier 2013:295–6). Here Durkheim took the battle to the anti-Dreyfusards claiming they attacked a straw man:

> It is indeed an easy game to denounce as an ideal without grandeur this crass commercialism which reduces society to nothing more than a vast apparatus of production and exchange…We quite agree that nothing is more deserved than that such doctrines be considered anarchical. But what is inadmissible is that they should reason as though this form of individualism was the only one which existed or was even possible. (Durkheim 1973:44)

Rejecting such a view of individualism as an 'egoistic cult of the self' (Durkheim 1973:45), Durkheim outlined his view of individualism providing a shared religion based on the sacred belief in the rights of individuals. In doing so Durkheim spelt out what led him and others to Dreyfus' cause:

> Whoever makes an attempt on a man's life, on a man's liberty, on a man's honour, inspires in us a feeling of horror analogous in every way to that which the believer experiences when he sees his idol profaned. Such an ethic is therefore not simply a hygienic discipline or a prudent economy or experience; it is a religion in which man is at once the worshiper and the god. (Durkheim 1973:46)

The anti-Dreyfusards were not only unjust in their actions, but they were in effect speaking blasphemies, an accusation which would have stung those rallying to the cause of religion. Reading 'Individualism and the Intellectuals' today is to encounter what is in effect one of the great documents of traditional public sociology.

This traditional public sociology is then shared by other writers we have discussed. Many of Mannheim's writings on the Third Way began life as radio broadcasts or newspaper articles (Mannheim 1943), Marcuse gained his reputation of 'father of the New Left' partly through his willingness to give public lectures and write for their publications (Marcuse 1969b) and Giddens has used his seat in the House of Lords to make media appearances, write for newspapers and produce books for a mass audience on topics such as climate change (Giddens 2011) and the European Union (Giddens 2013).

So Burawoy is correct to argue that traditional public sociology, befitting the name, has a long history. However, he could be said to exaggerate the newness of its organic counterpart since we have also seen plentiful examples of this throughout the book. Perhaps the best came from the work of Mead who, as we saw, utilised his working hypothesis idea of social reform through connection with Chicago-based organisations and social movements. To take one instance from Mead's work, his role in establishing the Immigrants Protection League would seem the archetypal 'organic' public sociology Burawoy favours given its goal of allowing new arrivals to Chicago access to civil society. As we also saw, Mead's standpoint of trying to provide space for the 'genius' in all, rather than seeing intellectuals as a particularly skilled elite, fits with the two-way, bottom-up ethos of organic public sociology. Indeed, during his life Mead was primarily known as and for his public activities rather than his academic work. Consequently, many of what we now consider Mead's 'academic' publications are in fact transcripts of public speeches, blurring the lines between 'professional' and 'public' sociology (Huebner 2014:25–39).

We can also see further examples of this. Du Bois is an obvious candidate given his role in activism and helping found the NAACP. As we saw, this shift to activism was partly based upon a rejection of professional sociology and the limits of knowledge in solving racism. What was required instead was action. A further example can be found in feminism. Perhaps more than any other sociological field, feminist researchers are likely to engage in organic public sociology (Acker 2005, Collins 2007). This reflects the nature of a discipline which believes that the personal is political and, like Marxism, is concerned with *praxis* (Rowbotham 1973). We saw instances of such activity in Chapter 7. This included James' work in co-founding the international Wages for Housework Campaign as well as Dworkin and MacKinnon's advocacy work for their anti-pornography law. Such activity continues in feminist sociology. It can be found, for example, in the US 'Sociologists for Women in Society' (SWS) group. This was an organisation inspired by the events of the 1969 ASA annual conference where, with their caucus banned from meeting at the conference, they met in the basement of a nearby church. The next year the SWS was founded to both challenge sexism within professional sociology and to provide space and support for work outside the academy (Feltey and Rushing 1998). Since 1995 this group has been awarding a 'Feminist Activism Award' to the sociologist who 'has made notable contributions to improving the lives of women in society' through their activist work (Sociologists for Women in Society 2014).

Therefore, organic public sociology also has a long history. This is especially the case in those fields of sociology focused on disadvantaged groups, such as ethnic minorities and women, a point we will return to below. Furthermore, it is possible to combine organic and traditional public sociology. For example, as mentioned in Chapter 7, James combined her work with the Wages for Housework campaign with the writing of books and media appearances. Consequently, not only do all forms of public sociology have a long history in the discipline but we can also see how sociologists move between them.

The above may leave the reader wondering what is exactly new about public sociology. This is indeed one of the criticisms raised against it, to which we now turn.

Criticisms of public sociology

Let us summarise what has come in the chapter thus far. We have seen that for Burawoy sociology is marked by a fourfold division of labour. In this division between professional, policy, critical and public sociology, different forms have been more dominant at particular points of time. However, in an era of neoliberalism and the increasing opposition between a left-wing sociology concerned with civil society and a right-wing society intent on marketisation, it is public sociology which should be, and increasingly is becoming, dominant. There are two ways of practising public sociology: a 'traditional' form which is based on a top-down relationship of communicating research findings beyond sociology by appearing in the media and writing for a mass audience and an 'organic' form which involves a bottom-up working with social movements and local communities. While, for Burawoy, traditional public sociology has a long history its organic form only truly becomes widespread following the turn to critical sociology in the 1970s. A survey of the sociologists considered in this book suggested that in fact both had a long history in sociology, with the organic form being especially strong in the feminist and black radical traditions.

Burawoy's intervention attracted a lot of attention and, inevitably, some of these were critical of his ideas. Since it would be impossible to cover all the critiques of public sociology, the following will focus on a selection which relate to the overall concern of this book. While some of these critics have taken issue with the principle behind Burawoy's advocacy, arguing that sociology should not be public, most are sympathetic to this sentiment but either disagree with how Burawoy expresses it or wish to highlight practical obstacles. These criticisms can be grouped into five categories.

The first, and perhaps major, criticism is that Burawoy assumes a political consensus in sociology which is not there. As we have seen, Burawoy argues being a public sociologist is defined by being broadly left wing, pro-civil society and anti-markets. Some, like Holmwood, are critical of the fact this reduces the plurality of sociology, since 'for Burawoy, the fragmentation of sociology is to be understood as simply a pejorative name for its multiplicity, *but multiplicity, rather than consensus, is the condition for a flourishing sociology*' (Holmwood 2007:52). Sociology has always had a variety of intellectual and political positions and to present consensus around one position is to remove what makes sociology unique as a discipline. We have seen such variety in this book with no one political position being shared by all the writers. Some have taken this criticism further, arguing that in fact Burawoy's anti-markets and anti-state position belies his Marxism rather than any conception of what sociology is (Calhoun 2005). Burawoy does indeed say that 'if public sociology is to have a progressive impact it will have to hold itself continuously accountable to some such vision of democratic socialism' (Burawoy 2005b:325). For Brady (2004) such a Marxist orientation can be seen in Burawoy's denigration of policy sociology. Despite being concerned with taking sociology beyond the academy and improving the world, this is somehow not 'public' in the same way as public sociology.

Others however see a more cynical reason for Burawoy turning to the language of 'public' sociology in recent years since, following the fall of communism, 'one hears of public sociologies more and more just as one hears of Marxist sociology less and less. Is this a coincidence?' (Nielsen 2004:1621). For these critics it is partly the implicit Marxism which is problematic, but *any* value system taken as universal would be problematic. Reflecting arguments from Weber in Chapter 1, these critics see such Marxist values as simply reflecting individual, rather than disciplinary, beliefs (Nielsen 2004, Boyns and Fletcher 2005) or unintentionally opening the door to all values – including ones like racism – being a legitimate part of sociological practice (Smith-Lovin 2007). Given the political diversity of sociology it may be argued that 'political neutrality is central to the corporate organisation of sociology, not because it secures objectivity, nor because social inquiry can, or should be, value-neutral' (Holmwood 2007:63, see also J. Turner 2005). While value-freedom may not be plausible, we should not seek to ascribe common political values to all sociologists as public sociology seems to do.

Such debates were, appropriately, played out publically a year before Burawoy gave his talk For Public Sociology. In 2003 the ASA balloted its members on whether it should oppose the Iraq War; 66 per cent voted in favour of this. Burawoy cites this as indication of the scissors movement with the increasingly cohesive and left-wing sociology differing from the rest of American society which, at this point, overwhelmingly supported the war (Burawoy 2005a:6). However, for Nielsen (2004:1624–5) this showed all that was wrong with public sociology. Firstly, there was not consensus; a third of members didn't support the resolution. Therefore, Burawoy is again exaggerating the dominance of his left-wing position. Secondly, it seems problematic to say a body like the ASA should take a position on the Iraq War; why would opposing the Iraq War be a condition of being a sociologist and member of the ASA? For Nielsen, the implication for the third who voted against the resolution is clear:

> They feel that the 'adoption' of such resolutions by the ASA abusively associates their name with a political opinion with which they disagree, represents contemptuous disregard for their minority opinion, and really aims at suppressing dissent among members under cover of a false unanimity. (Nielsen 2004:1624)

Such critics ask: can you not be a sociologist and be pro-Iraq War? And pro-markets? Or, more importantly, does one have to be pro- or anti-markets to be a sociologist? Surely you only need to be pro-sociology? Public sociology, by rejecting political neutrality, has the danger of removing the very possibility of future sociologists who hold right-wing views (Abbott 2007) and alienate those who already hold such views. A good example of this is Peter Berger, who argues that 'sociology is radical in its debunking analysis but conservative in its practical implications' (Berger 2011:176) and demonstrated such a belief by working for US tobacco companies to covertly research the 'anti-smoking' groups, including discovering the profile of the members and their motives (Berger 2011:169–75). Was Berger's work a form of 'organic' public sociology despite it emerging from a pro-market position?

While the first group of critics are those who wish to stay clear of public sociology, the second group are those who embrace it. As Patricia Hill Collins (2007) puts it, she and many others had long been practising 'the sociology that had no name', doing public sociology without having the word for it. Collins highlights that, as we saw above, this tended to be especially true of female and/or black and minority ethnic sociologists who were often driven to public engagement due to a mix of personal experience and research interests. While Collins and others (Acker 2005, Katz-Fishman and Scott 2005, Misztal 2009, Sprague and Laube 2009) see positives in this activity being given a name, they also have fears. Firstly, it could become 'yet another fad...that privileged sociologists can play at just as a cat toys with a mouse' (Collins 2007:106). Dominant figures in sociology, likely to be white men, may begin to dip in and out of public sociology or produce authoritative texts outlining how public sociology *should* be done; books will be written and seminars held on public sociology, but few will actually do it. As mentioned earlier, groups engaged in organic public sociology are often critical of others seeking to give such advice (Nyden et al. 2012). Alternatively, the opposite may happen; public sociology is seen as a 'good' thing but largely left to younger scholars – most likely women and/or black and minority ethnic sociologists – yet to 'establish' themselves and with less job security (Collins 2007). Here, the fact that universities are usually unwilling to consider public sociology when hiring candidates is an obstacle

(Stacey 2007). Therefore, naming a sociology which has been done for years, especially when that naming is done by someone as influential as Burawoy, could pose future problems.

A third set of critics are united in their belief that Burawoy gives sociology too much credit; there are two ways in which this is expressed. The first comes from what Tittle (2004) calls the 'arrogance' of public sociology. As we saw, much of Burawoy's defence for public sociology concerns our engagement in the civil sphere which is seen as a space of equal engagement allowing for the 'collective self-regulation of society' (Burawoy 2005d:386). Some public sociologists fully embrace this egalitarian principle, arguing that sociology has no unique access to knowledge (Nyden et al. 2012:13) and that it needs to more fully embrace the knowledge of 'lay' actors (Touraine 2007, Noy 2009) or at least recognise that such a distinction is not clear cut (Mesny 2009). However, Burawoy does not share this perspective and, as we have seen, argues that sociologists have a unique commitment to civil society, seemingly giving them a special position within this. For Tittle, there is a contradiction here which, in its claim sociologists are uniquely placed vis-à-vis other citizens, gives public sociology an air of arrogance and embraces 'a form of inequality that in other contexts Burawoy would probably abhor' (Tittle 2004:1643). A slightly friendlier though still critical point comes from Stacey (2007) who argues that Burawoy's claim of sociology's unique role in defending the civil sphere and humanity is 'insulting' to other subjects that may have a similar claim (such as anthropology, history and social policy), a point echoed by others (Aronwitz 2005). For example, a recent attempt has been made to justify a form of 'public criminology' on the basis of the democratic ideal outlined by Burawoy (Loader and Sparks 2011).

The fourth group of criticisms argue that being public is much more challenging than Burawoy makes out. There are multiple reasons for this; for example, as we have seen throughout this book, to be critical is one thing, and to suggest alternatives another. The latter inevitably involves practical questions. Both Mead and Mannheim were critical of liberal democracy, but their practical alternatives differed greatly; some feminists shared the view that pornography was negative, but only some held the view it should be banned. Therefore, to be public is to engage in practical questions. For some, this means that sociology could not live up to its promise because we do not yet have definite answers to the questions we ask; we do not know, for example, what exactly causes crime (Tittle 2004).

This then leads to two possible conclusions. The first is that sociologists should focus all their efforts on professional sociology, working until we have clear answers to key questions (Tittle 2004; Boyns and Fletcher 2005; J. Turner 2005). The second position, contrary to an earlier critique, argues that in fact Burawoy does not acknowledge how political public sociology would need to be (Aronwitz 2005; Etzoni 2005; Piven 2007; Wallerstein 2007). Partly in response to earlier critics Burawoy defends public sociology as able to 'support Christian Fundamentalism as it can Liberation Sociology or Communitarianism'

(Burawoy 2005a:8); the fact it is more likely to support left-wing goals simply reflects the position of individual sociologists in the scissors movement. For these critics this overlooks the fact that sociology operates in a highly political environment, whether this be media outlets with views to promote (Ericson 2005), funders who desire certain research studies (Piven 2007) or neoliberal governments suspicious both of sociology and the welfare state (Urry 2005). Therefore, to pretend public sociology can adopt different political positions is wishful thinking; it would have to, following Gouldner, adopt certain moral positions concerning what 'democracy' should be (Ossewaarde 2005; S. Turner 2005). In the view of Barbara Ehrenreich, who straddles the border of sociology and journalism, this may require sociologists to become more like journalists (Ehrenreich 2007).

The final criticism suggests that Burawoy exaggerates the public who are interested in what sociology has to say. Some note that in fact much of sociology is already public in the sense its findings are easily available and sociologists do appear in the media (Ericson 2005) rather 'the problem is that publics do not want to read them' (Scott 2005:408). Therefore, the goal is not simply to become public, but rather:

> The key task for public sociology, then, is to establish the means through which publics are motivated to take seriously and to engage with its academic products. This is a slow, incremental process in which people must be persuaded and enticed into reading sociology and, most importantly, thinking sociologically. A great deal can be achieved through the public that we encounter every day – our students – but there is a more difficult task of building a dialogue with the publics outside the universities. The advocacy of public sociology is a claim for autonomy combined with a claim for engagement – and that is its challenge. (Scott 2005:408)

Therefore, echoing Scott, some have encouraged Burawoy and public sociology to take an even greater account of how important teaching is to the mission of public sociology (Calhoun 2005, Stacey 2007, Noy 2009).

As mentioned above, this is just a selection of the many critiques offered of public sociology. However, they reflect some of the key themes which we have discussed throughout this book. These include the role of political values in sociology, the problems of inequality, the difficulties of moving from critique to alternative and the importance of spreading a sociological outlook. Burawoy has, in multiple spaces, responded to these criticisms (see Burawoy 2005c; d, 2007a; b). His main response has been that they reflect the division of sociological labour he outlined. Those wishing to pull up the drawbridge and devote their energies to value-free research and discovering final answers are defending professional sociology (Burawoy 2007b), while those seeking to further politicise the discipline are coming from critical sociology (Burawoy 2005d). This for Burawoy demonstrates the vibrancy and variety of sociology which he claims to celebrate (Burawoy 2005c). He does acknowledge the comments concerning the difficulty of public sociology, including who gets to do it (Burawoy 2007b) but argues that:

> even with all the obstacles – and there are many – public sociology is flourishing. It simply does not have a public profile but operates in the interstices of society in neighbourhoods, in schools, in classrooms, in factories, in short, wherever sociologists find themselves. The existence of a plurality of invisible public sociologies gives lie to the sceptics. To give it more vitality, more influence, more visibility, we need to recognize it. What better way to recognize it than naming it, and then placing it alongside and in relation to other sociologies and then introducing incentives. (Burawoy 2005c:426)

In many ways, this echoes what we have seen in this book. The obstacles in the way of being public sociologists have always been there and sociologists have endeavoured to offer their alternatives in different ways, whether by organic or traditional public sociology. What unites them is that sociology is able to, as Bauman put it, 'keep other options alive' (Bauman 2008:238). We shall return to this in the 'Conclusion' following this chapter.

Conclusion: the case of Pierre Bourdieu

This chapter has discussed the ways in which sociologists go about offering alternatives through the lens of Michael Burawoy's conception of 'public sociology'. As we have seen, Burawoy imagines a fourfold sociological division of labour among professional, policy, critical and public sociologies. While other forms have been emphasised at certain times, in the current neoliberal era it is public sociology, with its defence of a participatory and democratic civil sphere, which sociology should be engaged in. This can be practised in two ways: a top-down traditional public sociology which involves writing for a mass audience and appearing in the media and a bottom-up organic public sociology where sociologists work directly with social movements and community groups. For Burawoy it is the latter which is increasingly prominent and important in the current day. We saw that his conception of public sociology is one which has been shared by many of the sociologists discussed in this book. Furthermore, we saw that critics have emphasised various problems with public sociology, including the political values of sociology and sociologists, who would do it, practical problems with doing it and whether there is an audience for sociological findings. These criticisms, for Burawoy, reflect the division of sociological labour and the continued promise of public sociology.

Such ideas of public sociology play out in the case of Pierre Bourdieu. Before his death in 2002 Bourdieu had attained the position of a noted public intellectual in his native France and, in particular, was involved in anti-globalization politics (Bourdieu 1998, 2003). Bourdieu's early, pre-1990s, career had been spent in the field of professional sociology with texts such as *Outline of the The- ory of Practice* (1977) and *Distinction* (1984) bearing all the marks of this field. However, Bourdieu's later work included both traditional and organic public sociology. On the traditional side, we have *Weight of the World* (Bourdieu et al. 1999), a collection of interviews with everyday people suffering from social ills, as well as *Acts of Resistance* (1998) and *Firing Back* (2003), both of which are collections of short, polemical, pieces on contemporary political issues.

Acts of Resistance and *Firing Back* also indicate Bourdieu's organic public sociology since they are made up partly of transcripts from speeches at protests, strikes or occupations, reflecting his involvement with a variety of political groupings. Furthermore, he made an increasing number of media appear- ances to protest the increasingly neoliberal nature of the French state. His fame as a public intellectual increased to the extent that theatre groups began to perform some of the stories contained in *Weight of the World* (see Swartz 2003:799–814).

This shift in Bourdieu's work attracted major comment since Bourdieu's ear- lier writings had been critical of political activism on the part of intellectuals and had favoured building up sociology as a distinct scientific discipline (Swartz 2003:793). However, as noted by others (Schinkel 2003, Poupeau and Disce- polo 2008) Bourdieu had always written on political matters; what changed in the 1990s was the form and frequency of that writing and activity. To use the language of this chapter, while Bourdieu consistently wrote on politics, in this period he made the shift from professional to public sociology.

Why did Bourdieu make this shift? While due to a multitude of factors – including Bourdieu's and sociology's improved position in France – a major factor was the emergence of neoliberalism and what Bourdieu saw as the unwillingness of the French Socialist Party to combat it. Bourdieu spoke of neoliberalism as a theory based upon 'pure mathematical fiction' which is best conceived as 'a political programme of action' in which 'an immense *politi- cal operation* is being pursued … aimed at creating the conditions for realis- ing and operating of the "theory"; a *programme of methodical destruction of collectivities*' (Bourdieu 1998:94–6). As this indicates, Bourdieu conceived of neoliberalism as a project to destroy the gains of the welfare state or, as he also put it, as a 'neo-conservative revolution' in which 'a kind of radical capital- ism…with no restraint or disguise, but rationalised and driven to the limit of its economic efficiency by the introduction of new forms of domination' was becoming dominant (Bourdieu 2008:288). In pursuing this project a collection of actors, including intellectuals, have succeeded in presenting neoliberalism as an inevitability:

> we hear it said, all day long – and this is what gives the dominant dis- course its strength – that there is nothing to put forward in opposition to the neo-liberal view … that there is no alternative. (Bourdieu 1998:29)

To achieve this, the project of neoliberalism had been presented as the empirical reality of 'globalization' which:

> is a myth in the strong sense of the word, a powerful discourse, an *idée force*, an idea which has social force, which obtains belief. It is the main weapon in the battles against the gains of the welfare state. (Bourdieu 1998:34)

As we saw in Chapter 8, this led Bourdieu to be critical of Giddens' work and his links to New Labour. The result of such policies, documented in *Weight of the World*, was increased suffering measured in poverty, poor health, crime rates and insufficient housing. While the 'right hand' of the state was busy making cuts to welfare spending it was unaware of the costs to the 'left hand' of the state in terms of social work and care (Bourdieu 1998:1–10).

Therefore, Bourdieu's entry to public sociology was based upon his professional sociology work documenting the suffering of neoliberal times. Indeed, he justified it on this very basis:

> As I see it, the scholar has no choice today: if he is convinced that there is a correlation between neoliberal policies and crime rates, all the sins of what Durkheim would have called anomie, how can he avoid saying so? It is not just that there is nothing to reproach him for in this, he should even be congratulated. (Bourdieu 2008:381)

Neoliberalism and globalization had created a 'policy of depoliticisation' in which the lack of supposed alternatives had reduced the space for democratic debate and discussion (Bourdieu 2003:38–52). Therefore, Bourdieu's intervention is intended to generate this debate. In doing so, it shows what 'the practice of social science can do for democratic life' by questioning the legitimacy of political claims and helping 'open up the possibility for social transformation' (Swartz 2013:234). For example, he advocates new forms of European and global opposition movements, perhaps emerging from the trade unions, which reject these economic forces and instead seek to 'subordinate them to truly universal ends' (Bourdieu 2003:96).

Bourdieu's case could seem to echo Burawoy's claim that public sociology emerges in response to neoliberalism and seeks to generate democratic debate and a strong civil society by using the findings from professional sociology. But it is also a more complex picture. As we have seen, Bourdieu's desire to 'go public' was partly shaped by the way in which other intellectuals – including some influential in sociology such as Giddens and Beck (Bourdieu 2008:385) as well as Alan Touraine (Swartz 2003:804) and Jean Baudrillard (Bourdieu 1998:32) – had not, in his view, challenged the increased dominance of neoliberalism and rather had become complicit in it. Therefore, Bourdieu's case also reflects claims that public sociology is not, as Burawoy claims, universally instigated by an alliance of sociology and civil society against marketisation. Therefore, there is a need to acknowledge such political plurality. We should also acknowledge, given some of the criticisms of Burawoy, that Bourdieu's powerful position in French sociology gave him a public stage perhaps not available to others (Swartz 2003). Nevertheless, there is one moral which can perhaps be taken from the case of Bourdieu, for which we must once more turn to the work of Bauman.

Just after Bourdieu's death, Bauman (2002) published an article on his 'political turn'. Bauman places Bourdieu in a history of sociology which seeks to define our vision of the social world in which others (politicians, journalists, economists and so on) are also active. These were the groups, and their role in the policy of depoliticisation, who Bourdieu contested in hoping to break the inevitability of neoliberalism. Such a position means that:

> Inserted, by choice or by the nature of things, in the competitive struggle over the substance and shape of world visions, sociology cannot but carve itself upon the reality which it investigates; it transforms human world as it goes on examining its credentials...by doing things that by their very nature are not neutral, the sociologist is already responsible for the shape of the world s/he investigates. Entering political battle is nothing more, yet nothing less either, than assuming responsibility for that responsibility; that step is an ethical demand and a moral act. It is also a 'citizen duty'. (Bauman 2002:186)

Here Bauman draws a link between 'vita contemplativa' (the action all sociologists do in contemplating the social world) and 'vita activa' (acting in that social world publically). Given that sociologists are interested in shared understandings and the condition of that social world, such interventions are somewhat inevitable. Therefore, Bourdieu reflects the tradition outlined in this book of sociologists intervening actively and publically. However, this does not mean, as also shown in this book, that we can proclaim there is a correct or universal political position for sociologists to take or even that all individual sociologists will take up such public activity. This will instead be shaped by factors including their personal political beliefs, position and relation to institutions such as the state.

It is this final point which we shall consider further in the 'Conclusion'. Having traced our history of alternatives in sociology, and considered the role of sociologists in offering them, we could be said to have come full circle. Indeed, many have argued Burawoy's arguments reflect the earlier arguments between Weber and those who followed him, such as Becker and Gouldner (Ossewaarde 2005, Scott 2005). Therefore, the question remaining from our discussion is, what can we learn about the nature of sociology and its alternatives from the ideas outlined in this book?

Conclusion: Sociology and Alternatives

This book has discussed three questions: (1) should sociology offer alternatives? (2) what alternatives has sociology offered? (3) how has/should sociology offer alternatives? As we have seen, these are interlinked. While in Chapter 1 we discussed the value-freedom debates in response to the first question, the concern for what sociology is 'for' – including whether it should offer alternatives – has been a common concern. Furthermore, during the discussion of alternatives, how they should be offered was never far from the surface, as in the discussions in chapters covering Du Bois and James concerning the links of academia and activism. Indeed, the tripartite definition of sociological alternatives provided in the 'Introduction' – a critique, an alternative and a justification for how the alternative solves the critique – has often necessitated this.

To further explore the key elements of sociological alternatives, this conclusion will consider seven themes which could be found throughout this book and the history of social theory it has traced.

The importance of inequality to critique

Many of the critiques in this book take inequality as their focus. This reflects a common idea of sociology being a discipline especially concerned with inequality, most notably class. Indeed, it has been claimed that 'sociology has only one independent variable: class' (Stinchcombe quoted in Wright 1979:3). We may question the contemporary relevance of this claim, indicated by the fact that while there were alternatives which emphasised economic equality, others emphasised differing forms of equality.

In the first category here we can locate Durkheim, for whom economic inequality was one of the key elements of his critique. This led him to claim that inheritance was a pathological social fact and 'contrary to the spirit of individualism' (Durkheim 1992:217). However, for others it was more complicated. While class was a key factor in the construction of Marx's alternative this was not necessarily a push for greater equality – as the 'right to inequality' in the first stage of communism indicated. Meanwhile, while Lefebvre and Marcuse shared the Marxist vision of a classless society they differed on the role of the working class in constructing such an alternative. Furthermore, for Mannheim it was not inequality which was the problem but rather the insufficient mechanisms for creating a 'new ruling class' and stable middle class.

We have also seen a focus on different forms of inequality, whether these be of race (Du Bois), gender (Dworkin) or lifestyles (Giddens). Therefore, while the sociological concern with inequality has been indicated by the alternatives offered in this book, it would be inaccurate to say simply that sociological alternatives universally hope to remove inequality and construct a classless society.

The link of the critique and the alternative

To what extent could the alternatives discussed in this book be combined? Could we, for example, have Du Bois' black economic segregation alongside Beck's cosmopolitan states? Or Mead's everyday democracy alongside Dworkin's campaign to ban pornography? This returns us to the importance of the fact that alternatives begin with a critique. In the terms of Levitas (2007), 'looking for the green' of a utopian reconstruction of society first requires 'looking for the blue' and finding problems with our current one. Therefore, all the alternatives have emerged as an attempt to solve particular problems. It is on this standard by which they can be judged.

We have seen how different critiques can shape divergent alternatives. The most prominent example of this came from Du Bois where a change in his critique (from a concern with forms of education towards economic exploitation) shaped a new alternative in his economic cooperatives. As was suggested, if you agreed with Du Bois' first critique then his second alternative was dangerous and unnecessary. While if we accept his second critique, then the first alternative was pointless. We can also see such divergence between theorists who were otherwise similar. Marcuse's critique that the working class had been co-opted into the happy consciousness of capitalism opened up divisions between his alternative and that of Lefebvre which emphasised class action. Beck's claim that 'methodological nationalism' was no longer viable raised issues for an alternative such as Giddens' Third Way which retained a focus on the nation state. Finally, Dworkin's claim that pornography was 'the DNA' of male dominance, for other feminists, exaggerated its role in causing, rather than being a symptom of, patriarchy.

Consequently, whether alternatives are compatible is perhaps better phrased as whether critiques are complementary. It is when the latter is true, such as in the example of Mead and Dworkin – whose critiques are focused on different elements – that combination is more plausible than when critiques attempt to attack similar problems, like those of Marcuse and Lefebvre.

The willingness (or lack thereof) to provide a blueprint

There has been a tension throughout this book concerning the willingness of theorists to clearly state their alternative and, in the most extreme form, draft a blueprint. This began with our first alternative and Marx's claim that since the proletariat will create communism he would not provide 'recipes for the cook-shops of the future' (Marx 1996a:17). Those inspired by Marx, notably

Lefebvre and Marcuse, shared this view though for slightly different reasons. As we also saw, for some readings of utopianism a blueprint was unnecessary or even dangerous, creating what Sargisson (2012) termed the 'dangerous fools' who claim to have all the answers. Instead utopias are orientation points used for the education of desire and conceiving of ultimate goals (Levitas) or can be found by extrapolating from already existing practices (Wright). Finally, a blueprint was largely unnecessary for Mead since he spent his time attempting to create his alternative via everyday forms of democracy.

However, we also found some dedicated blueprint constructors. Dworkin and MacKinnon wrote their policy into a law which, as we saw, had varying forms of success in North America. Giddens, given his link to the Labour Party, also had to be clear on what policies could be enacted and achieved via his Third Way. While Durkheim, Du Bois, James and others provided at least partial blueprints, perhaps the prime constructor of maps for the future was Mannheim who devoted most of Parts II and III (roughly 200 pages) of his *Freedom, Power and Democratic Planning* to his blueprint.

Why do these differences exist? As indicated above, one reason could be who is seen as the agent of change. When a particular group, whether this is the proletariat or the new subject, is seen to create the new society then responsibility for constructing an alternative shifts to them. A more telling explanation concerns the place of intellectuals. Those with the most detailed blueprints also tended to be those who suggested that intellectuals as a group had a key role to play in the construction of alternatives. Again, Mannheim is the best example of this with his conception of the new ruling class as effectively the 'sociologist king', but there are other examples. Giddens argued that, as an 'intellectual in politics', his main goal was to translate sociological ideas into political practice. Durkheim also saw sociologists as having a 'constant preoccupation' with 'practical questions' which led him to his advocacy of the corporations (Durkheim 1982:160).

While these positions created the space for developing blueprints, others provided less space. Engels warned against the 'individual man of genius', the utopian intellectual seen to have all the answers who became a potential dictator (Engels 1984:112), a concern also shared by Weber who raised such a claim against Marx and Engels (Weber 1918). Also, Mead saw the development of the 'genius' in all as a key part of his alternative and was critical of what he termed 'the academic attitude of creating problems for Doctor's theses' which often didn't help solve social problems (Mead 1938:326) and led him to be critical of Marxism (Mead 1899b). Therefore, the willingness to construct blueprints more often than not reflects the role the writer imagines sociologists to play. Interestingly, despite Marx's unwillingness it has often been a supposed Marxist tendency towards blueprint construction which others have defined themselves against.

Historically, and beyond sociology, intellectuals have not always had a positive relationship with publics. The claim for intellectuals having the interests of the exploited at heart has often manifested itself as a commendation of the ignorant 'masses' in need of help (Carey 1992). The involvement of social scientists in regimes such as Nazism (Ingrao 2013), apartheid South Africa (Connell 2007:99) and, especially in Britain, empire (Steinmetz 2013) is another reason to think carefully about whether such a relationship is necessarily positive.

The distinction between legislators and interpreters

Such debates introduce another distinction concerning the role of sociologists. At the end of Chapter 5 I introduced Bauman's (1987) separation between legislators and interpreters. The former were those who, seeing lay actors as 'dumb' (Bauman 2011:163), sought to provide universal claims enacted by the nation state. This, through re-educating the populace, could become the basis of a new, more rational order. Interpreters instead seek to translate intellectual claims into the concerns of everyday actors. This is done in a conversation, as part of which such actors can reject, accept or modify the claims of sociologists to match their everyday concerns.

Initially it would seem the willingness to construct blueprints would map unproblematically onto this distinction. However, upon further analysis, this is not the case. For example, while James' wages for housework campaign provided at least a partial blueprint it is not true, given her links to social movements, that she imagined lay actors as needing manipulating by elites. The same can be said of Du Bois, especially during his second alternative. In many ways, these providers of blueprints can nevertheless perhaps more accurately be seen as interpreters akin to Mead.

Others do fit this legislator role. Mannheim was initially introduced as an indicator of this but Giddens is probably the ideal. While his critique initially emphasised reflexive actors as 'clever people' his alternative and eventual position in the House of Lords has made him a literal legislator. Beck's methodological cosmopolitanism could also be said to be located in this category with its focus on developing a new, intellectually informed, way of viewing the world and, thereafter, developing alternatives.

Therefore, the role of intellectuals is not a straightforward question in sociology. It is divided internally by ideas of their roles in developing alternatives and externally by relations with social movements and lay actors. It is these factors, and many more, which shape not just the willingness to offer blueprints but the details of the offer.

The significance of socialism as a 'counter-culture'

Tom Bottomore once claimed 'that a close connection exists between sociology and socialism is evident' (Bottomore 1984:1). On the basis of this book there is mixed evidence for such a statement. In support we have the fact that many alternatives have claimed socialism/communism as their end goal (Marx and

Engels, late Du Bois, Lefebvre, Marcuse, James) or, in the case of Durkheim (Gane 1984) and Mead (Shalin 1988), have been proclaimed as socialist by others. Furthermore, those seeking to imagine sociology as utopian have suggested links to socialism, whether this is Levitas' claim that it allows for dignity and grace (Levitas 2013:217) or Wright's idea of using socialism as a compass to judge the value of alternatives (Wright 2006). Finally, as we saw in the previous chapter, Burawoy makes explicit links to the idea of public sociology, with its critique of the market and the state, as a socialist endeavour.

So, initially, there seems strong evidence for the claim of a link between sociology and socialism. However, it is also notable how often socialism has been rejected. Weber's claim for value-freedom was especially strong when discussing the tendency for intellectuals to become 'disciples' of the 'crusading leader and faith' of socialism (Weber 1921:125). For Weber, such intellectuals were 'emotionally unfit for everyday life or averse to it and its demands, and who therefore hunger and thirst after the great revolutionary miracle' (Weber 1918:298). Furthermore, Mead, Mannheim, Giddens and Beck created alternatives in at least partial opposition to socialism, while this barely figured in the debates on pornography (beyond the Marxist critics). Finally, as already discussed, Burawoy was heavily criticised for the socialist sympathies of public sociology, specifically in the claim that this marginalises the intellectual and political plurality of sociology.

Sociology has never been purely socialist with liberal (Collini 1979) and conservative (Strasser 1976) trends also present. Indeed, it is possible to find all these trends in the legacy of one theorist. For example, while this book presented Durkheim's alternative as broadly socialist, some have claimed that his sociology demonstrates far-right and authoritarian tendencies (see Desan and Heilbron 2015 for an overview of this debate). Furthermore, national context is significant in the political positioning in sociology. To provide one comparison, while Canadian sociology has a long-term left-wing tendency partly reflecting the impetus of movements of the 1960s which so inspired Marcuse in sociology's institutional birth (McLaughlin 2005), Irish sociology was long dominated by the Catholic church and therefore limited in its ability to discuss left-wing, especially Marxist, writings (Fanning and Hess 2015). Of course, claiming an inherent or organic link between sociology and socialism can also marginalise the fact that countries under Soviet control had a Marxist–Leninist line imposed on their sociological practice (Mucha and Keen 2010:132–3).

Perhaps a better way of looking at this is to turn to another of Bauman's concepts – that of socialism as a 'counter-culture' to capitalism (Bauman 1976b). Namely, wherever capitalism exists then socialism will exist, at least as an idea, as its opposite. This would explain why many of the alternatives discussed here – all of which were written in the context of a capitalist society of some form – have utilised a form of socialism. It would also help explain why the non-socialist alternatives of Mannheim, Giddens and Beck have had to draw a distinction between their ideas and socialism. This was done either by decrying it as part of the problem (for Mannheim) or seeing it as irrelevant for late/second modernity in which those advocating socialism are 'like blind people discussing colours' (Beck 1997:137). Therefore, any discussion of alternatives, when placed in a capitalist society, is inevitably going to encounter the question of socialism even if such an encounter involves rejection.

The forgotten history of public sociology

In the 'Introduction' I spoke of this book providing a different reading of the history of social theory as a normative enterprise concerned with offering alternatives. Hopefully the reader has found this a valuable story. A different reading could say this is a history of public sociology. As we saw in the last chapter, it is possible to place the writers discussed in this book within the traditional and organic categories developed by Burawoy, which I will not repeat here.

A wider point is what we might call sociology's 'presentism' (Inglis 2014b) or desire for 'newness'. While Burawoy did mention writers like Du Bois and Durkheim as early advocates of public sociology, his work, along with other attempts to discuss the purpose and value of sociology, tends to see this as a reimagining of the discipline. Furthermore, when some unique 'founders' of public sociology are invoked by Burawoy, such as Robert Owen, they tend not to be used for insight on what led them to become public and their theoretical positions but rather 'invoked' as 'symbolic' justification for positions held in the present, furthering this tendency towards presentism (Pūras 2014:63). This involves some lack of appreciation for sociology's history. As we have seen, there are many writers throughout this book who have practised public sociology in different ways: as legislators, as interpreters, linked to social movements or to governments, as part of campaigning groups, crafting laws, and so on. To take one example, it seems Mead would have much to tell us about the value and means of doing public sociology. Alas, it is very rare to see his name mentioned in debates on public sociology – Aronwitz's passing reference (2005:336) being an exception.

It could be argued that this lack of knowledge of sociology's history is negative in and of itself for those seeking to lay claim to what sociology should be. As Durkheim and Fauconnet (1905:229) suggested, sociology spends a lot of time debating what it should be, without reference to what it actually is and has been. However, there is a wider point here which returns us to the discussion of the previous chapter. As we saw there, for some critics of Burawoy the sudden 'discovery' of public sociology threatened to marginalise its history. As Collins (2007) puts it, some had for a long time been practising the 'sociology that had no name'; many of whom tended to be women and/or ethnic minorities. The case of Bourdieu demonstrates some of these complexities. I can only claim to have touched upon such writers in this book, but a proper discussion of public sociology would seek inspiration from the varied writers who populate public sociology's (forgotten) past, such as Jane Addams, Emily Greene Balch, G.D.H. Cole, Clara Cahill Park, Erich Fromm, Herbert Marcuse, Patrick Geddes, Selma James, Pierre Bourdieu, Viola Klein and George Herbert Mead alongside the often-invoked names of Durkheim and Du Bois.

The need for a nuanced discussion concerning what sociology is 'for'

This brings us to the final point. As indicated above, there are frequent attempts to claim what sociology is 'for' or 'pro'. We have seen examples of this throughout. Chapter 5 mentioned claims for sociology being pro-democracy which were also found in Chapter 10 alongside ideas that it is inherently anti-marketisation and pro-civil sphere. In Chapter 1 we saw claims that sociology was pro-the Underdog (Becker) or opposed to the intolerance of human suffering (Gouldner). Throughout we have also seen claims that sociology is somehow inevitably left-wing in its focus. Or, at the least, individual sociologists tend to be left-wing. Indeed, this has reached its apex in claims of the close connection between sociology and socialism. From a different perspective, our discussion of Mannheim also came with the suggestion that sociology is a tool for understanding how to develop common values and develop the obedience towards them. We could also point to other claims such as that sociology is 'the study of all forms of resistance to power' (Touraine 2007:71), hope for a better future (Back 2007:167, Levitas 2007) or that it is concerned with developing 'intellectual liberation' (Berger 1963:198). At the most extreme end is the claim that 'liberation sociology' is the 'real sociology, the sociology that can help bring a more just social world' (Feagin et al. 2015:244–5).

Amid these claims there is often a collapsing of what sociology teaches and the way it allows you to see with the world with a supposed normative goal of sociology. Sociology can be, and often is, a critical discipline concerned with highlighting inequalities and lack of human flourishing. However, it can equally be a discipline concerned with control, defining normality and repression. To use the terms of Bauman (1976a), sociology can be the 'science of unfreedom' just as much as sociologists wish it to be the 'science of freedom'.

So, based upon this discussion, what is sociology 'for'? This returns to the 'Introduction' and my reference to Cole's claim that his students were attending his social theory lectures due to a desire to change the world. We have seen throughout this book how a sociological outlook has helped many to create a vision of an alternative world and how social theory has inspired many to say that things cannot stay like this. For Levitas, by being 'critical' sociology inevitably holds some conception of the good society; this was why sociology had an inherently utopian element. However, we have not found an agreement on the normative end, the type of society, which sociology is for. In this normative sense, sociology is not inherently 'for' anything. This is not a cause for worry or fear but rather is to be celebrated.

Sociology may help, as Bauman once put it, to 'keep other options alive' (Bauman 2008:238) without necessarily being for one of those options or even seeing them as more enticing than the status quo. Perhaps, when we face the question of what sociology is for, the best answer is that 'sociology is passionate about the social'; it argues that 'social life is awesome, amazing and often horrendous, sometimes to be celebrated and sometimes to lead to disenchantment' (Plummer 2010:206). It is this amazement with social life, its ups, its downs, its forms of oppression and potential liberation which has led many sociologists, like those discussed in this book, to seek out a different world: a sociological alternative.

Bibliography

Abbott, A. (2007) 'For Humanist Sociology', in D. Clawson et al. (eds), *Public Sociology*. Berkeley: University of California Press, pp. 195–209.

Acker, J. (2004) 'Gender, Capitalism and Globalization', *Critical Sociology*, 30 (1): 17–41.

Acker, J. (2005) 'Comments on Burawoy on Public Sociology', *Critical Sociology*, 31 (3): 327–31.

Ackerman, B. and Alstott, A. (2004) 'Why Stakeholding', *Politics & Society*, 32 (1):42–60.

Addams, J. (1910) *Twenty Years at Hull-House*. New York: Macmillan.

Adorno, T. (1991) *The Culture Industry: Selected Essays on Mass Culture*. London: Routledge.

Anderson, R.J., Hughes, J.A. and Sharrock, W.W. (1985) *The Sociology Game: An Introduction to Sociological Reasoning*. London: Longman.

Aronwitz, S. (2005) 'Comments on Michael Burawoy's "The Critical Turn to Public Sociology"', *Critical Sociology*, 31 (3): 333–8.

Avineri, S. (1968) *The Social and Political Thought of Karl Marx*. Cambridge: Cambridge University Press.

Back, L. (2007) *The Art of Listening*. London: Berg.

Batiuk, E. and Sacks, H. (1981) 'George Herbert Mead and Karl Marx: Exploring Consciousness and Community', *Symbolic Interaction*, 4 (2): 207–23.

Bauman, Z. (1976a) *Towards a Critical Sociology*. London: Routledge.

Bauman, Z. (1976b) *Socialism: The Active Utopia*. London: Routledge.

Bauman, Z. (1978) *Hermeneutics and Social Science*. London: Routledge.

Bauman, Z. (1987) *Legislators and Interpreters: On Modernity, Post-Modernity and Intellectuals*. Cambridge: Polity Press.

Bauman, Z. (1999) *In Search of Politics*. Cambridge: Polity Press.

Bauman, Z. (2002) 'Pierre Bourdieu. Or the Dialectics of Vita Contemplativa and Vita Activa', *Revue Internationale de Philosophie*, 2002/2 (220): 179–93.

Bauman, Z. (2003) 'Utopia with No Topos', *History of the Human Sciences*, 16 (1): 11–25.

Bauman, Z. (2007a) *Consuming Life*. Cambridge: Polity Press.

Bauman, Z. (2007b) 'Britain after Blair, or Thatcherism Consolidated', in G. Hassan (ed.), *After Blair: Politics after the New Labour Decade*. London: Lawrence and Wishart, pp. 60–74.

Bauman, Z. (2008) 'Bauman on Bauman – Pro Domo Sua', in M.H. Jacobsen and P. Poder (eds), *The Sociology of Zygmunt Bauman: Challenges and Critique*. Hampshire: Ashgate, pp. 231–40.

Bauman, Z. (2011) *Collateral Damage: Social Inequalities in a Global Age*. Cambridge: Polity Press.

Bauman, Z. and Welzer, H. (2002) 'On the Rationality of Evil: An Interview with Zygmunt Bauman', *Thesis Eleven*, 70: 100–12.

Beck, U. (1992) *Risk Society: Towards a New Modernity*. London: Sage.

Beck, U. (1995) *Ecological Politics in an Age of Risk*. Cambridge: Polity Press.

Beck, U. (1997) *The Reinvention of Politics: Rethinking Modernity in the Global Social Order*. Cambridge: Polity Press.

Beck, U. (2000a) *What is Globalization?* Cambridge: Polity Press.

Beck, U. (2000b) *The Brave New World of Work*. Cambridge: Polity Press.

Beck, U. (2000c) 'Democratization of Democracy – Third Way Policy Needs to Redefine Work', *The European Legacy: Towards New Paradigms*, 5 (2): 177–81.

Beck, U. (2002) 'The Terrorist Threat: World Risk Society Revisited', *Theory, Culture and Society*, 19 (4): 39–55.

Beck, U. (2005a) 'Inequality and Recognition: Pan-European Social Conflict and Their Political Dynamics', in A. Giddens and P. Diamond (eds), *The New Egalitarianism*. Cambridge: Polity Press, pp. 120–42.

Beck, U. (2005b) 'The Cosmopolitan State: Redefining Power in the Global Age', *International Journal of Politics, Culture and Society*, 18 (3/4): 143–59.

Beck, U. (2005c) *Power in the Global Age*. Cambridge: Polity Press.

Beck, U. (2006a) *Cosmopolitan Vision*. Cambridge: Polity Press.

Beck, U. (2006b) 'Living in the World Risk Society', *Economy and Society*, 35 (3): 329–45.

Beck, U. (2007) 'The Cosmopolitan Condition: Why Methodological Nationalism Fails', *Theory, Culture and Society*, 24 (7–8): 286–90.

Beck, U. (2008) 'Climate Change and Globalization Are Reinforcing Global Inequalities: High Time for a New Social Democratic Era', *Globalizations*, 5 (1): 78–80.

Beck, U. (2009) *World at Risk*. Cambridge: Polity Press.

Beck, U. (2010a) 'Remapping Social Inequalities in an Age of Climate Change: For a Cosmopolitan Renewal of Sociology', *Global Networks*, 10 (2): 168–81.

Beck, U. (2010b) 'Climate for Change, or How to Create a Green Modernity', *Theory, Culture and Society*, 27 (2–3): 254–66.

Beck, U. (2012a) 'Redefining the Sociological Project: The Cosmopolitan Challenge', *Sociology*, 46 (1): 7–12.

Beck, U. (2012b) *Twenty Observations on a World in Turmoil*. Cambridge: Polity Press.

Beck, U. (2013a) 'Why "Class" is Too Soft a Category to Capture the Explosiveness of Social Inequality at the Beginning of the Twenty-First Century', *British Journal of Sociology*, 64 (1): 63–74.

Beck, U. (2013b) *German Europe*. Cambridge: Polity Press.

Beck, U. (2015) 'Emancipatory Catastrophism: What Does It Mean to Climate Change and Sociology?', *Current Sociology*, 63 (1): 75–88.

Beck, U. and Beck-Gernsheim, E. (1995) *The Normal Chaos of Love*. Cambridge: Polity Press.

Beck, U. and Beck-Gernsheim, E. (2002) *Individualization: Institutionalised Individualism and Its Social and Political Consequences*. London: Sage.

Beck, U. and Beck-Gernsheim, E. (2014) *Distant Love: Personal Life in the Global Age*. Cambridge: Polity Press.

Beck, U. and Grande, E. (2007) *Cosmopolitan Europe*. Cambridge: Polity Press.

Beck, U. and Grande, E. (2010) 'Varieties of Second Modernity: The Cosmopolitan Turn in Social and Political Theory and Research', *British Journal of Sociology*, 61 (3): 409–43.

Beck, U. and Levy, D. (2013) 'Cosmopolitan Nations: Re-imagining Collectivity in World Risk Society', *Theory, Culture and Society*, 30 (2): 3–31.

Beck, U., Giddens, A. and Lash, S. (1994) *Reflexive Modernization: Politics, Tradition and Aesthetics in the Modern Social Order.* Cambridge: Polity Press.

Becker, H. (1967) 'Whose Side Are We On?', *Social Problems*, 14 (3): 239–47.

Benería, L. (1999) 'Globalization, Gender and the Davos Man', *Feminist Economics*, 5 (3): 61–83.

Benn, M. (1998) *Madonna and Child: Towards a New Politics of Parenthood.* London: Jonathan Cape.

Benston, M. (1980) 'The Political Economy of Women's Liberation', in E. Malos (ed.), *The Politics of Housework.* London: Allison and Busby, pp. 119–29.

Benton, T. (1996) 'Marxism and Natural Limits: An Ecological Critique and Reconstruction', in T. Benton (ed.), *The Greening of Marxism.* New York: The Guilford Press, pp. 157–83.

Benton, T. (2002) 'Sociological Theory and Ecological Politics: Reflexive Modernization or Green Socialism?', in R. Dunlap, F. Buttel, P. Dickens and A. Gijswijt (eds), *Sociological Theory and the Environment: Classical Foundations, Contemporary Insights.* Oxford: Rowman and Littlefield Publishers, pp. 252–73.

Berger, P. (1963) *Invitation to Sociology: A Humanistic Perspective.* London: Penguin.

Berger, P. (2011) *Adventures of an Accidental Sociologist: How to Explain the World without Becoming a Bore.* New York: Prometheus Books.

Bergman, H. et al. (2014) 'What about the Future? The Troubled Relationship between Futures and Feminism', *NORA – Nordic Journal of Feminist and Gender Research*, 22 (1): 63–9.

Bergmann, B. (1986) *The Economic Emergence of Women.* New York: Basic Books.

Bergmann, B. (2004) 'A Swedish-Style Welfare State or Basic Income: Which Should Have Priority?', *Politics & Society*, 32 (1): 107–18.

Bernstein, R. (1988) 'Negativity: Themes and Variations', in R. Pippin, A. Feenberg and C. Webel (eds), *Marcuse: Critical Theory and the Promise of Utopia.* Hampshire: Macmillan, pp. 13–28.

Bhambra, G. (2007) *Rethinking Modernity: Postcolonialism and the Sociological Imagination.* Hampshire: Palgrave Macmillan.

Bhambra, G. (2014) 'A Sociological Dilemma: Race, Segregation and US Sociology', *Current Sociology*, 62 (4): 472–92.

Black, A. (1984) *Guilds and Civil Society in European Political Thought from the Twelfth Century to the Present.* London: Methuen.

Black, D. (2014) 'On the Almost Inconceivable Misunderstandings Concerning the Subject of Value-Free Social Science', *British Journal of Sociology*, 64 (4): 763–80.

Blair, T. (1998) *The Third Way: New Politics for the New Century.* London: Fabian Society.

Bloch, E. (1986) *The Principle of Hope.* Oxford: Basil Blackwell.

Blumer, H. (1969) *Symbolic Interactionism: Perspective and Method.* Berkeley: University of California Press.

Boltanski, L. (2011) *On Critique: A Sociology of Emancipation.* Cambridge: Polity Press.

Bottomore, T. (1984) *Sociology and Socialism.* New York: St. Martin's Press.

Bourdieu, P. (1977) *Outline of a Theory of Practice.* Cambridge: Cambridge University Press.

Bourdieu, P. (1984) *Distinction: A Social Critique of the Judgement of Taste.* London: Routledge.

Bourdieu, P. (1998) *Acts of Resistance: Against the New Myths of Our Time*. Cambridge: Polity Press.

Bourdieu, P. (2003) *Firing Back: Against the Tyranny of the Market 2*. London: Verso.

Bourdieu, P. (2008) *Political Interventions: Social Science and Political Action*. London: Verso.

Bourdieu, P. and Passeron, J.-C. (1977) *Reproduction in Education, Society and Culture*. London: Sage.

Bourdieu, P. and Wacquant, L. (2001) 'New Liberal Speak: Notes on the New Planetary Vulgate', *Radical Philosophy*, 105 (January/February): 1–6.

Bourdieu, P. et al. (1999) *The Weight of the World: Social Suffering in Contemporary Society*. Cambridge: Polity Press.

Boyle, K. (ed.) (2010a) *Everyday Pornography*. London: Routledge.

Boyle, K. (2010b) 'Introduction: Everyday Pornography', in K. Boyle (ed.), *Everyday Pornography*. London: Routledge, pp. 1–13.

Boyns, D. and Fletcher, J. (2005) 'Reflections on Public Sociology: Public Relations, Disciplinary Identity, and the Strong Program in Professional Sociology', *The American Sociologist*, 36 (3–4): 5–26.

Brady, D. (2004) 'Why Public Sociology May Fail', *Social Forces*, 82 (4): 1629–38.

Brenner, N. and Elden, S. (2009) 'Introduction: State, Space, World', in N. Brenner and S. Elden (eds), *Henri Lefebvre: State, Space, World Selected Essays*. Minneapolis: University of Minnesota Press, pp. 1–48.

Bronner, S. (1988) 'Between Art and Utopia: Reconsidering the Aesthetic Theory of Herbert Marcuse', in R. Pippin, A. Feenberg and C. Webel (eds), *Marcuse: Critical Theory and the Promise of Utopia*. Hampshire: Macmillan, pp. 107–40.

Brown, W. (1995) *States of Injury: Power and Freedom in Late Modernity*. Princeton, NJ: Princeton University Press.

Brown, W. (2001) *Politics Out of History*. Princeton, NJ: Princeton University Press.

Bryant, C. and Jary, D. (2001) 'Anthony Giddens: A Global Social Theorist', in C. Bryant and D. Jary (eds), *The Contemporary Giddens: Social Theory in a Globalizing Age*. Hampshire: Palgrave Macmillan, pp. 3–39.

Bryson, V. (1999) *Feminist Debates: Issues of Theory and Political Practice*. Hampshire: Palgrave Macmillan.

Burawoy, M. (2005a) 'For Public Sociology', *American Sociological Review*, 70 (1): 4–28.

Burawoy, M. (2005b) 'The Critical Turn to Public Sociology', *Critical Sociology*, 31 (3): 313–26.

Burawoy, M. (2005c) 'Response: Public Sociology: Populist Fad or Path to Renewal?', *British Journal of Sociology*, 56 (3): 417–32.

Burawoy, M. (2005d) 'Rejoinder: Toward a Critical Public Sociology', *Critical Sociology*, 31 (3): 379–90.

Burawoy, M. (2007a) 'Public Sociology vs. the Market', *Socio-Economic Review*, 5 (2): 356–67.

Burawoy, M. (2007b) 'The Field of Sociology: Its Power and Its Promise', in D. Clawson et al. (eds), *Public Sociology*. Berkeley: University of California Press, pp. 241–58.

Burawoy, M. (2010) 'Forging Global Sociology from Below', in S. Patel (ed.), *The ISA Handbook of Diverse Sociological Traditions*. London: Sage, pp. 52–65.

Burawoy, M. and Wright, E.O. (2001) 'Sociological Marxism', in J. Turner (ed.), *Handbook of Sociological Theory*. New York: Springer, pp. 459–86.

Cahill, A. (2001) *Rethinking Rape*. Ithaca: Cornell University Press.

Calhoun, C. (1995) *Critical Social Theory: Culture, History and the Challenge of Difference*. Oxford: Wiley-Blackwell.

Calhoun, C. (2005) 'The Promise of Public Sociology', *British Journal of Sociology*, 56 (3): 355–63.

Calhoun, C. et al. (eds) (2012) *Classical Sociological Theory*. 3rd Edn. Oxford: Wiley-Blackwell.

Carey, J. (1992) *The Intellectuals and the Masses: Pride and Prejudice among the Literary Intelligentsia, 1880–1939*. London: Faber and Faber.

Castree, N. (2010) 'The Paradoxical Professor Giddens', *Sociological Review*, 58 (1): 156–62.

Cheney, G. (1999) *Values at Work: Employee Participation Meets Market Pressures at Mondragón*. Ithaca: ILR Press.

Chernilo, D. (2006) 'Social Theory's Methodological Nationalism: Myth and Reality', *European Journal of Social Theory*, 9 (1): 5–22.

Cladis, M. (1995) 'Education, Virtue and Democracy in the Work of Emile Durkheim', *Journal of Moral Education*, 24 (1): 37–52.

Cohen, J. and Rogers, J. (eds) (1995) *Associations and Democracy*. London: Verso.

Cohen, S. and Taylor, L. (1992) *Escape Attempts: The Theory and Practice of Resistance to Everyday Life*. 2nd Edn. London: Routledge.

Cole, G.D.H. (1920) *Guild Socialism Restated*. London: Routledge.

Cole, G.D.H. (1929) *The Next Ten Years in British Social and Economic Policy*. London: Macmillan.

Cole, G.D.H. (1930) *The Life of Robert Owen*. London: Macmillan.

Cole, G.D.H. (1935) *Principles of Economic Planning*. London: Macmillan.

Cole, G.D.H. (1947) 'Sociology and Politics in the Twentieth Century', in G.D.H. Cole (1950), *Essays in Social Theory*. London: Macmillan, pp. 17–30.

Cole, G.D.H. (1950) *The Subject-Matter of Social Theory*. Lecture, Cole Collection, Nuffield College, University of Oxford. Box 53, Document E3/3/2/1-10.

Cole, G.D.H. (1954) *A History of Socialist Thought: Volume II, Marxism and Anarchism 1850–1890*. London: Macmillan.

Cole, G.D.H. (1957) 'Sociology and Social Policy', *British Journal of Sociology*, 8 (2): 158–71.

Collini, S. (1979) *Liberalism & Sociology: L.T. Hobhouse and Political Argument in England 1880–1914*. Cambridge: Cambridge University Press.

Collins, P.H. (2000) *Black Feminist Thought: Knowledge, Consciousness and the Politics of Empowerment*. London: Routledge.

Collins, P.H. (2007) 'Going Public: Doing the Sociology That Had No Name', in D. Clawson et al. (eds), *Public Sociology*. Berkeley: University of California Press, pp. 101–13.

Connell, R. (2007) *Southern Theory: The Global Dynamics of Knowledge in Social Science*. Cambridge: Polity Press.

Cook, G. (1993) *George Herbert Mead: The Making of a Social Pragmatist*. Chicago: University of Illinois Press.

Coser, L. (1960) 'Durkheim's Conservatism and Its Implication for His Sociological Theory', in K. Wolff (ed.), *Emile Durkheim, 1858–1917*. Columbus: Ohio State University Press, pp. 211–32.

Crenshaw, K. (1991) 'Mapping the Margins: Intersectionality, Identity Politics and Violence against Women of Color', *Stanford Law Review*, 43 (6): 1241–99.

Cristi, M. (2012) 'Durkheim on Moral Individualism, Social Justice, and Rights: A Gendered Construction of Rights', *Canadian Journal of Sociology*, 37 (4): 409–38.

Cushman, T. (2012) 'Intellectuals and Resentment towards Capitalism', *Society*, 49 (3): 247–55.

Dahrendorf, R. (1968) *Essays in the Theory of Society*. London: Routledge.

Dahrendorf, R. (1995) *LSE: A History of the London School of Economics and Political Science 1895–1995*. Oxford: Oxford University Press.

Dalla Costa, M. (1974) 'A General Strike', in W. Edmond and S. Fleming (eds) (1975), *All Work and No Pay: Women, Housework and the Wages Due*. London: Power of Women Collective and the Falling Wall Press, pp. 125–7.

Dalla Costa, M. and James, S. (1972) *The Power of Women and the Subversion of Community*. Bristol: Falling Wall Press.

Davies, B. (1994) 'Durkheim and the Sociology of Education in Britain', *British Journal of Sociology of Education*, 15 (1): 3–25.

Dawson, M. (2013) *Late Modernity, Individualization and Socialism: An Associational Critique of Neoliberalism*. Hampshire: Palgrave Macmillan.

Dawson, M. and Masquelier, C. (2015) 'G.D.H. Cole: Sociology, Politics, Empowerment and "How to Be Socially Good"', in A. Law and E.R. Lybeck (eds), *Sociological Amnesia: Cross-Currents in Disciplinary History*. Farnham: Ashgate, pp. 125–40.

Deegan, M. (1988) *Jane Addams and the Men of the Chicago School, 1892–1918*. Oxford: Transaction Books.

Deegan, M. (2006) 'The Human Drama Behind the Study of People as Potato Bugs: The Curious Marriage of Robert E. Park and Clara Cahill Park', *Journal of Classical Sociology*, 6 (1): 101–22.

Deegan, M. (2007) 'Jane Addams', in J. Scott (ed.), *Fifty Key Sociologists: The Formative Theorists*. London: Routledge, pp. 3–8.

Deegan, M. (2013) 'Jane Addams, the Hull-House School of Sociology, and Social Justice, 1892–1935', *Humanity & Society*, 37 (3): 248–58.

Deegan, M. and Berger, J. (1978) 'George Herbert Mead and Social Reform: His Work and Writings', *Journal of the History of Behavioural Sciences*, 14 (4): 362–73.

DeMarco, J. (1983) *The Social Thought of W.E.B. DuBois*. Lanham, MD: University Press of America.

Dennis, A., Philburn, R. and Smith, G. (2013) *Sociologies of Interaction*. Cambridge: Polity Press.

Desan, M.H. and Heilbron, J. (2015) 'Young Durkheimians and the Temptation of Fascism: The Case of Marcel Déat', *History of the Human Sciences*, 28 (3): 22–50.

Diamond, P. and Giddens, A. (2005) 'The New Egalitarianism: Economic Inequality in the UK', in A. Giddens and P. Diamond (eds), *The New Egalitarianism*. Cambridge: Polity Press, pp. 101–19.

Dines, G. (2010) *Pornland: How Porn Has Hijacked Our Sexuality*. London: Beacon Press.

Draper, H. (1961) 'Marx and the Dictatorship of the Proletariat', *New Politics*, 1 (2): 91–104.

Du Bois, W.E.B. (1897) 'The Conservation of Races', in W.E.B. Du Bois (1986), *W.E.B. Du Bois: Writings*. New York: The Library of America, pp. 815–26.

Du Bois, W.E.B. (1898) 'Careers Open to College-Bred Negroes', in W.E.B. Du Bois (1986), *W.E.B. Du Bois: Writings*. New York: The Library of America, pp. 827–41.

Du Bois, W.E.B. (1903) 'The Talented Tenth', in W.E.B. Du Bois (1986), *W.E.B. Du Bois: Writings*. New York: The Library of America, pp. 842–61.

Du Bois, W.E.B. (1933) 'The Negro College', in W.E.B. Du Bois (1986), *W.E.B. Du Bois: Writings*. New York: The Library of America, pp. 1010–19.

Du Bois, W.E.B. (1934) 'Segregation in the North', in W.E.B. Du Bois (1986), *W.E.B. Du Bois: Writings*. New York: The Library of America, pp. 1239–48.

Du Bois, W.E.B. (1944) 'My Evolving Program for Negro Freedom', in R. Logan (ed.), *What the Negro Wants*. Chapel Hill: University of North Carolina Press, pp. 31–70.

Du Bois, W.E.B. (1952a) 'The Trial', in W.E.B. Du Bois (1986), *W.E.B. Du Bois: Writings.* New York: The Library of America, pp. 1071–92.

Du Bois, W.E.B. (1952b) 'The Acquittal', in W.E.B. Du Bois (1986), *W.E.B. Du Bois: Writings.* New York: The Library of America, pp. 1093–109.

Du Bois, W.E.B. (1956) *Black Reconstruction in America.* New York: S.A. Russell Company.

Du Bois, W.E.B. (1958a) 'Towards a Socialist America', in H. Alfred (ed.), *Towards a Socialist America.* New York: Peace Publications, pp. 179–91.

Du Bois, W.E.B. (1958b) 'A Vista of Ninety Fruitful Years', in W.E.B. Du Bois (1986), *W.E.B. Du Bois: Writings.* New York: The Library of America, pp. 1110–13.

Du Bois, W.E.B. (1984) *Dusk of Dawn: An Essay toward an Autobiography of a Race Concept.* London: Transaction Publishers.

Du Bois, W.E.B. (1994) *The Souls of Black Folk.* New York: Dover.

Du Bois, W.E.B. (1996) *The Philadelphia Negro: A Social Study.* Philadelphia: University of Pennsylvania Press.

Du Bois, W.E.B. (2000) 'Sociology Hesitant', *Boundary,* 27 (3): 37–44.

Du Bois, W.E.B. (2003) *Darkwater: Voices from Within the Veil.* Amherst: Humanity Books.

Durkheim, E. (1885) 'Social Property and Democracy: Review of Alfred Fouille, *La Propriete et la Democratie* (Paris, 1884)', in E. Durkheim (1986), *Durkheim on Politics and the State.* Stanford: Stanford University Press, pp. 86–96.

Durkheim, E. (1899) 'Review of Saverio Merlino: *Forms et Essence du Socialisme* (Paris, 1897)', in E. Durkheim (1986), *Durkheim on Politics and the State.* Stanford: Stanford University Press, pp. 136–45.

Durkheim, E. (1908) 'A Debate on Civil Service Unions', in E. Durkheim (1986), *Durkheim on Politics and the State.* Stanford: Stanford University Press, pp. 145–53.

Durkheim, E. (1952) *Suicide.* London: Routledge.

Durkheim, E. (1953) *Sociology and Philosophy.* London: Routledge.

Durkheim, E. (1959) *Socialism and Saint-Simon.* London: Routledge.

Durkheim, E. (1961) *Moral Education: A Study in the Theory & Application of the Sociology of Education.* New York: Free Press.

Durkheim, E. (1973) 'Individualism and the Intellectuals', in E. Durkheim, *On Morality and Society.* Chicago: University of Chicago Press, pp. 43–57.

Durkheim, E. (1982) *The Rules of Sociological Method.* Hampshire: Macmillan.

Durkheim, E. (1984) *The Division of Labour in Society.* Hampshire: Macmillan.

Durkheim, E. (1992) *Professional Ethics and Civic Morals.* London: Routledge.

Durkheim, E. (1995) 'Durkheim and Moral Education for Children: A Recently Discovered Lecture', *Journal of Moral Education,* 24 (1): 26–36.

Durkheim, E. (2009) 'The Politics of the Future', *Durkheimian Studies,* 15: 3–6.

Durkheim, E. and Fauconnet, P. (1905) 'Sociology and the Social Sciences', in Sociological Society *Sociological Papers 1904.* London: Macmillan, pp. 258–80.

Durkin, K. (2014) *The Radical Humanism of Erich Fromm.* Hampshire: Palgrave Macmillan.

Dworkin, A. (1987) *Intercourse.* New York: Basic Books.

Dworkin, A. (1989) *Pornography: Men Possessing Women.* London: Penguin.

Ehrenreich, B. (2007) 'A Journalist's Plea', in D. Clawson et al. (eds), *Public Sociology.* Berkeley: University of California Press, pp. 231–8.

Elden, S. (2004) *Understanding Henri Lefebvre: Theory and the Possible.* London: Continuum.

Eldridge, J. (1990) 'Sociology in Britain: A Going Concern', in C. Bryant and H. Becker (eds), *What Has Sociology Achieved?* London: Macmillan, pp. 157–78.

Eldridge, J. (2000) 'Sociology and the Third Way', in J. Eldridge et al. (eds), *For Sociology: Legacies and Prospects.* Durham: Sociology Press, pp. 131–44.

Elshtain, J.B. (1981) *Public Man, Private Woman.* Princeton, NJ: Princeton University Press.

Engels, F. (1958) *The Condition of the Working Class in England.* Oxford: Basil Blackwell.

Engels, F. (1978) *The Origin of the Family, Private Property and the State.* Peking: Foreign Languages Press.

Engels, F. (1984) 'Socialism: Utopian and Scientific', in L.S. Feuer (ed.), *Karl Marx & Friedrich Engels: Basic Writings on Politics and Philosophy.* Aylesbury: Fontana/Collins, pp. 109–52.

Engels, F. (1990) 'Introduction to Karl Marx's *The Civil War in France*', in K. Marx and F. Engels, *Karl Marx and Frederick Engels Collected Works: Volume 27.* London: Lawrence & Wishart, pp. 179–91.

Ericson, R. (2005) 'Publicising Sociology', *British Journal of Sociology*, 56 (3): 365–72.

Etzoni, A. (2005) 'Bookmarks for Public Sociologists', *British Journal of Sociology*, 56 (3): 373–8.

European Parliament (2013) 'Equality in the Boardroom', *European Parliament*, http://www.europarl.europa.eu/news/en/top-stories/content/20131015TST22325/html/Equality-in-the-boardroom, date accessed: 24 February 2014.

Fanning, B. and Hess, A. (2015) *Sociology in Ireland: A Short History.* Hampshire: Palgrave Macmillan.

Feagin, J., Vera, H. and Ducey, K. (2015) *Liberation Sociology.* 3rd Edn. Boulder: Paradigm.

Fedrici, S. (1980) 'Wages against Housework', in E. Malos (ed.), *The Politics of Housework.* London: Allison and Busby, pp. 253–61.

Felski, R. (1999/2000) 'The Invention of Everyday Life', *New Formations*, 39: 15–31.

Feltey, K and Rushing, B. (1998) 'Women and Power in Sociology: SWS as an Arena of Change', *Sociological Spectrum*, 18 (3): 211–28.

Fisher, B.M. and Strauss, A.L. (1979) 'George Herbert Mead and the Chicago Tradition of Sociology', *Symbolic Interaction*, 2 (1): 9–26.

Fitzpatrick, T. (1999) *Freedom and Security: An Introduction to the Basic Income Debate.* Hampshire: Macmillan.

Foster, J.B. (2000) *Marx's Ecology: Materialism and Nature.* New York: Monthly Review Press.

Fournier, M. (2013) *Émile Durkheim: A Biography.* Cambridge: Polity Press.

Freud, S. (2002) *Civilization and Its Discontents.* London: Penguin Press.

Fraser, N. (1997) *Justice Interruptus: Critical Reflections on the 'Postsocialist' Condition.* London: Routledge.

Friedan, B. (1963) *The Feminine Mystique.* London: Penguin Press.

Friedman, M. (2013) 'The Case for a Negative Income Tax: A View from the Right', in Widerquist, K. et al. (eds), *Basic Income: An Anthology of Contemporary Research.* Oxford: Wiley-Blackwell, pp. 11–16.

Fromm, E. (1956) *The Sane Society.* London: Routledge.

Fromm, E. (1981) 'The Psychological Aspects of the Guaranteed Income', in E. Fromm *On Disobedience and Other Essays.* New York: The Seabury Press, pp. 91–101.

Fukuyama, F. (1992) *The End of History and the Last Man.* London: Hamish Hamilton.

Fung, A. and Wright, E.O. (eds) (2003) *Deepening Democracy: Innovations in Empowered Participatory Governance*. London: Verso.

Gane, M. (1984) 'Institutional Socialism and the Sociological Critique of Communism (Introduction to Durkheim and Mauss)', *Economy and Society*, 13 (3): 304–30.

Gane, N. and Back, L. (2012) 'C. Wright Mills 50 Years On: The Promise and Craft of Sociology Revisited', *Theory, Culture and Society*, 29 (7–8): 399–421.

Gardiner, M. (2012) 'Henri Lefebvre and the "Sociology of Boredom"', *Theory, Culture and Society*, 29 (2): 37–62.

Garrett, P. (2008) 'Helping Labour to Win Again? Anthony Giddens' Programme for the New Prime Minister', *Critical Social Policy*, 28 (2): 235–45.

Geoghegan, V. (1987) *Utopianism and Marxism*. London: Methuen.

Giddens, A. (1971) *Capitalism and Modern Social Theory*. Cambridge: Cambridge University Press.

Giddens, A. (1981) *A Contemporary Critique of Historical Materialism: Power, Property and the State*. London: Macmillan.

Giddens, A. (1982) 'Class Division, Class Conflict and Citizenship Rights', in A. Giddens *Profiles and Critique in Social Theory*. London: Macmillan, pp. 164–80.

Giddens, A. (1984) *The Constitution of Society: Outline of the Theory of Structuration*. Cambridge: Polity Press.

Giddens, A. (1990) *The Consequences of Modernity*. Cambridge: Polity Press.

Giddens, A. (1991) *Modernity and Self-Identity: Self and Society in the Late Modern Age*. Cambridge: Polity Press.

Giddens, A. (1992) *The Transformation of Intimacy*. Cambridge: Polity Press.

Giddens, A. (1994a) *Beyond Left and Right: The Future of Radical Politics*. Cambridge: Polity Press.

Giddens, A. (1994b) 'Living in a Post-Traditional Society', in U. Beck, A. Giddens and S. Lash (eds), *Reflexive Modernisation: Politics, Tradition and Aesthetics in the Modern Social Order*. Cambridge: Polity Press, pp. 56–109.

Giddens, A. (1995) 'Introduction', in A. Giddens (ed.), *Politics, Sociology and Social Theory: Encounters with Classical and Contemporary Social Thought*. Cambridge: Polity Press, pp. 1–14.

Giddens, A. (1998a) *The Third Way: The Renewal of Social Democracy*. Cambridge: Polity Press.

Giddens, A. (1998b) 'Risk Society: The Context of British Politics', in J. Franklin (ed.), *The Politics of Risk Society*. Cambridge: Polity Press, pp. 23–34.

Giddens, A. (2000) *The Third Way and Its Critics*. Cambridge: Polity Press.

Giddens, A. (2001) 'Introduction', in A. Giddens (ed.), *The Global Third Way Debate*. Cambridge: Polity Press, 1–22.

Giddens, A. (2002) *Where Now for New Labour?* Cambridge: Polity Press.

Giddens, A. (2004) 'Did They Foul Up My Third Way?', *New Statesman*, 7 June.

Giddens, A. (2007a) *Over to You, Mr. Brown: How New Labour Can Win Again*. Cambridge: Polity Press.

Giddens, A. (2007b) 'An Intellectual in Politics: A Talk by Professor Lord Giddens', *Twenty-First Century Society: Journal of the Academy of Social Sciences*, 2 (2): 121–9.

Giddens, A. (2007c) 'My Chat with the Colonel', *Guardian*, 9 March, http://www.theguardian.com/commentisfree/2007/mar/09/comment.libya, date accessed: 4 May 2014.

Giddens, A. (2011) *The Politics of Climate Change*. Cambridge: Polity Press.

Giddens, A. (2013) *Turbulent and Mighty Continent: What Future for Europe?* Cambridge: Polity Press.

Giddens, A., Bleicher, J. and Featherstone, M. (1982) 'Historical Materialism Today: An Interview with Anthony Giddens', *Theory, Culture & Society*, 1 (2): 63–77.

Giddens, A., Bryant, C. and Jary, D. (2001) 'The Reflexive Giddens', in C. Bryant and D. Jary (eds), *The Contemporary Giddens: Social Theory in a Globalizing Age*. Hampshire: Palgrave Macmillan, pp. 229–67.

Gillies, V. (2005) 'Raising the "Meritocracy": Parenting and the Individualization of Social Class', *Sociology*, 39 (5): 835–53.

Gilroy, P. (1993) *Black Atlantic: Modernity and Double Consciousness*. London: Verso.

Gornick, J. and Meyers, M. (eds) (2009) *Gender Equality: Transforming Family Divisons of Labour*. London: Verso.

Gorz, A. (1999) *Reclaiming Work: Beyond the Wage-Based Society*. Cambridge: Polity Press.

Gouldner, A. (1962) 'Anti-Minotaur: The Myth of a Value-Free Sociology', *Social Problems*, 9 (3): 199–213.

Gouldner, A. (1968) 'The Sociologist as Partisan', *The American Sociologist*, 3 (2): 103–16.

Graeber, D. (2002) 'The New Anarchists', *New Left Review*, 13: 61–73.

Habermas, J. (1985) *The Theory of Communicative Action Volume One: Reason and the Rationalization of Society*. Cambridge: Polity Press.

Habermas, J. (1987) *The Theory of Communicative Action Volume Two: Lifeworld and System: The Critique of Functionalist Reason*. Cambridge: Polity Press.

Habermas, J. (2000) *The Postnational Constellation: Political Essays*. Cambridge: Polity Press.

Hall, S. (2011) 'The Neo-Liberal Revolution', *Cultural Studies*, 25 (6): 705–28.

Halsey, A.H. (2004) *A History of Sociology in Britain: Science, Literature and Society*. Oxford: Oxford University Press.

Hammersley, M. (1999) 'Sociology, What's It For? A Critique of Gouldner', *Sociological Research Online*, 4 (3), http://www.socresonline.org.uk/4/3/hammersley.html, date accessed: 23 March 2015.

Hammersley, M. (2005) 'Should Social Science Be Critical?', *Philosophy of the Social Sciences*, 35 (2): 175–95.

Haraway, D. (2004) 'Situated Knowledges: The Science Question in Feminism and the Privilege of Partial Perspective', in S. Harding (ed.), *The Feminist Standpoint Theory Reader: Intellectual and Political Controversies*. London: Routledge, pp. 81–102.

Harding, S. (1987) 'Introduction: Is There a Feminist Methodology?', in S. Harding (ed.), *Feminism and Methodology*. Milton Keynes: Open University Press, pp. 1–14.

Harrington, A. (2005) *Modern Social Theory: An Introduction*. Oxford: Oxford University Press.

Harvey, D. (1991) 'Afterword', in H. Lefebvre (1991a), *The Production of Space*. Oxford: Blackwell, pp. 425–34.

Harvey, D. (2005) *A Brief History of Neoliberalism*. Oxford: Oxford University Press.

Hawkins, M.J. (1994) 'Durkheim on Occupational Corporations: An Exegesis and Interpretation', *Journal of the History of Ideas*, 55 (3): 461–81.

Held, D. (2000) 'Regulating Globalization? The Reinvention of Politics', *International Sociology*, 15 (2): 394–408.

Held, D. (2006) *Models of Democracy*. 3rd Edn. Cambridge: Polity Press.

Held, D. et al. (1999) *Global Transformations*. Cambridge: Polity Press.

Highmore, B. (2002) *Everyday Life and Cultural Theory*. London: Routledge.

Hirst, P. (1994) *Associative Democracy: New Forms of Economic and Social Governance*. Cambridge: Polity Press.

Hobsbawm, E. (1998) 'On the *Communist Manifesto*', in E. Hobsbawm (2011), *How to Change the World: Tales of Marx and Marxism*. London: Abacus, pp. 101–20.

Hochschild, A. (1989) *The Second Shift: Working Parents and the Revolution at Home*. New York: Viking.

Hochschild, A. (2003) *The Commercialization of Intimate Life*. Berkeley: University of California Press.

Holloway, J. (2010) *Crack Capitalism*. London: Pluto Press.

Holmes, R. (2014) *Eleanor Marx: A Life*. London: Bloomsbury.

Holmwood, J. (2007) 'Sociology as Public Discourse and Professional Practice: A Critique of Michael Burawoy', *Sociological Theory*, 25 (1): 46–66.

Holton, R. (2009) *Cosmopolitanisms: New Thinking and New Directions*. Hampshire: Palgrave Macmillan.

Horne, A. (2007) *The Fall of Paris: The Siege and the Commune 1870–71*. London: Penguin.

Hornstein, S. (2009) 'On Totalitarianism: The Continuing Relevance of Herbert Marcuse', in G. Bhambra and I. Demir (eds), *1968 in Retrospect: History, Theory, Alterity*. Hampshire: Palgrave Macmillan, pp. 87–99.

Huebner, D. (2014) *Becoming Mead: The Social Process of Academic Knowledge*. Chicago: University of Chicago Press.

Inglis, D. (2014a) 'Cosmopolitanism's Sociology and Sociology's Cosmopolitanism: Retelling the History of Cosmopolitan Theory from Stoicism to Durkheim and Beyond', *Distinktion: Scandinavian Journal of Social Theory*, 15 (1): 69–87.

Inglis, D. (2014b) 'What Is Worth Defending in Sociology Today? Presentism, Historical Vision and the Uses of Sociology', *Cultural Sociology*, 8 (1): 99–118.

Inglis, D. and Thorpe, C. (2012) *An Invitation to Social Theory*. Cambridge: Polity Press.

Ingrao, C. (2013) *Believe and Destroy: Intellectuals in the SS War Machine*. Cambridge: Polity Press.

Jackson, T. (2009) *Prosperity without Growth: Economics for a Finite Planet*. London: Earthscan.

James, S. (1975) 'Wageless of the World', in W. Edmond and S. Fleming (eds), *All Work and No Pay: Women, Housework and the Wages Due*. London: Power of Women Collective and the Falling Wall Press, pp. 25–34.

James, S. (2012) *Sex, Race and Class: The Perspective of Winning*. London: Merlin Press.

Joas, H. (1997) *G.H. Mead: A Contemporary Re-Examination of His Thought*. Cambridge, MA: MIT Press.

Katz, B. (1982) *Herbert Marcuse and the Art of Liberation*. London: New Left Books.

Katz-Fishman, W. and Scott, J. (2005) 'Comments on Burawoy: A View from the Bottom-Up', *Critical Sociology*, 31 (3): 371–74.

Kettler, D. and Meja, V. (1988) 'The Reconstitution of Political Life: The Contemporary Relevance of Karl Mannheim's Political Project', *Polity*, 20 (4): 623–47.

Kettler, D., Meja, V. and Stehr, N. (1984) *Karl Mannheim*. Chichester: Ellis Horwood.

Korgen, K., White, J. and White, S. (eds) (2011) *Sociologists in Action: Sociology, Social Change and Social Justice*. London: Sage.

Kudomi, Y. (1996) 'Karl Mannheim in Britain: An Interim Research Report', *Hitotsubashi Journal of Social Studies*, 28 (2): 43–56.

Kumar, K. (1987) *Utopia and Anti-Utopia in Modern Times*. Oxford: Basil Blackwell.

Kumar, K. (1991) *Utopianism*. Milton Keynes: Open University Press.

Labour Women's Network (2014) 'All-Women Shortlists', *Labour Women's Network*, http://www.lwn.org.uk/all_women_shortlists, date accessed: 24 February 2014.

Landes, J. (1980) 'Wages for Housework: Political and Theoretical Considerations', in E. Malos (ed.), *The Politics of Housework*. London: Allison and Busby, pp. 262–74.

Lanning, T. (2013) *Great Expectations: Exploring the Promise of Gender Equality*. London: Institute for Public Policy Research.

Larsson, A. and Magdalenić, S. (2015) *Sociology in Sweden: A History*. Hampshire: Palgrave Macmillan.

Latouche, S. (2009) *Farewell to Growth*. Cambridge: Polity Press.

Law, A. (2014) *Social Theory for Today: Making Sense of Social Worlds*. London: Sage.

Lefebvre, H. (1964a) 'The Withering Away of the State: The Sources of Marxist-Leninist State Theory', in N. Brenner and S. Elden (eds) (2009), *Henri Lefebvre: State, Space, World Selected Essays*. Minneapolis: University of Minnesota Press, pp. 69–94.

Lefebvre, H. (1964b) 'The State and Society', in N. Brenner and S. Elden (eds) (2009), *Henri Lefebvre: State, Space, World Selected Essays*. Minneapolis: University of Minnesota Press, pp. 51–68.

Lefebvre, H. (1966) 'Theoretical Problems of *Autogestion*', in N. Brenner and S. Elden (eds) (2009), *Henri Lefebvre: State, Space, World Selected Essays*. Minneapolis: University of Minnesota Press, pp. 138–52.

Lefebvre, H. (1968) *The Sociology of Marx*. London: Allen Lane.

Lefebvre, H. (1971) *Everyday Life in the Modern World*. London: Continuum.

Lefebvre, H. (1976a) *The Survival of Capitalism: Reproduction of the Relations of Production*. London: Allison and Busby.

Lefebvre, H. (1976b) '"It Is the World That Has Changed": Interview with *Autogestion et socialisme*', in N. Brenner and S. Elden (eds) (2009), *Henri Lefebvre: State, Space, World Selected Essays*. Minneapolis: University of Minnesota Press, pp. 153–64.

Lefebvre, H. (1988) 'Towards a Leftist Cultural Politics: Remarks Occasioned by the Centenary of Marx's Death', in C. Nelson and L. Grossberg (eds), *Marxism and the Interpretation of Culture*. Hampshire: Macmillan Education, pp. 75–88.

Lefebvre, H. (1990) 'From the Social Pact to the Contract of Citizenship', in H. Lefebvre (2003), *Key Writings*. London: Continuum, pp. 238–54.

Lefebvre, H. (1991a) *The Production of Space*. Oxford: Blackwell.

Lefebvre, H. (1991b) *Critique of Everyday Life: Volume 1*. London: Verso.

Lefebvre, H. (1995) *Introduction to Modernity*. London: Verso.

Lefebvre, H. (2002) *Critique of Everyday Life, Volume 2: Foundations for a Sociology of the Everyday*. London: Verso.

Lefebvre, H. (2005) *Critique of Everyday Life, Volume 3: From Modernity to Modernism*. London: Verso.

Leggett, W. (2005) *After New Labour*. Hampshire: Palgrave Macmillan.

Lemert, C. (2008) 'W.E.B. Du Bois', in G. Ritzer (ed.), *Blackwell Companion to Major Classical Social Theorists*. Oxford: Blackwell, pp. 333–54.

Lenin, V.I. (1932) *State and Revolution*. New York: International Publishers.

Lenin, V.I. (1962) 'Lessons of the Commune', in V.I. Lenin, *Collected Works: Volume 13*. London: Lawrence and Wishart, pp. 475–478.

Levine, A. (1995) 'Democratic Corporatism and/versus Socialism', in J. Cohen and J. Rogers (eds), *Associations and Democracy*. London: Verso, pp. 157–66.

Levitas, R. (1979) 'Sociology and Utopia', *Sociology*, 13 (1): 19–33.

Levitas, R. (1986) 'Competition and Compliance: The Utopias of the New Right', in R. Levitas (ed.), *The Ideology of the New Right*. Cambridge: Polity Press, pp. 80–106.

Levitas, R. (2000a) 'For Utopia: The (Limits of the) Utopian Function in Late Capitalist Society', *Critical Review of International Social and Political Philosophy*, 3 (2–3): 25–43.

Levitas, R. (2000b) 'Discourses of Risk and Utopia', in B. Adam, U. Beck and J. Van Loon (eds), *The Risk Society and Beyond*. London: Sage, pp. 198–210.

Levitas, R. (2001) 'Against Work: A Utopian Excursion into Social Policy', *Critical Social Policy*, 21 (4): 449–65.

Levitas, R. (2003) 'The Elusive Idea of Utopia', *History of the Human Sciences*, 16 (1): 1–10.

Levitas, R. (2005a) *The Imaginary Reconstruction of Society: Or, Why Sociologists and Others Should Take Utopia More Seriously*, Inaugural lecture delivered at the University of Bristol, 24 October 2005, http://www.bris.ac.uk/spais/files/inaugural.pdf

Levitas, R. (2005b) *The Inclusive Society? Social Exclusion and New Labour*. Hampshire: Palgrave Macmillan.

Levitas, R. (2005c) *Morris, Hammersmith and Utopia*. London: William Morris Society.

Levitas, R. (2007) 'Looking for the Blue: The Necessity of Utopia', *Journal of Political Ideologies*, 12 (3): 286–306.

Levitas, R. (2010) 'Back to the Future: Wells, Sociology, Utopia and Method', *Sociological Review*, 58 (4): 530–47.

Levitas, R. (2012) 'The Just's Umbrella: Austerity and the Big Society, Coalition Policy and Beyond', *Critical Social Policy*, 32 (3): 320–42.

Levitas, R. (2013) *Utopia as Method: The Imaginary Reconstruction of Society*. Hampshire: Palgrave Macmillan.

Levy, A. (2006) *Female Chauvinist Pigs: Women and the Rise of Raunch Culture*. London: Pocket Books.

Lister, R. (1999) 'What Welfare Provisions Do Women Need to Become Full Citizens?', in S. Walby (ed.), *New Agendas for Women*. Hampshire: Palgrave Macmillan, pp. 17–31.

Loader, C. (1985) *The Intellectual Development of Karl Mannheim: Culture, Politics, and Planning*. Cambridge: Cambridge University Press.

Loader, I. and Sparks, R. (2011) *Public Criminology?* London: Routledge.

Loyal, S. (2003) *The Sociology of Anthony Giddens*. London: Pluto Press.

Lubasz, H. (1976) 'Marx's Initial Problematic: The Problem of Poverty', *Political Studies*, 24 (1): 24–42.

Lukes, S. (1973) *Émile Durkheim: His Life and Work*. London: Penguin.

Lumsden, K. (2012) '"You Are What You Research": Research Partisanship and the Sociology of the "Underdog"', *Qualitative Research*, 13 (1): 3–18.

Lynch, A. (2012) *Porn Chic: Exploring the Countours of Raunch Eroticism*. London: Berg.

MacKinnon, C. (1982) 'Feminism, Marxism, Method and the State: An Agenda for Theory', *Feminist Theory*, 7 (3): 515–44.

MacKinnon, C. (1989) 'Sexuality, Pornography and Method: Pleasure under Patriarchy', *Ethics*, 99 (2): 314–46.

MacKinnon, C. (1991) 'Pornography as Defamation and Discrimination' *Boston University Law Review*, 71 (5): 793–818.

MacKinnon, C. (1997) 'Rape: On Coercion and Consent', in K. Conboy, N. Medina and S. Stanbury (eds), *Writing on the Body: Female Embodiment and Feminist Theory.* New York: Columbia University Press, 42–58.

MacKinnon, C. and Dworkin, A. (1994) 'Statement by Catherine A. MacKinnon and Andrea Dworkin Regarding Canadian Customs and Legal Approaches to Pornography', *No Status Quo*, http://www.nostatusquo.com/ACLU/dworkin/Ordinance-Canada.html, date accessed: 12 February 2014.

MacKinnon, C. and Dworkin, A. (1997) *In Harm's Way: The Pornography Civil Rights Hearings.* Harvard, MA: Harvard University Press.

MacIntyre, A. (1970) *Marcuse.* London: Fontana.

Magubane, Z. (2014) 'Science, Reform, and the 'Science of Reform': Booker T Washington, Robert Park, and the Making of a "Science of Society"', *Current Sociology*, 62 (4): 568–83.

Mannheim, K. (1936) *Ideology and Utopia: An Introduction to the Sociology of Knowledge.* New York: Harvest Books.

Mannheim, K. (1938) 'Planned Society and the Problem of Human Personality: A Sociological Analysis', in K. Mannheim (1953), *Essays on Sociology and Social Psychology.* London: Routledge, 255–310.

Mannheim, K. (1943) *Diagnosis of Our Time: Wartime Essays of a Sociologist.* London: Routledge.

Mannheim, K. (1951) *Freedom, Power and Democratic Planning.* London: Routledge.

Marable, M. (1986) *W.E.B. Du Bois: Black Radical Democrat.* Boston, MA: Twayne Publishers.

Marcuse, H. (1956) *Eros and Civilization: A Philosophical Inquiry into Freud.* London: Routledge.

Marcuse, H. (1958) *Soviet Marxism: A Critical Analysis.* London: Routledge.

Marcuse, H. (1964) *One-Dimensional Man: Studies in the Ideology of Advanced Industrial Society.* London: Routledge.

Marcuse, H. (1967) 'The End of Utopia', in H. Marcuse (1970), *Five Lectures.* Boston: Beacon Press, pp. 62–82.

Marcuse, H. (1968) 'Liberation from the Affluent Society', in D. Cooper (ed.), *The Dialectics of Liberation.* Harmondsworth: Penguin, pp. 175–92.

Marcuse, H. (1969a) *An Essay on Liberation.* London: Allen Lane.

Marcuse, H. (1969b) 'On the New Left', in H. Marcuse (2005), *The New Left and the 1960s: Collected Papers of Herbert Marcuse Volume Three.* London: Routledge, pp. 122–7.

Marcuse, H. (1974) 'Marxism and Feminism', in H. Marcuse (2005), *The New Left and the 1960s: Collected Papers of Herbert Marcuse Volume Three.* London: Routledge, pp. 165–72.

Marshall, B. and Witz, A. (eds) (2004) *Engendering the Social: Feminist Encounters with Sociological Theory.* Milton Keynes: Open University Press.

Martell, L. (1994) *Ecology and Society: An Introduction.* Cambridge: Polity Press.

Martell, L. (2010) *The Sociology of Globalization.* Cambridge: Polity Press.

Marx, K. (1976) *Capital: Volume 1.* London: Penguin.

Marx, K. (1978) 'The Class Struggles in France, 1948–50', in K. Marx and F. Engels, *Karl Marx and Frederick Engels Collected Works: Volume 10.* London: Lawrence & Wishart, pp. 45–146.

Marx, K. (1992a) 'Economic and Philosophical Manuscripts', in K. Marx, *Early Writings.* London: Penguin, pp. 279–400.

Marx, K. (1992b) 'Concerning Feuerbach', in K. Marx, *Early Writings*. London: Penguin, pp. 421–3.

Marx, K. (1992c) 'Preface to a Contribution to the Critique of Political Economy', in K. Marx, *Early Writings*. London: Penguin, pp. 424–8.

Marx, K. (1996a) 'Afterword to the Second German Edition', in K. Marx and F. Engels, *Karl Marx and Frederick Engels Collected Works: Volume 35*. London: Lawrence & Wishart, pp. 12–22.

Marx, K. (1996b) 'The Civil War in France', in K. Marx, *Later Political Writings*. Cambridge: Cambridge University Press, pp. 163–207.

Marx, K. (1996c) 'Critique of the Gotha Programme', in K. Marx, *Later Political Writings*. Cambridge: Cambridge University Press, pp. 208–26.

Marx, K. (2007) *Dispatches for the New York Tribune: Selected Journalism of Karl Marx*. London: Penguin.

Marx, K. and Engels, F. (1992) *The Communist Manifesto*. Oxford: Oxford University Press.

Marx, K. and Engels, F. (1998) *The German Ideology*. New York: Prometheus Books.

Marx, K. and Landor, R. (1962) 'The Curtain Raised: Interview with Karl Marx, the Head of L'Internationale', *New Politics*, 2 (3): 128–33.

McDonald, L. (1997) 'Classical Social Theory with the Women Founders Included', in C. Camic (ed.), *Reclaiming the Sociological Classics: The State of the Scholarship*. Oxford: Blackwell, pp. 112–41.

McGregor, S (1989) 'Rape, Pornography and Capitalism', *International Socialism*, 45: 3–31.

McLaughlin, N. (2005) 'Canada's Impossible Science: Historical and Institutional Origins of the Coming Crisis in Anglo-Canadian Sociology', *Canadian Journal of Sociology*, 30 (1): 1–40.

Mead, G.H. (1899a) 'The Working Hypothesis in Social Reform', *American Journal of Sociology*, 5 (3): 367–71.

Mead, G.H. (1899b) 'Review of the Psychology of Socialism by Gustave LeBon', *American Journal of Sociology*, 5 (3): 404–12.

Mead, G.H. (1907) 'Review of New Ideals of Peace by Jane Addams', *American Journal of Sociology*, 13 (1): 121–8.

Mead, G.H. (1907–8) 'The Social Settlement: Its Basis and Function' *University of Chicago Review*, 12, 108–10.

Mead, G.H. (1913) 'The Social Self', in G.H. Mead (1964a), *Selected Writings*. Chicago: University of Chicago Press, pp. 142–9.

Mead, G.H. (1915) 'Natural Rights and the Theory of the Political Institution', in G.H. Mead (1964a), *Selected Writings*. Chicago: University of Chicago Press, pp. 150–70.

Mead, G.H. (1929) 'National Mindedness and International Mindedness', *International Journal of Ethics*, 39 (4): 385–407.

Mead, G.H. (1930) 'Philanthropy from the Point of View of Ethics', in G.H. Mead (1964a), *Selected Writings*. Chicago: University of Chicago Press, pp. 392–407.

Mead, G.H. (1934) *Mind, Self & Society from the Standpoint of a Social Behaviourist*. Chicago: University of Chicago Press.

Mead, G.H. (1936) 'The Problem of Society – How We Become Selves', in G.H. Mead (1964b), *On Social Psychology*. Chicago: University of Chicago Press, pp. 19–42.

Mead, G.H. (1938) 'History and the Experimental Method', in G.H. Mead (1964b), *On Social Psychology*. Chicago: University of Chicago Press, pp. 319–27.

Mead, G.H. (1987a) 'Democracy's Issues in the World War', *Symbolic Interaction*, 10 (2): 275–6.

Mead, G.H. (1987b) 'Mead's Letter', *Symbolic Interaction*, 10 (2): 271–4.

Mead, G.H. (2011) 'On the State and Social Control', in G.H. Mead, *A Reader*. London: Routledge, 86–8.

Merton, R.K. (1973) *The Sociology of Science: Theoretical and Empirical Investigations*. Chicago: University of Chicago Press.

Mesny, A. (2009) 'What do "We" Know that "They" Don't? Sociologists' versus Nonsociologists' Knowledge', *Canadian Journal of Sociology*, 34 (3): 671–95.

Meštrović, S. (1991) *The Coming Fin De Siècle: An Application of Durkheim's Sociology to Modernity and Postmodernism*. London: Routledge.

Michels, R. (1991) *Political Parties: A Sociological Study of the Oligarchic Tendencies of Modern Democracy*. London: Transaction.

Miles, M. (2012) *Herbert Marcuse: An Aesthetics of Liberation*. London: Pluto Press.

Mills, C.W. (1951) *Blue Collar: The American Middle Class*. Oxford: Oxford University Press.

Mills, C.W. (1956) *The Power Elite*. Oxford: Oxford University Press.

Mills, C.W. (1959) *The Sociological Imagination*. Oxford: Oxford University Press.

Misztal, B. (2009) 'A Nobel Trinity: Jane Addams, Emily Greene Balch and Alva Myrdal', *The American Sociologist*, 40 (4): 332–53.

Moghadam, V. (2005) *Globalizing Women: Transnational Feminist Networks*. Baltimore, MD: John Hopkins University Press.

Molyneux, M. (1991) 'The "Woman Question" in the Age of Perestroika', in R. Blackburn (ed.) *After the Fall: The Failure of Communism and the Future of Socialism*. London: Verso, pp. 47–77.

Mommsen, W. (1974) *Max Weber and German Politics, 1890–1920*. Chicago: University of Chicago Press.

Mondragón (2015) 'The Mondragón Corporation', *Mondragón*, http://www.mondragon-corporation.com/eng/, date accessed: 13 January 2015.

Morris, A. (2015) *The Scholar Denied: W.E.B. Du Bois and the Birth of Modern Sociology*. Oakland, CA: University of California Press.

Morris, L. (1994) *Dangerous Classes: The Underclass and Social Citizenship*. London: Routledge.

Morris, W. (2004) *News from Nowhere and Other Writings*. London: Penguin.

Mouzelis, N. (2008) *Modern and Postmodern Social Theorizing: Bridging the Divide*. Cambridge: Cambridge University Press.

Mucha, J. and Keen, M. (2010) 'Post-Communist Democratization and the Practice of Sociology in Central and Eastern Europe', in S. Patel (ed.), *The ISA Handbook of Diverse Sociological Traditions*. London: Sage, pp. 129–38.

Muller, H. (1993) 'Durkheim's Political Sociology', in S. Turner (ed.), *Emile Durkheim: Sociologist and Moralist*. London: Routledge, pp. 95–110.

Nielsen, F. (2004) 'The Vacant "We": Remarks on Public Sociology', *Social Forces*, 82 (4): 1619–27.

Nimtz, A. (2014) *Lenin's Electoral Strategy from 1907 to the October Revolution of 1917*. Hampshire: Palgrave Macmillan.

Noy, D. (2009) 'Contradictions of Public Sociology: A View from a Graduate Student at Berkeley', *The American Sociologist*, 40 (4): 235–48.

Nyden, P., Hossfield, L. and Nyden, G. (eds) (2012) *Public Sociology: Research, Action and Change*. London: Sage.

O'Connor, J. (1996) 'The Second Contradiction of Capitalism', in T. Benton (ed.), *The Greening of Marxism*. New York: The Guilford Press, pp. 197–221.

Oakley, A. (1974) *Housewife*. London: Penguin.

Ollman, B. (1976) *Alienation: Marx's Conception of Man in Capitalist Society*. Cambridge: Cambridge University Press.

Ollman, B. (1977) 'Marx's Vision of Communism: A Reconstruction', *Critique: Journal of Socialist Theory*, 8 (1): 4–41.

Ossewaarde, M. (2005) 'Sociology Back to the Publics', *Sociology*, 41 (5): 799–812.

Pateman, C. (1988) *The Sexual Contract*. Cambridge: Polity Press.

Pateman, C. (2004) 'Democratising Citizenship: Some Advantages of a Basic Income', *Politics and Society*, 32 (1): 89–105.

Phipps, A. (2014) *The Politics of the Body*. Cambridge: Polity Press.

Piketty, T. (2014) *Capital in the Twenty-First Century*. Harvard, MA: Harvard University Press.

Piven, F.F. (2007) 'From Public Sociology to Politicized Sociologist', in D. Clawson et al. (eds), *Public Sociology*. Berkeley: University of California Press, pp. 158–66.

Plummer, K. (2010) *Sociology: The Basics*. London: Routledge.

Poupeau, F. and Discepolo, T. (2008) 'Introduction: A Specific Kind of Political Commitment', in P. Bourdieu, *Political Interventions: Social Science and Political Action*. London: Verso, pp. xiii–vi.

Power, N. (2009) *One Dimensional Woman*. Winchester: Zero Books.

Pūras, A. (2014) 'Robert Owen in the History of the Social Sciences: Three Presentist Views', *Journal of the History of Behavioral Sciences*, 50 (1): 58–78.

Ray, L. (2007) *Globalization and Everyday Life*. London: Routledge.

Reed, A. (1985) 'W.E.B. Du Bois: A Perspective on the Basis of His Political Thought', *Political Theory*, 13 (3): 431–56.

Remmling, G. (1975) *The Sociology of Karl Mannheim*. London: Routledge.

Renwick, C. (2012) *British Sociology's Lost Biological Roots: A History of Futures Past*. Hampshire: Palgrave Macmillan.

Rocquin, B. (2014) 'British Sociology in the Inter-War Years', in J. Holmwood and J. Scott (eds), *Palgrave Handbook of Sociology*. Hampshire: Palgrave Macmillan, pp. 189–210.

Rowbotham, S. (1973) *Woman's Consciousness, Man's World*. London: Penguin.

Rudwick, E. (1969) 'Note on a Forgotten Black Sociologist: W.E.B. Du Bois and the Sociological Profession', *The American Sociologist*, 4 (4): 303–6.

Rustin, M. (1995) 'The Future of Post-Socialism', *Radical Philosophy*, 74 (November/December): 17–27.

Said, E. (1994) *Representations of the Intellectual*. London: Vintage Books.

Salam, S. (2007) 'Selma James and the Wages for Housework Campaign', *New Beginnings: A Journal of Independent Labor*, http://nbjournal.org/2007/07/selma-james-and-the-wages-for-housework-campaign/

Sanderson, D. (1943) 'Sociology as a Means to Democracy', *American Sociological Review*, 8 (1): 1–9.

Sargisson, L. (1996) *Contemporary Feminist Utopianism*. London: Routledge.

Sargisson, L. (2012) *Fool's Gold? Utopianism in the Twenty-First Century*. Hampshire: Palgrave Macmillan.

Sassoon, D. (2010) *One Hundred Years of Socialism: The West European Left in the Twentieth Century*. London: I.B. Tauris.

Saunders, P. (1995) 'Might Britain Be a Meritocracy?', *Sociology*, 29 (1): 23–41.

Saunders, P. (2011) 'Academic Sociology and Social Policy Think Tanks in Britain and Australia: A Personal Reflection', *Sociological Research Online*, 16 (3), http://www.socresonline.org.uk/16/3/10.html, date accessed: 25 April 2014.

Sayer, A. (2009) 'Who's Afraid of Critical Social Science?', *Current Sociology*, 57 (6): 767–86.

Sayer, A. (2011) *Why Things Matter to People: Social Science, Values and Ethical Life*. Cambridge: Cambridge University Press.

Schinkel, W. (2003) 'Pierre Bourdieu's Political Turn?', *Theory, Culture & Society*, 20 (6): 69–93.

Scott, J. (2005) 'Who Will Speak and Who Will Listen? Comments on Burawoy and Public Sociology', *British Journal of Sociology*, 56 (3): 405–9.

Scott, J. and Bromley, R. (2013) *Envisioning Sociology: Victor Branford, Patrick Geddes, and the Quest for Social Reconstruction*. Albany: State University of New York Press.

Scott, J. and Marshall, G. (2005) *Oxford Dictionary of Sociology*. Oxford: Oxford University Press.

Screpanti, E. (2007) *Libertarian Communism: Marx, Engels and the Political Economy of Freedom* Hampshire: Palgrave Macmillan.

Segal, L. (1990) 'Pornography and Violence: What the "Experts" Really Say', *Feminist*, 36, 29–41.

Segal, L. (1991) 'Whose Left? Socialism, Feminism and the Future', in R. Blackburn (ed.) *After the Fall: The Failure of Communism and the Future of Socialism*. London: Verso, pp. 274–86.

Segal, L. (1993) 'False Promises – Anti-Pornography Feminism', *Socialist Register*, 29, 92–105.

Seubert, V. (1991) 'Sociology and Value Neutrality: Limiting Sociology to the Empirical Level', *American Sociologist*, 22 (3/4): 210–20.

Shalin, D. (1988) 'G.H. Mead, Socialism and the Progressive Agenda', *American Journal of Sociology*, 93 (4): 913–51.

Shils, E. (1997) 'Karl Mannheim', in E. Shils, *Portraits: A Gallery of Intellectuals*. Chicago: University of Chicago Press, pp. 202–18.

Silva, F.C. (2007a) 'Re-Examining Mead: G.H. Mead on the 'Material Reproduction of Society', *Journal of Classical Sociology*, 7 (3): 291–313.

Silva, F.C. (2007b) *G.H. Mead: A Critical Introduction*. Cambridge: Polity Press.

Silva, F.C. (2010) 'School and Democracy: A Reassessment of G.H. Mead's Educational Ideas', *Ethics and Politics*, 12 (1): 181–94.

Sirianni, C. (1984) 'Justice and the Division of Labour: A Reconsideration of Durkheim's *Division of Labour in Society*', *Sociological Review*, 32 (3): 449–70.

Sklair, L. (2009) 'The Emancipatory Potential of Generic Globalization', *Globalizations*, 6 (4): 525–39.

Smith, A. (2015) 'Rethinking the 'Everyday' in 'Ethnicity and Everyday Life'', *Ethnic and Racial Studies*, 38 (7): 1137–51.

Smith, D. (1987) *The Everyday World as Problematic: A Feminist Sociology*. Milton Keynes: Open University Press.

Smith, D. (2005) *Institutional Ethnography: A Sociology for People*. Oxford: Rowman and Littlefield Publishing.

Smith, P. and Alexander J.C. (2005) 'Introduction: The new Durkheim', in J.C Alexander and P. Smith (eds), *Cambridge Companion to Durkheim*. Cambridge: Cambridge University Press, pp. 1–37.

Smith-Lovin, L. (2007) 'Do We Need a Public Sociology? It Depends on What You Mean by *Sociology*', in D. Clawson et al. (eds), *Public Sociology*. Berkeley: University of California Press, pp. 124–34.

Sociologists for Women in Society (2014) 'Feminist Activism Award', http://www.socwomen.org/feminist-activism-award-2/, date accessed: 4 May 2014.

Sørenson, M. and Christiansen, A. (2013) *Ulrich Beck: An Introduction to the Theory of Second Modernity and the Risk Society*. London: Routledge.

Sprague, J. and Laube, H. (2009) 'Institutional Barriers to Doing Public Sociology: Experiences of Feminists in the Academy', *The American Sociologist*, 40 (4): 249–71.

Squires, J. (2007) *The New Politics of Gender Equality*. Hampshire: Palgrave Macmillan.

Stacey, J. (2007) 'If I Were the Goddess of Sociological Things', in D. Clawson et al. (eds), *Public Sociology*. Berkeley: University of California Press, pp. 91–100.

Standing, G. (2011) *The Precariat: The New Dangerous Class*. London: Bloomsbury.

Stanley, L. and Wise, S. (1990) 'Method, Methodology and Epistemology in Feminist Research Processes', in L. Stanley (ed.), *Feminist Praxis: Research, Theory and Epistemology in Feminist Sociology*. London: Routledge, pp. 20–60.

Stedman Jones, S. (2001) *Durkheim Reconsidered*. Cambridge: Polity Press.

Steinmetz, G. (2013) 'A Child of Empire: British Sociology and Colonialism', *Journal of the History of the Behavioural Sciences*, 49 (4): 353–78.

Stop Porn Culture (2014) 'About Stop Porn Culture International', http://stoppornculture.org/about/about-stop-porn-culture-international/, date accessed: 4 May 2014.

Strasser, H. (1976) *The Normative Structure of Sociology: Conservative and Emancipatory Themes in Social Thought*. London: Routledge.

Strossen, N. (2000) *Defending Pornography: Free Speech, Sex and the Fight for Women's Rights*. London: Abacus.

Sullivan, A. (2001) 'Cultural Capital and Educational Attainment', *Sociology*, 35 (4): 893–912.

Swartz, D. (2003) 'From Critical Sociology to Public Intellectual: Pierre Bourdieu and Politics', *Theory and Society*, 32 (5–6): 791–823.

Swartz, D. (2013) *Symbolic Power, Politics, and Intellectuals: The Political Sociology of Pierre Bourdieu*. Chicago: University of Chicago Press.

Thorpe, C. and Jacobsen, B. (2013) 'Life Politics, Nature and the State: Giddens' Sociological Theory and *The Politics of Climate Change*', *British Journal of Sociology*, 64 (1): 99–122.

Tittle, C. (2004) 'The Arrogance of Public Sociology', *Social Forces*, 82 (4): 1639–43.

Tong, R.P. (1998) *Feminist Thought*. 2nd Edn. Oxford: Westview Press.

Touraine, A. (2007) 'Public Sociology and the End of Society', in D. Clawson et al. (eds), *Public Sociology*. Berkeley: University of California Press, pp. 67–78.

Trebitsch, M. (1991) 'Preface', in H. Lefebvre (1991b), *Critique of Everyday Life: Volume 1*. London: Verso, pp. ix–xxviii.

Turner, C. (2010) *Investigating Sociological Theory*. London: Sage.

Turner, J. (2005) 'Is Public Sociology such a Good Idea?', *The American Sociologist*, 36 (3–4): 27–45.

Turner, S. (2005) 'Public Sociology and Democratic Theory', *Sociology*, 41 (5): 785–98.

Turner, S. (2014) *American Sociology: From Pre-Disciplinary to Post-Normal*. Hampshire: Palgrave Macmillan.

Urry, J. (2005) 'The Good News and the Bad News', *Critical Sociology*, 31 (3): 375–8.

Urry, J. (2008) 'Climate Change, Travel and Complex Futures', *British Journal of Sociology*, 59 (2): 261–79.

Van Parijs, P. (1995) *Real Freedom for All. What (If Anything) Can Justify Capitalism?* Oxford: Oxford University Press.

Venn, C. (2006) *The Postcolonial Challenge: Towards Alternative Worlds.* London: Sage.

Walaszek, Z. (1977) 'Recent Developments in Polish Sociology', *Annual Review of Sociology,* 3: 331–62.

Walby, S. (1990) *Theorizing Patriarchy.* Oxford: Blackwell.

Walby, S. (2000) 'Gender, Globalisation and Democracy', *Gender and Development,* 8 (1): 20–8.

Walby, S. (2011) *The Future of Feminism.* Cambridge: Polity Press.

Wallerstein, I. (2007) 'The Sociologist and the Public Sphere', in D. Clawson et al. (eds), *Public Sociology.* Berkeley: University of California Press, pp. 169–75.

Walter, N. (2010) *Living Dolls: The Return of Sexism.* London: Virago.

Warren, M. (2001) *Democracy and Association.* Princeton, NJ: Princeton University Press.

Weber, M. (1895) 'The Nation State and Economic Policy', in P. Lassman and D. Speirs (eds) (1994), *Weber: Political Writings.* Cambridge: Cambridge University Press, pp. 1–28.

Weber, M. (1918) 'Socialism', in P. Lassman and D. Speirs (eds) (1994), *Weber: Political Writings.* Cambridge: Cambridge University Press, pp. 272–303.

Weber, M. (1921) 'Politics as a Vocation', in H.H. Gerth & C.W. Mills (eds) (1991), *From Max Weber: Essays in Sociology.* London: Routledge, pp. 77–128.

Weber, M. (1922) 'Science as a Vocation', in H.H. Gerth & C.W. Mills (eds) (1991), *From Max Weber: Essays in Sociology.* London: Routledge, pp. 129–56.

Weber, M. (1930) *The Protestant Ethic and the Spirit of Capitalism.* London: Routledge.

Weber, M. (1949a) 'The Meaning of "Ethical Neutrality" in Economics and Sociology', in E. Shils and H. Finch (eds), *The Methodology of the Social Sciences.* London: Transactions Publishers, pp. 1–47.

Weber, M. (1949b) '"Objectivity" in Social Science and Social Policy', in E. Shils and H. Finch (eds), *The Methodology of the Social Sciences.* London: Transactions Publishers, pp. 49–112.

Wells, H.G. (1907) 'The So-Called Science of Sociology', in *Sociological Society, Sociological Papers 1906.* London: Macmillan, pp. 357–69.

Wheen, F. (1999) *Karl Marx: A Life.* London: W.W. Norton and Company.

White, M. (2013) *The Manipulation of Choice: Ethics and Libertarian Paternalism.* Hampshire: Palgrave Macmillan.

White, S. (2004) 'The Citizens' Stake and Paternalism', *Politics and Society,* 32 (1): 61–78.

Whitty, G. (1997) 'Social Theory and Education Policy: The Legacy of Karl Mannheim', *British Journal of Sociology of Education,* 18 (2): 149–63.

Williams, R. (2006) 'The Early Social Science of W.E.B. Du Bois', *Du Bois Review,* 3 (2): 365–94.

Witz, A. and Marshall, B. (2004) 'Introduction: Feminist Encounters with Sociological Theory', in B. Marshall and A. Witz (eds), *Engendering the Social: Feminist Encounters with Sociological Theory.* Milton Keynes: Open University Press, pp. 1–16.

Wright, E.O. (1979) *Class Structure and Income Determination.* New York: Academic Press.

Wright, E.O. (1985) *Classes.* London: Verso.

Wright, E.O. (1997) *Class Counts.* London: Verso.

Wright, E.O. (2000) 'Reducing Income and Wealth Inequalities: Real Utopian Proposals', *Contemporary Sociology,* 29 (1): 143–56.

Wright, E.O. (2004) 'Basic Income, Stakeholder Grants and Class Analysis', *Politics and Society*, 32 (1): 79–87.

Wright, E.O. (2006) 'Compass Points: Towards a Socialist Alternative', *New Left Review*, 41 (Sep–Oct): 93–124.

Wright, E.O. (2010) *Envisioning Real Utopias*. London: Verso.

Wyatt, C. (2006) 'A Recipe for a Cookshop of the Future: G.D.H. Cole and the Conundrum of Sovereignty', *Capital and Class*, 30 (3): 93–123.

Young, B. (2001) 'The Mistress and the Maid in the Global Economy', *Socialist Register*, 37: 315–27.

Young, M, (1961) *The Rise of the Meritocracy*. Harmondsworth: Penguin.

Index